100
Years
100 Men

Edwards & Broughton's plant and offices located on Raleigh's North Boulevard (US 1 North).

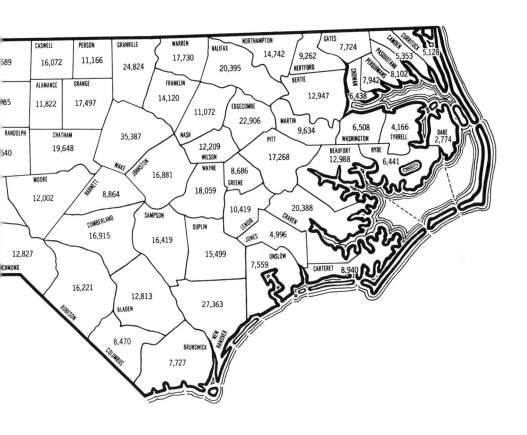

North Carolina Counties
and Population Figures at
the Beginning of the 1870's

100 Years 100 Men

1871-1971

Edited by

Christopher Crittenden
William S. Powell
Robert H. Woody

PRINTED AND BOUND IN THE UNITED STATES OF AMERICA,
RALEIGH, NORTH CAROLINA, EDWARDS & BROUGHTON COMPANY

Dedication

To the people of the Edwards & Broughton Company, past and present. These people ARE our past, our present, and our future.

Foreword

In 1968, as the 100th anniversary of the company approached, its officers began discussing ways to commemorate it. Since the publication of *A History of Printing in North Carolina*, by George Washington Paschal, on the company's 75th anniversary, had been so well received, naturally the idea of another book immediately came to mind. After much thought the decision was made to publish a book containing condensed biographies of the men and women who had done the most for the State of North Carolina in the past 100 years, to be called *100 Years—100 Men*.

Dr. Robert Woody of the History Department of Duke University; Mr. William S. Powell, Director of the North Carolina Collection at the University of North Carolina; and Dr. Christopher Crittenden, then Director of the North Carolina Department of Archives and History, agreed to act as editors.

It was their task to select these 100 men and women and supervise the writing of the biographies.

The selections had all been made before the untimely death of Dr. Crittenden.

The rules were very simple: What had they done for

North Carolina? Service to the Nation or other parts thereof was to have no bearing on the selections; merely their
contribution to the State. The board of editors was given
complete freedom in their choice.

We are sure that many of our readers will not agree
with some of the choices that have been made. They will,
no doubt, ask why this person was included when that person was omitted. We have no excuses to make. We think
our editors have done an outstanding job.

The writing of the biographies was done, under the supervision of Mr. Powell, by Mr. Gary Trawick and Mr. Paul
Wyche, to whom we owe much.

The quotations from the poems of John Charles McNeill
are used by permission of the University of North Carolina
Press, Chapel Hill, N. C.

For helping us procure pictures, we express thanks to
the University of North Carolina Library, the State Department of Archives and History and to members of the families of those pictured.

The biographies of Mr. Edwards and Mr. Broughton appearing in the Appendix are reprinted in full from "A
History of Printing in North Carolina" by George Washington Paschal, published in 1946. Dr. Charles Lee Smith's
biography, with some editing and updating to the time of
his death, also is from this work.

It is our hope that this book will give you pleasant reading as well as furthering your knowledge of these outstanding men and women.

—EDWARDS & BROUGHTON COMPANY

Table of Contents

100 Years 100 Men

A. B. Andrews

Alexander Boyd Andrews was born in Franklin County, North Carolina, on July 23, 1841, the son of William J. and Virginia Hawkins Andrews.

Andrews received his formal education at the Henderson Male Academy. At the age of seventeen he stopped school to become a clerk for his uncle, P. B. Hawkins, who was under contract to construct a portion of the Blue Ridge Railway.

Shortly after the completion of the Blue Ridge, the Civil War broke out and he enlisted in the Confederate Army. He rose to the rank of captain and in September, 1863, was severely wounded at Jacks Shop, Virginia. In the fall of 1864 he was retired from active duty.

At the war's end, Andrews borrowed $100 with which he leased and equipped a ferry which he personally operated across the Roanoke River at Weldon, North Carolina. In July, 1867, he accepted the position of superintendent of the Raleigh and Gaston Railroad, and the next year he also became the superintendent of the Chatham Railroad.

In 1871 the Richmond and Danville Railroad Company obtained a lease on the North Carolina Railroad which ran from Charlotte to Goldsboro. In 1875 the officials of the company offered Andrews the superintendency of the line and he accepted. He thus left the employment of the Raleigh and Gaston. From 1878 until 1880 he also served as superintendent of the Atlantic and North Carolina Railroad.

Perhaps the greatest service A. B. Andrews rendered to North Carolina was in connection with the completion of the Western North Carolina Railroad. This railroad had been organized in 1855 and by the time the war came had been completed almost to Morganton. The war stopped all progress in completing it. The railroad was sold in 1881 to a New York syndicate headed by William J. Best, and under the terms of sale the road was to be completed to Paint Rock and Murphy. Best chose Andrews as president and builder of the railroad, but after making one payment to the state he was unable to fulfill the contract. Andrews persuaded the directors of the Richmond and Danville Railroad to take over the Best contract. With their financial backing, he set out to finish the railroad, and this he did. Under his management the railroad paid the debt owed the state under the Best contract and in 1884 made a single payment of $600,000 which relieved the State of levying any public taxes that year. This railroad, built over, around, and through mountains, is due much of the credit fc the development of western North Carolina.

The Richmond and Danville promoted Andrews to third vice president in 1886 and to second vice president in 1889. Three years later the company became insolvent and was placed in the hands of receivers. The receivers appointed Andrews their general agent, and he continued to participate in the management of the railroad until all the lines were purchased by the Southern Railway Company which was organized in June, 1894. At the first meeting of the Southern Railway, Andrews was elected second vice president and the next year became first vice president, a position he held until his death.

In addition to his other duties, Andrews was president of the Charlotte, Columbia, and Augusta Railroad Company, of the Columbia and Oxford and Henderson, the Atlantic, Tennessee and Ohio, the Statesville and Western, and the Piedmont Railroad Company. All of these were brought into the Southern Railway system in 1894. After the organization of Southern Railway, he was president of a number of independent railroads which operated within the Southern system.

Besides his railroad interests, Andrews was a director of the Sloss-Sheffield Steel and Iron Company of Birmingham, Alabama, and was an organizer and director of the Citizens National Bank of Raleigh.

He served on the board of aldermen of both Henderson and Raleigh. He was one of the commissioners from North Carolina to the Columbian Exposition at Chicago. He served on the Executive Committee of the Board of Trustees of the University of North Carolina. He was a Mason, member of the Capital Club at Raleigh, and a Shriner. His political affiliation was with the Democratic party and his religious affiliation was with the Episcopal Church.

He was married on September 1, 1869, to Julia M. Johnston, the daughter of Colonel William and Mrs. Anna Johnston of Charlotte. Five children were born of this marriage: William J. Andrews, Alexander B. Andrews, Jr., Jane Hawkins Andrews, who married William M. Marks, John H. Andrews, and Graham H. Andrews.

He died April 17, 1915, and is buried in Oakwood Cemetery, Raleigh.

A portrait of A. B. Andrews is owned by the State of North Carolina and hangs in Raleigh.

For additional information concerning A. B. Andrews, see: *Biographical History of North Carolina*, volume 1, edited by Samuel A. Ashe.

2

Charles B. Aycock

Charles Brantley Aycock was born in Wayne County, North Carolina, November 1, 1859, the son of Benjamin and Serena Hooks Aycock. It is believed that young Aycock received his first formal education at the Nahunta Academy. After studying locally from 1867 to 1872, he attended the Wilson Collegiate Institute for three years. Following the death of his father in 1875, he remained at home and taught school for part of the year in Fremont. The next year he attended an academy in Kinston. In 1877 he entered the University of North Carolina and was graduated three years later. During his last year he read law under Dr. Kemp Battle.

Aycock returned to his home county after leaving the University and continued to study law as an apprentice under A. K. Smedes. In 1881 he received his license to practice. That same year Aycock and Frank Arthur Daniels opened a partnership in Goldsboro.

Immediately following his return to Wayne County, Charles began to take an active part in politics. He rapidly rose to a high position in the local political circles and in 1890 made an unsuccessful bid for the Democratic nomination for Congress from the Third District. In 1892 he worked for the election of Grover Cleveland for president.

In recognition of his service, he was appointed United States Attorney for the District of Eastern North Carolina.

Aycock's prominence as a political leader in the state of North Carolina was assured by his role in the White Supremacy campaign of 1898. During this campaign he spoke to one hundred thousand people in the course of making over one hundred speeches in seventy-five of the state's counties. Due in large measure to his efforts, the machinery of the state government was returned to Democratic control.

When the Democratic State Convention met to choose a candidate for governor in 1900, Charles B. Aycock was the logical choice. He won the nomination with little opposition and went on to win the general election by the largest majority ever given to a candidate for governor until that time. He was inaugurated on January 15, 1901.

The state took many strides forward during Aycock's administration, but perhaps the most important were those in the field of education. When he took office few districts in the state maintained even the four-months school term required by the state constitution. During his administration the annual school appropriation was raised by the legislature to $200,000, double the previous amount. Of this, $5,000 in 1901, and $7,500 in 1903, was set aside for libraries in rural schools, not one of which had a library prior to this time. Within two years, 429 of these libraries were established. The State Board of Education was required to select textbooks, instead of leaving this up to each local school board. Standards were set for schoolhouses and the standards for teachers were raised. Appropriations were increased for certain of the state's institutions of higher learning. A normal school was established at Boone, now Appalachian State University. The state literary fund was made available as a loan fund to counties for the construction of new school buildings. The Governor's greatest effort for education in the state came from his personal appeals to the people of the state to improve local schools.

Accomplishments outside the educational field were also achieved during Aycock's term in office. Among these some of the more important were the following: the passage of a bill restricting the sale and manufacture of intoxicants to incorporated towns where police supervision was available; the authorization of a $300,000 bond issue to prevent a curtailment of the state's programs; and the passage of a child labor law.

After his term as governor, Aycock returned to Goldsboro, but after a short time he moved to Raleigh and practiced law with Judge Robert T. Winston.

C. B. Aycock was a Mason, Odd Fellow, and Knight of Pythias, and a member of the Baptist Church.

Aycock and Varina Woodard were married on May 25, 1881. Three children were born of this union; two died in childhood. Mrs. Aycock died in 1889 and Aycock married her sister, Cora, in January of 1891. Seven children were born to Charles and Cora Aycock.

Charles B. Aycock died April 4, 1912. On that night he was speaking in Birmingham, Alabama, in the Jefferson Theater. The last word he ever spoke was "education." Following these words, ". . . sometimes on Sundays they would ask me down to the churches to talk, and I always talked about education . . . , " he simply dropped dead. He is buried in Oakwood Cemetery, Raleigh, North Carolina.

There is a statue of Aycock on the capitol grounds and a portrait of him in the governor's office in Raleigh.

For additional information concerning Charles B. Aycock, see: *The Life and Speeches of Charles Brantley Aycock,* by R. D. W. Connor and Clarence Poe, and *Charles Brantley Aycock,* by Oliver H. Orr, Jr. His papers can be found in the North Carolina Department of Archives and History.

Josiah William Bailey

Josiah William Bailey was born in Warrenton, North Carolina, on September 14, 1873; but he was reared in Raleigh and received his early education there, where his father, the Reverend Christopher Thomas Bailey, a Baptist minister, edited the *Biblical Recorder*. His mother was Annie Sarah Bailey.

Bailey attended the public schools of Raleigh and the Raleigh Male Academy, also known as the Morson and Denson School. He then matriculated at Wake Forest College, graduating in 1893 with a Bachelor of Arts degree.

After his graduation, Bailey returned to Raleigh and took over editorship of the *Biblical Recorder*, official publication of the Baptist State Convention.

After ten years in the editorship, Bailey acquired an interest in law, and he took private lessons from Dean Samuel F. Mordecai of Trinity College (now Duke University). In 1907 he re-entered Wake Forest College, this time in the Law School. Finishing the following year, he began the practice of law in Raleigh.

Bailey's interest in politics began when he was editor of the *Recorder* and he became active in this field when he took up the practice of law, playing a leading part in city and county Democratic political battles early in the century.

He served as a presidential elector-at-large in 1908 and as a member of the constitutional commission for North Carolina in 1913-14.

Bailey was a strong supporter of Woodrow Wilson, campaigning for him in the state, and in 1913, President Wilson appointed him Collector of Internal Revenue for North Carolina. He served in this capacity throughout Wilson's two terms in office.

In 1924 Bailey ran for governor in the Democratic primary but was defeated by Angus W. McLean. Entering no more political races until 1930, he ran against and defeated Senator F. M. Simmons in the primary, and Republican George M. Pritchard in the general elections.

Not long after taking office, Senator Bailey became classed as a conservative and he clashed frequently with the liberal wing of the Democratic party. When Franklin D. Roosevelt came into office in 1933, it soon became apparent that Senator Bailey's views did not often coincide with the fundamental policies of the New Deal. Though he did vote for many of Roosevelt's measures, and supported the President each time he came up for re-election, a number of Congressional battles saw Bailey on the opposite side from the administration's supporters. He took a leading part in the bitter Congressional fight which led to rejection of Roosevelt's proposal for re-organizing the Federal judiciary. As an advocate of states rights, he took part in filibusters that beat the anti-lynching bill in 1938, and the Fair Employment Practices Act of 1946. He spoke out vigorously against the Bankhead Bill which would limit the production of cotton. In 1936 and again in 1942 Bailey easily defeated his Republican opponents for re-election.

In the Senate, Bailey was a member of the committees on Finance, Claims and Post Offices and Post Roads. He served as chairman of the Claims Committee before becoming head of the Commerce Committee in 1939.

While still serving as editor of the *Biblical Recorder*, Bailey traveled widely throughout the state in the interest of Baptist affairs, becoming well known as a Bible scholar and as a speaker. He taught Sunday school classes for some 25 years. He was a consistent crusader against the liquor traffic, and for years was a leading figure in the North Carolina division of the Anti-Saloon League.

Bailey was an avid fan of the outdoor life, with a good deal of knowledge about birds and trees. He had a keen skill in fishing, and this gave him his one constant recreation.

On August 15, 1916, Bailey was married to Edith Walker Pou, daughter of James H. Pou, Raleigh attorney. To them were born five children: James Hinton Pou, Annie Elizabeth Pou, Josiah William, Jr., Edith Pou, and Sallie Bailey.

Senator Bailey died on December 15, 1946, and is buried in Oakwood Cemetery in Raleigh.

For additional information on Josiah W. Bailey see: *Senator Josiah William Bailey of North Carolina: A Political Biography*, by John Robert Moore.

Kemp Plummer Battle

Kemp Plummer Battle was born on a farm in Franklin County, North Carolina, December 19, 1831. He was the son of William Horn Battle and Lucy Martin Plummer.

Battle attended the Louisburg Female Academy until he was eight years old, at which time his father moved to Raleigh, where he attended the Raleigh Male Academy. In 1843 Judge Battle moved again, this time to Chapel Hill, and young Kemp prepared for college at the village school there. He entered the University of North Carolina at the age of thirteen, and was graduated in 1849 at seventeen, sharing the valedictory with two others.

After graduation, Battle was elected tutor of mathematics at the University, in which capacity he served for four years. During this time he studied law under his father. Receiving his license in 1854, he at once began practice in Raleigh.

In 1860 he was a Whig candidate for the House of Commons in Wake County, and though himself defeated, he aided in bringing into the House a Whig majority by his campaign pamphlet, *Ad Valorem Taxation Explained by Questions and Answers.*

During the presidential campaign of 1860, Battle was president of the Wake County Union Club, but when the Civil War broke out, he actively embraced the cause of the

South, and was elected a member of the Secession Convention. Foreseeing that the Confederacy would need fuel for its navy and its factories, he was instrumental in the building of a railroad to the coal fields of Chatham.

Battle was elected State Treasurer in 1865 and served until being turned out of office in 1868 by operation of the Reconstruction Acts. He was a member of the North Carolina Constitutional Convention of 1868.

In 1862 he was made a trustee of the University and soon thereafter was placed on its executive committee. In 1867 the University entered the darkest period of its history. There was a lack of money and a lack of students and its professors were fast resigning. Finally it closed its doors.

By 1874, the University had been for eight years nothing but a pathetic reminder of better days in North Carolina, but from its decay came Battle's greatest work. By constitutional amendment, the University was given back to its old-time friends. Battle, one of the new trustees, was elected secretary and treasurer, and on his recommendation, successful application was made to the General Assembly for $7,500 a year. With this amount as a beginning, he began a movement to reopen the University. Its buildings were decaying and the campus was growing up in weeds, but Battle appealed to its friends, who gladly answered his call, giving him $800 with which to make repairs.

In September, 1875, the doors were thrown open and sixty-nine students were enrolled. After one year, it was seen that a president was needed and Battle accepted the position.

Under his direction the number of students steadily increased, instruction in all departments was widened and deepened, new departments were added, new laboratories were built and new buildings were constructed. He gathered about him an outstanding faculty. Under him several literary and scientific societies were organized and the University railroad was completed.

In 1881 Battle secured from the legislature an annual appropriation of $20,000, the first annual appropriation ever given to the University by the state. Again at his urging, the General Assembly authorized the establishment of a Normal School in connection with the University to train teachers for the common schools of the state.

In 1891 he resigned as president and was at once elected Alumni Professor of History. In 1907 he became emeritus Professor of History, retiring on a Carnegie pension to take up active work on his monumental two volume *History of the University of North Carolina*. Besides this, Battle was also author of *The Trials and Judicial Proceedings of the New Testament* and a *History of the North Carolina Supreme Court*. He wrote a *History of the Parish of the Chapel of the Cross* and a *History of Christ Church Parish, Raleigh,* as well as numerous articles for law reviews, magazines, and newspapers and a large manuscript volume of "Personal Reminiscences."

Besides offices already referred to, Battle was Director of the Insane Asylum, State Superintendent of Public Instruction, president of the State Agricultural Society, the Chatham Railroad, and founder and director of Citizens National Bank of Raleigh.

Battle was married on November 28, 1855 to a distant kinswoman, Martha Ann Battle, daughter of James S. Battle of Edgecombe County. They had five children: Kemp P., Jr., Thomas H., Herbert B., William J., and Nellie.

Dr. Battle died on February 4, 1919 and is buried in Raleigh.

For additional information on Kemp P. Battle see: *Memories of an Old-Time Tar Heel,* by Kemp Battle, edited by his son, William James Battle.

William Henry Belk

William Henry Belk was born June 2, 1862 in Lancaster
County, South Carolina. His father, Abel Nelson Washington Belk, was drowned by Sherman's raiders in 1865 for
refusing to divulge the whereabouts of his father's gold mine.
His mother was Sarah Narcissus Walkup.

Belk got his first training in books at home from his
mother, who had been educated at Carolina Female Academy
in Ansonville, North Carolina. Later he attended the local
one-room schoolhouse. In 1873 the family moved to Monroe,
North Carolina and Belk attended school there and in nearby
Mecklenburg County. He did not attend college because of
lack of money.

At the age of fourteen, Belk went to work in a dry goods
store at a salary of $5 per month and after three months
had saved $14.85, his expenses running a nickel per month.
The next quarter, he got a raise to $25 and before long
another raise to $50 per quarter.

At the end of eleven years, when he had become head
man in the store, confidential clerk and buyer, he was raised
to $40 per month. The next year, when he was 26 years
old, Belk decided to establish his own business.

With $750 that he had saved and $500 that he borrowed
at 10 per cent interest and $3,000 worth of merchandise

that he traded for, Belk opened for business in Monroe on May 29, 1888. He called his store the "New York Racket," because he thought that it "sounded big."

A little more than six months later he had paid off the three thousand dollars for the stock and the five hundred dollars for the loan. With his slogan of "Belk Sells It for Less" he had paid off the money he had borrowed, was in the clear on salaries, rent, and other expenses, and had shown a clear profit of thirty-three hundred dollars.

Three years later, Belk persuaded his brother, John Montgomery Belk, a practicing physician, to give up his profession and join in the mercantile venture. They worked as a team from that time until the death of Dr. Belk in 1928.

Their policy was totally unheard of before the turn of the century. Merchandise was clearly marked, and it sold at that price; there would be no more haggling at the counter. Belk's policy was to sell good merchandise, and whenever possible, to sell it for less. If a customer bought an article, took it home, and found that it was not what he wanted, he could return it and get his money back. This was enough of a new thing in itself, but his other merchandising idea was far more radical. He sold for cash only. He would have no accounts to record, no notes to accept, no mortgages on farm crops and animals to foreclose, and no customers distressed and angry because he had dispossessed them of their property.

The business continued to grow, not spectacularly, but steadily. There was no work about the store that he did not do, and he demanded more of himself than of any of those who worked for him.

In 1892, Belk opened a second store in Chester, South Carolina, with Alex Kluttz as a partner under the firm name Kluttz and Belk. A year later this second store was followed by a third, this time in Union, South Carolina, with Reece

P. Harry as co-owner and manager. On September 25, 1895, the Belks opened their store in Charlotte and called it Belk Brothers Company.

As the years went on, new Belk stores began to fan out through the Southeast. Belk followed a consistent plan of watching for promising young men who were honest, willing to work, and striving for a chance. By linking his name and his support to each business, he helped it on to successful service to its home community. The training of so large a number of good solid businessmen in many communities was one of the great services of Belk's life. Today, there are some 415 Belk-related stores in seventeen southeastern states and Puerto Rico.

Besides being North Carolina's "merchant prince," Belk was a devout member of the Presbyterian Church. He was greatly interested in Presbyterian Junior College (now consolidated with Flora Macdonald College into St. Andrews Presbyterian College) in Maxton, and he contributed heavily to its work. Other special interests included Presbyterian Hospital in Charlotte and the Presbyterian Orphans' Home at Barium Springs. He and his brother John established a hospital in Tai-Chow, China, known as the "Sarah Walkup Belk Memorial Hospital" in honor of their mother. Through the John M. Belk Memorial Fund, he assisted some 335 churches and manses in their building programs. Portions of the store profits as well as personal income was used for these and other philanthropic purposes.

On June 9, 1915, Belk married Mary Lenora Irwin, and to them were born six children: William Henry, Jr., Sarah, John, Irwin, Henderson, and Tom.

Belk died on February 21, 1952, and is buried in Elmwood Cemetery in Charlotte.

For additional information on William H. Belk see: *William Henry Belk, Merchant of the South,* by LeGette Blythe.

3

Harriet Morehead Berry

Harriet Morehead Berry was born in Hillsboro, North Carolina, on July 23, 1879. She was the daughter of Dr. John Berry and Mary Strayhorn Berry.

Miss Berry was graduated from the State Normal College, now the University of North Carolina at Greensboro, and then taught school for three years. She then returned to the State Normal for a business course, after which, in 1901, she became stenographer and statistician for the United States Geological Survey at Chapel Hill.

In 1902 the North Carolina Good Roads Association was organized and Miss Berry attended the first meeting in the capacity of stenographer. Her work with the Association during the next eighteen years brought her to the forefront of the good roads movement in the State.

Her work with the Geological Survey amounted to a continuous study of the natural resources and needs of North Carolina. She wrote and edited many of the papers, reports, and press releases issued by the Geological Survey. In connection with either the Geological Survey or the Good Roads Association she helped put on the exhibitions for North Carolina at county, state, national, and international fairs, road congresses, and commercial congresses.

She rose within the ranks of the Geological Survey until

she was named acting director when Colonel Joseph Hyde Pratt was called to active military duty during World War I. In this capacity she directed all the activities of the agency and was called to Washington by President Woodrow Wilson for conferences on minerals needed in the war effort.

She also rose within the Goods Roads Association until she was made assistant secretary in 1912 and placed in charge of promotion of good roads. In 1915 the General Assembly adopted a bill, which she had written, which established the first State Highway Commission. The work of the Commission was mainly to advise counties and townships on road building and not to undertake the work directly themselves.

Miss Berry decided that the only way the state could obtain an adequate system of roads was for it to take over the road building function from the counties and towns. She submitted a plan for a state highway system to the General Assembly in 1917, but it was dismissed without much consideration. By the time the next Legislature met in 1919 the idea of good roads had been planted in the minds of the people of the state and a number of road bills were introduced into the Assembly. While not a legislator, Miss Berry was very much in evidence at the state capitol, fighting for those road bills she thought good and against those she believed bad. However, when the Legislature adjourned, not much of substance had been accomplished.

After gaining the approval of the Executive Committee of the Good Roads Association, she wrote a bill which would create a state system of highways, and she set out to sell it to the public. In 1920 she became Executive Secretary of the Association and that same year obtained a year's leave of absence from the Geological Survey in which to campaign for her bill.

The bill which Miss Berry had written, which had under-

gone a few minor changes by the Legislature Committee of
the Good Roads Association, became the basis for the
Doughton-Connor-Bowie Bill which was passed by the 1921
General Assembly. The act authorized the State Highway
Commission to undertake the construction of a state system
of highways which would connect all the county seats and
principal cities in the state. To finance this undertaking,
the act authorized the issuance of $50,000,000 of State
bonds. This act and later enabling acts resulted in North
Carolina having the largest system of state-owned and main-
tained highways in the nation. For her part in this work
Miss Berry has become known as the "Mother of Good
Roads" in North Carolina.

For the remainder of her life her chief occupation was
as Superintendent of Credit Unions under the State Department of Agriculture. The purpose of the unions was to provide a better means of credit to farmers and thereby help
eradicate the crop lien system in North Carolina.

During World War I Miss Berry served on the North
Carolina Committee of Women in Industry, participated in
the Orange County Liberty Loan Drive, and helped organize
the Chapel Hill Community Club. She was an officer in
the Equal Suffrage League on both a state and local level.
Her political affiliation was with the Democratic party and
she served on both her County and State Executive Committees and was elected as a delegate-at-large to the Democratic National Convention in 1924.

She died March 24, 1940, and is buried in Chapel Hill.

For additional information concerning Miss Berry, see:
The memorial address given by Mrs. Henry Cromartie at the
plaque dedication ceremony on October 25, 1962, in the
State Highway Building, Raleigh.

Thomas W. Bickett

Thomas Walter Bickett was born in Monroe, North Carolina, on February 28, 1869. He was the son of Thomas Winchester Bickett and his wife, Mary A. Covington.

His college preparation was acquired in the public schools and in 1886 he entered Wake Forest College, from which he received the A.B. degree in 1890. His family was not able to pay his college expenses. Bickett therefore financed his own education by working and incurring some debts.

After his graduation Bickett took a teaching position at Marion but remained there only a very short time before going to Winston-Salem to teach at West End School. After teaching for two years Bickett entered the law school of the University of North Carolina and the next year, 1893, received his diploma and was licensed to practice. He first practiced with his uncle, D. A. Covington, in Monroe, but after about six months he moved to Danbury, North Carolina, and formed a partnership with A. M. Stack. In 1895 he went to Louisburg, North Carolina, where he soon established himself as a capable member of the bar.

In 1907 he was elected to the General Assembly as a representative from Franklin County. While in the legislature he served as chairman of the Committee on Insane Asylums and in this capacity introduced a bill which would require the state to care for the insane and specifying that jails no longer be used to house the mentally ill. This bill, known as the Bickett Bill, passed and committed the state to spend $500,000 for the purchase of land and the construction of buildings in which to care for the insane.

Bickett first came to state-wide attention at the State Democratic Convention of 1908 in Charlotte. He made a nominating speech for Ashley Horne for governor and while he did not succeed in securing the nomination for Horne, he so impressed the convention that he was nominated for attorney general. He won the election and in 1912 was re-elected to the post. Bickett's record as attorney general is perhaps best illustrated by a portion of an editorial that appeared in the Raleigh *News and Observer* on November 11, 1915: "The record of Attorney General Thomas W. Bickett before the United States Supreme Court is one of which he can well be proud. Since coming into the high office which he holds he has had occasion to argue five different cases before the Supreme Court as the guardian of the state's legal rights, and he has won every one of them."

In 1916 Bickett received the nomination of the Democratic party as a candidate for governor and was elected to the office by a large majority of the voters. He was inaugurated on January 11, 1917.

In his inaugural address Bickett advocated forty-three measures he wished to see adopted by the legislature, and of these, thirty-five were adopted by the next Assembly. One of the main aims of his administration was to transform tenants into landlords. It was his belief that one who owned land was a more avid defender of freedom than those who merely rented. The children of the state materially benefitted from Bickett's proposals such as: the establishment of a juvenile court system; the strengthening of the child labor law; the provision of greater services by the county and state health departments; the provision of the six-month school term; the inclusion of home economics, manual training, and agriculture in the public school curriculum; and the raising of the compulsory school age to fourteen. Bickett received the nickname, "the pardoning governor," because he regularly visited the prisons to examine the cases of prisoners who might have a rightful claim to the exercise of executive clemency. The rural areas of the state were greatly aided by legislation encouraging the creation of credit unions, an act which brought an end to the crop lien system which had kept the farmers of the state in perpetual debt. Bickett also led a personal crusade for the improvement of the tax system which resulted in a more equitable distribution of the burdens of government. He used his personal influence to encourage the Liberty Loan campaign during World War I and personally went to areas of the state to explain the federal draft regulations and reasons for American involvement in the war where these were misunderstood.

After his term in office ended, he associated himself with J. S. Manning and Garland S. Ferguson in the practice of law in Raleigh.

Governor Bickett was a Mason and a member of the Episcopal Church.

He married Fannie N. Yarborough, of Louisburg, on November 29, 1898. She was the daughter of Colonel William M. Yarborough. Three children were born of this union.

Bickett died on December 28, 1921 and is buried in Louisburg.

A portrait of Governor Bickett is owned by the State of North Carolina and hangs in Raleigh.

For additional information concerning Thomas W. Bickett, see: *Public Letters and Papers of Thomas Walter Bickett*, edited by R. B. House.

William K. Boyd

William Kenneth Boyd was born at Curryville, Missouri, on January 10, 1879. He was the son of Harvey Marshall Boyd and his wife, Mary Elizabeth Black.

His family moved to western North Carolina while he was yet a boy and it was here that he received his elementary education. When he reached college age he entered Weaver College at Weaverville, North Carolina, which he attended for two years. In 1895 he entered Trinity College (now Duke University) from which he was graduated two years later. He continued his studies at Trinity and in 1898 was awarded the Master of Arts degree.

From 1898 to 1900 Boyd served as master of history at Trinity Park School. He then spent one year studying at Columbia University before returning to Trinity and the position of adjunct professor of history. In 1902 he continued his studies at Columbia and having acquired an interest in the early church, he wrote his doctoral dissertation on "The Ecclesiastical Edicts of the Theodosian Code." He was a member of the editorial staff of the *Encyclopedia Britannica* during 1904-05. His next position was as instructor of history at Dartmouth College for one academic year. Columbia awarded Boyd the Ph.D. degree in 1906, after which he returned to Trinity as professor of history, a position in which he continued until his death. He also taught the first half of the 1927-28 school year at Harvard as visiting lecturer. He received the Harrison Fellowship for research at the University of Pennsylvania for 1921-22.

Dr. Boyd was aware that if history were to be accurately written and recorded, it was necessary to use the original records as source materials. To this end he collected, from his student days, Southern Americana for the University. At his death this collection contained over 25,000 books and pamphlets, 83,000 newspapers, and 300,000 manuscripts. The bulk of this material is contained in the George Washington Flowers Collection at Duke University, which was established by William Washington Flowers in memory of his father. During the last years of his life Boyd was able to concentrate on building up this collection and was so successful that at his death the collection was one of the most complete in its field.

Professor Boyd was one of the first to seek the establishment of a university press as one of the necessary agencies of the university. He wrote or edited a number of books. Among these are: editor, *The Autobiography of Brantley York*, 1910; editor, *Memoirs of W. W. Holden*, 1911; editor, *Military Reminiscences of Gen. Wm. R. Boggs, C.S.A.*, 1913; *History of North Carolina: the Federal Period, 1783-1860*, 1919; *The Story of Durham: City of the New South*, 1925; and editor, *William Byrd's Histories of the Dividing Line Betwixt Virginia and North Carolina, with Introduction and Notes*, 1929. He worked with others on several books: with J. G. de Roulhac Hamilton, *A Syllabus of North Carolina History*, 1913; with Robert P. Brooks, *A Selected Bibliography and Syllabus of the History of the South, 1584-1876*, 1918; and with Smith Burnham, *A History of the United States for Schools*, 1921. He contributed many articles and reviews to scholarly journals and for several years was a member of the editorial board of the *South Atlantic Quarterly*.

The Duke Art Association was organized by Boyd in 1930 and he served as its president until his death. From 1929 to 1933 he served as the first director of Duke libraries. In this capacity he worked long and hard to transform a college library into a university library.

Boyd was a member of the following organizations: the committee on intellectual cooperation between Duke University and the University of North Carolina, the North Carolina Historical Commission, Committee on Inter-Racial Relations, North Carolina Historical Monument Association, the American Historical Association, the Southern Historical Association, and the North Carolina State Literary and Historical Association. He was a member of the Phi Beta Kappa society. His political affiliation was with the Democratic party and his religious affiliation was with the Methodist Episcopal Church, South.

He was married on December 22, 1908, to Pat LeGrand of Rockingham, North Carolina. One daughter was born of this union, Mary Elizabeth. His first wife died and Boyd married Marion Colley of Washington, Georgia, on August 11, 1930.

He died on January 19, 1938, and is buried in Maplewood Cemetery, Durham, North Carolina.

For additional information concerning William K. Boyd, see: *Duke University Alumni Register*, XXIV (January, 1938) 11-13, and *The National Cyclopaedia of American Biography*, volume 28.

Eugene C. Branson

Eugene Cunningham Branson was born in Morehead City, North Carolina, on August 6, 1861. He was one of seven children born to a Methodist minister, Levi Branson, and his wife, Edith Cunningham.

There is little known about Eugene's preliminary education. In 1877 he entered Trinity College (now Duke University) from which he was graduated with an M.A. degree. He then entered Peabody College in Nashville, Tennessee, from which he received another M.A. degree.

Upon leaving college he took a position as principal of a high school in Raleigh. He stayed here only a short time before he moved to Wilson to teach in the public schools and later to serve as superintendent. In 1885 the first public school system in Georgia was established at Athens, and Branson was called to organize it and to become its first superintendent. After spending several years in this position he accepted an offer to become professor of pedagogy at the Normal and Industrial College at Milledgeville, Georgia. He stayed there only a short time before going to the State Normal College at Athens where he also filled the position of professor of pedagogy. In 1900, at the age of 39, he was elevated to the presidency of the Georgia State Normal College, a position which he held for twelve years.

In 1912 he stepped down from the presidency and became professor of rural economics and sociology. This was a completely new field, and Branson even had to coin the name—there was nothing in the nation like it. In his new position he began to study the people of Georgia and sought a way that the depressed economic conditions of the state and the South might be improved. Edward Kidder Graham, President of the University of North Carolina, invited Branson in 1914 to return to his native state and establish a program at the Chapel Hill institution like the one he had begun in Georgia. This offer was accepted. After he had been at the University five years, he was awarded a Kenan Professorship.

Branson was able to expand his idea at the University because of the greater facilities given him with which to work. One of his first programs after reaching Chapel Hill was the inauguration of a "Know Your Own State" movement, it being his belief that one who knew his state would have a greater pride in her possibilities. He stressed this idea in his classroom. Other vehicles for the conveyance of his theme were the North Carolina Club, the *University News Letter*, the Seminar Library of the Department of Rural Social Economics, and social and economic studies of North Carolina and the South.

At the first meeting of the North Carolina Club, Branson was elected president and Frank P. Graham was elected secretary. At subsequent meetings papers concerned with social, economic, and civic problems in North Carolina were read and discussed. The results of these were published annually in yearbooks and these were made available to interested citizens.

The *University News Letter* was a single sheet which was published weekly and consisted mainly of facts about county affairs. Its purpose was to acquaint the people of North

Carolina with the state's resources and problems. The esteem which it acquired is evidenced by the fact that its subscription list grew to over 18,000.

Branson and his staff made exhaustive studies of 61 North Carolina counties. These studies were made primarily for Governor McLean's commission on county government. This commission and the State Association of County Commissioners made many recommendations to the General Assembly based on the studies, many of which were enacted into law.

In addition to these time-consuming undertakings, Branson found time to publish a number of books, monographs, and articles in scholarly journals. His first books were textbooks for the public schools which he edited while at the Georgia State Normal College. *Farm Life Abroad* (1924) was perhaps his most extensive work.

Branson was a member of a great number of official boards and commissions, all of which had as their purpose some humanitarian goal. Before leaving the state he was the youngest member of the Watauga Club, a group of leading cultural and political figures in Raleigh. His religious affiliation was with the Presbyterian Church.

He was married on September 27, 1889, to Lottie Lanier, of West Point, Georgia. Four children were born of this marriage: Frank Lanier Branson, Edith Lanier Branson, Phillip Lanier Branson, and Elizabeth Lanier Branson.

He died March 3, 1933, and is buried in the old Chapel Hill Cemetery.

For additional information concerning Eugene C. Branson, see: *Eugene Cunningham Branson, Humanitarian,* by Lanier Branson, and *The Kenan Professorships,* edited by A. C. Howell.

A portrait of E. C. Branson is owned by the Branson family.

4

Eugene C. Brooks

Eugene Clyde Brooks was born in Greene County, North Carolina, December 3, 1871. He was the son of Edward Jones Brooks and his wife, Martha Eleanor Brooks.

After attending a private school conducted on his father's farm, Brooks later attended the Phillips Public School and the Bethel Academy. In September, 1890, he entered Trinity College, now Duke University, from which he was graduated in 1894 with an A.B. degree and a Phi Beta Kappa key.

Upon leaving Trinity, Brooks took a job in Washington, D. C., as a correspondent for the Raleigh *News and Observer.* He left Washington to work with the Wilson, North Carolina, *Mirror,* but returned after only a very short period when he received an appointment as a clerk in the Treasury Department.

In 1897 he again returned to his native state and took a teaching position in Kernersville, Forsyth County. Before becoming superintendent of the Monroe schools in June, 1900, he served for short periods as principal of the Ormondsville School in Pitt County and the Kinston graded schools.

In the summer of 1902 he became involved with education on a state-wide basis when he was appointed secretary of the Educational Campaign Committee which was composed of Governor Charles B. Aycock, Charles D. McIver, and James Y. Joyner.

Brooks was elected superintendent of the Goldsboro city schools in 1904 and remained in this position for three years. When Trinity College established a department of education in 1907, E. C. Brooks was chosen as its head. He remained at Trinity until 1919.

In 1906 Brooks founded the *North Carolina Journal of Education*, a magazine for teachers. He served as editor of the periodical until 1923. The name was later changed to *North Carolina Education.*

Brooks was appointed Superintendent of Public Instruction by Governor Thomas W. Bickett upon the resignation of James Y. Joyner. He assumed the office on January 1, 1919, and served until June 10, 1923. There were many important accomplishments to his credit in the field of education during this period. Some of the more important are: six-month school terms were begun; the state began furnishing transportation for rural students; the public laws were recodified; vocational education was begun under the provisions of the national Smith-Hughes Act; salary schedules for teachers, principals, and superintendents were inaugurated; the regulations for certification were strengthened; and the consolidation of schools was begun.

Brooks resigned as Superintendent in 1923 to become president of the North Carolina State College of Agriculture and Engineering, now North Carolina State University. He continued to head this institution until 1934, although in 1931 it was consolidated with the University of North Carolina and North Carolina College for Women to form the greater University of North Carolina, and his title was changed to vice president. Under his leadership the college expanded the scope of its services. Within the school of engineering, courses in construction, ceramics, mining, sanitary and aeronautical engineering were begun; a division of forestry was established within the school of agriculture; a program of college extension work was started; and a textile school, school of science and business, and a school of education were created.

He also was the author of a large number of published works, the most notable of which are: *Woodrow Wilson as President, the Story of Cotton and the Development of the Cotton States,* the *Story of Corn,* the *Life of Braxton Craven, Education for Democracy, Stories of South America,* and *Our Dual Government.* He also edited a volume of *North Carolina Poems.*

Eugene Brooks served as chairman of the governor's committee to study the needs of county government. He served as president of the North Carolina Teachers' Assembly, president of the Association of Southern Agricultural Workers, and president of the North Carolina College Conference. He was appointed by the American Historical Association to the committee of eight to rewrite the courses of history for the elementary schools in America. He served as state director of the National Education Association and on the North Carolina Park Commission. He was elected in 1948 to the North Carolina Educational Hall of Fame posthumously. He was a member of the Methodist Church.

On December 19, 1900, he married Ida Myrtle Sapp of Kernersville, North Carolina. Three children were born to them: Martha Eleanor, Eugene Clyde, and Sarah Vass.

Eugene Brooks died in Raleigh on October 18, 1947. He is buried in Maplewood Cemetery in Durham.

A portrait of Brooks is owned by North Carolina State University at Raleigh.

For additional information concerning Eugene Clyde Brooks, see: *Eugene Clyde Brooks—Educator and Public Servant,* by Willard B. Gatewood, Jr.

J. Melville Broughton

Joseph Melville Broughton was born in Raleigh, North Carolina, November 17, 1888, the son of J. M. Broughton and Sallie Harris Broughton.

As a boy Broughton attended the public schools of Raleigh. In 1906 he completed his pre-college education when he graduated from Hugh Morson Academy.

From Hugh Morson Academy Broughton went to Wake Forest College to begin work on a Bachelor of Arts degree, which he received in 1910. In addition to his academic work Melville Broughton was a member of the debate council, member of the college senate, president of the Y.M.C.A., assistant editor of the weekly and its athletic editor, president of the junior class, and editor of *The Student*, a college magazine. He also played right guard on the football team.

Broughton also studied law while at Wake Forest and was admitted to the bar in 1910. In 1912-13 he continued his legal education at Harvard Law School. Even though he was admitted to the bar in 1910, he did not begin practice for several years. After leaving Wake Forest, he was principal of Bunn High School in Franklin County for two years, and from this position, he became a staff reporter for the *Winston-Salem Journal* for a short time. Finally in 1914 he returned to Raleigh and began the practice of law.

In spite of his business and professional activities, Broughton found time to participate in the political affairs of his state and county. From 1922 to 1929 he was a member of the Raleigh School Board and was twice city attorney for Raleigh. He was elected in 1926, and re-elected in 1928, as state Senator from Wake County. In 1933 he was president of the Wake County Bar Association, and in 1936 he was president of the North Carolina Bar Association. When the 1936 Democratic State Convention met, J. Melville Broughton was its keynote speaker.

While serving in the Senate, Broughton made unsuccessful efforts to have the school term extended from six to eight months. He introduced and sponsored the Australian Ballot Act, which received the approval of the General Assembly. He also served as chairman of the joint committee which drafted the Workmen's Compensation Act for North Carolina.

In the 1940 Democratic primary in North Carolina, Broughton received the largest number of votes of any of the seven candidates running for governor. He did not, however, receive enough votes to prevent a second primary. Lieutenant Governor Wilkins P. Horton, who was second in the primary, chose to withdraw—keeping Broughton from having to run a second time for the Democratic nomination. As in the past, the Republicans offered little opposition, and Broughton was elected governor in November, 1940.

The administration of Melville Broughton occurred during a difficult period. He had not been in office a full year when Pearl Harbor was attacked and the United States was forced to enter World War II as an active participant. In spite of the hardships imposed upon him as a war governor, Broughton did not abandon his programs designed for the betterment of the state. Some of the more important achievements of his administration were: the establishment of the Teachers' and State Employees' Retirement System of North Carolina; the enactment of legislation providing for a nine-month school term for the public schools of the state; and an act providing for the addition of the twelfth grade to the public schools. Also during his administration North Carolina became the first state in the South to give aid to public libraries, and a movement was launched for a broad medical care and hospital program for the state.

During the 1944 National Democratic Convention, Melville Broughton was nominated for the Vice Presidency. On the first ballot he ranked sixth among a field of sixteen.

On January 3, 1949, Broughton began a term as a United States Senator from North Carolina. He won his Senate seat in a heated campaign against an incumbent, William B. Umstead, who had previously been appointed to the position.

Broughton was a member of the Civitan Club, Masons, Junior Order, Modern Woodmen, and the Raleigh Elks Club. He served on the boards of trustees of Wake Forest College, the University of North Carolina, Shaw University, and the Olivia Raney Library of Raleigh. He was an outstanding Baptist layman and taught a men's Bible class for over a quarter century.

He was married to Alice Harper Willson, daughter of William W. Willson, on December 14, 1916. Four children were born to Melville and Alice Broughton. They are Alice Willson Broughton, Joseph Melville Broughton, Jr., Robert Bain Broughton, and Woodson Harris Broughton.

Senator Broughton died March 6, 1949, only two months after he had taken his seat as North Carolina's junior Senator, and is buried in Raleigh.

For additional information concerning Joseph Melville Broughton, see: *Addresses and Papers of Governor Joseph Melville Broughton, 1941-1945*, edited by David Leroy Corbitt.

Marion Butler

Marion Butler was born in Sampson County, about ten miles from Clinton, North Carolina, on May 20, 1863. He was the son of Wiley Butler and Romelia Ferrell.

Marion's mother was his chief source of educational instruction, and it was through her that he was prepared for college. He also attended Salem High School which was located in the community. At the age of eighteen he entered the University of North Carolina and was graduated four years later.

Around the middle of the 1880's a depression brought hard times to the farmers of the South. To help the financial conditions of those who depended upon agriculture for their livelihood, the Farmers' Alliance was organized. A local lodge was established and Butler was elected its president. He then purchased the *Clinton Caucasian*, a weekly newspaper, and threw the support of his paper behind the cause of the farmers. In 1891 he was chosen first vice president of the National Alliance; and in 1894, upon the death of Colonel L. L. Polk, he was chosen president of the national organization.

In 1890, at the age of 27, he was elected to the state senate. The issue of a state commission to control railroad freight rates and fares was the dominant issue in his cam-

paign and while in the senate he was instrumental in securing the passage of a bill which accomplished this. He was
also instrumental in the adoption of a bill establishing the
Normal and Industrial School for Women (now the University of North Carolina at Greensboro), a bill which
Charles D. McIver and Edwin Alderman had earlier sought.
There had been for many years a drive to cut off public
funds to the University. Butler led the fight against this
measure and he prevented its enactment.

The Farmers' Alliance during its early years sought to
accomplish its goals through the existing political parties.
The Alliance became very powerful and almost dominated
the Democratic party in the state. Differences existed, however, between the leaders of the Democratic party and the
leaders of the Alliance and these finally led to a split and
the formation of the People's party or Populist party. In
the election of 1894 the Populists and the Republicans established a fusion which gave them control of the state legislature. Butler, as state committee chairman, planned and
organized the fusion between the two parties. His reward
came when the legislature met and elected him and Jeter C.
Pritchard to the United States Senate.

As a member of the national Senate, Butler sponsored
legislation which created a system of free mail delivery
service in the rural areas of the nation. For these efforts he
has been called "the Father of Rural Free Delivery." When
Butler introduced this measure in the Senate it received
very unfavorable reaction, but after his explanation of how
it was to work and the benefits it would provide, Congress
appropriated $50,000 to test the system in a limited area.
These tests proved successful and the system was expanded
to the entire nation.

Butler, as a member of the Senate Naval Committee,
urged an appropriation for the building of submarines. His

proposal was opposed even by the Navy Department, but through his persistence an appropriation was made and the United States became the first nation in the world to build a modern submarine.

Butler was defeated for re-election to the Senate by F. M. Simmons of New Bern in one of North Carolina's most memorable elections. In this election the Democrats regained power in the state and shortly thereafter the Populist party faded from existence. In 1904 Butler affiliated with the Republican party and served as a delegate to the Republican National Conventions of 1912, 1916, 1920 and 1924.

While serving in the United States Senate, Butler completed the law course at the University of North Carolina which had been interrupted years before by the death of his father and was admitted to the Bar in 1899. After his defeat for re-election to the Senate, he entered into the practice of law and remained in this profession until his death.

Butler was a member of the Board of Trustees of the University of North Carolina and served on the executive committee. His religious affiliation was with the Episcopal Church.

He was married on August 31, 1893, to Florence Faison. Five children were born of this marriage; Mrs. Huntington Cairns, Mrs. Thomas D. Woodson, Marion, Jr., Wiley, and Edward.

He died June 3, 1938, in Washington, D. C., and is buried in Clinton, North Carolina.

A portrait of Butler is owned by the University of North Carolina and hangs in Chapel Hill.

For additional information concerning Marion Butler, see: *Biographical History of North Carolina,* volume 8, edited by S. A. Ashe and *The New Carolina Magazine,* March, 1921, published by the University of North Carolina.

Joseph P. Caldwell

Joseph Pearson Caldwell was born in Statesville, North Carolina, on June 16, 1853. He was the son of Joseph P. Caldwell, a lawyer, and Amanda McCullock Caldwell.

The elder Caldwell died when his son was only two weeks old. Because of this and the difficulties brought on by the Civil War, young Caldwell's educational opportunities were limited. Most of his training was the result of the teaching of his sister, Janie Caldwell, and a little time spent in night school.

At the age of fourteen he went to work for the *Iredell Express*, the first newspaper published in Iredell County. It was in the office of this newspaper that he learned the mechanical aspects of publishing a newspaper. He was to remain a newspaperman for the rest of his life. In the latter part of the 1860's he was hired by Colonel Charles R. Jones as a printer for the *Statesville Intelligencer*, a weekly. While working with the *Intelligencer* he began writing for the newspaper as well as doing mechanical work. During the day he would do his mechanical chores and at night he would write the local news.

A few years later Colonel Johnstone Jones, publisher of the *Charlotte Observer*, offered Caldwell a position as a reporter for that paper. He accepted the offer and went to

Charlotte in November, 1872. This being a daily, he was given a greater opportunity to develop his writing skills. Caldwell soon gained recognition as a capable newspaperman and in 1875 was offered a job with the *Wilmington Star*, which he intended to accept, until he was persuaded to remain with the *Observer*. The next year he went to Raleigh where he assumed the position of city editor of the *Raleigh News*. He remained in the Capital City only one year and then returned to Charlotte and the *Observer*. His year in Raleigh proved beneficial if for no reason other than the opportunity it gave him to meet some of the more important men of the state. On his return to the *Observer* Caldwell was made assistant editorial writer.

In January, 1880, he returned to Iredell County and purchased *The Landmark*, a weekly journal which had been established as the successor of the *Intelligencer*. He worked in his native city for twelve years and built *The Landmark* into one of the leading papers in the state. During this period he ventured into the active political arena for a short time. In 1886 he was elected mayor of Statesville by the board of aldermen to fill an unexpired term and upon completion of this term was elected to a two-year term. While he was mayor Statesville's first sidewalk paving was laid and its first electric lights installed. This was the only elected office he ever held.

In January, 1892, Caldwell and D. A. Tompkins entered into a partnership and purchased *The Chronicle*, the morning daily newspaper in Charlotte which had been established as the successor of the *Observer*. Only a short time after assuming control of the paper Caldwell changed the name back to the *Observer*. For about eighteen years he edited and published the *Observer* and during this time built it into the leading daily in North Carolina. As the head of the paper he assumed full control over it and supervised its operation from the gathering of the news, through the printing of the paper, and to its delivery to the readers.

As an editor, Caldwell understood the necessity for freedom of the press. His boldness in asserting this principle is perhaps best shown in his stand on the silver question. The popular view in North Carolina favored the free coinage of silver, but Caldwell did not hold this belief. His feelings were so strong that when the Democratic party chose as its candidate for president William Jennings Bryan, who stood for the free coinage of silver, Caldwell refused to support him. This caused many people in the state, many friends included, to accuse him of deserting the Democratic party and turning to the Republican party. In spite of these accusations, he refused to alter his position.

Caldwell served as a member of the board of directors of the State Hospital in Morganton and for a number of years was president of the board. He served as a member of the State Democratic Committee and in 1892 was elected as a delegate to the National Democratic Convention, serving as chairman of the delegation. He also served as president of the North Carolina Press Association.

He was married on June 14, 1877, to Margaret Spratt. Three children were born of this marriage: Mrs. D. H. McCollough, Mrs. Julia A. Taliaferro, and Frank Caldwell. His first wife died in 1893 and Caldwell married Addie Williams on January 4, 1908. One daughter, Adelaide, was born of this marriage.

He died November 22, 1911, and is buried in Oakwood Cemetery in Statesville, North Carolina.

A portrait of J. P. Caldwell is owned by the Museum of History in Raleigh.

For additional information concerning Joseph P. Caldwell, see: *Joseph Pearson Caldwell, 1853-1911*, by H. E. C. (Red Buck) Bryant.

5

Leslie H. Campbell

Leslie Hartwell Campbell was born at Buies Creek, North Carolina, on April 3, 1892, the son of James Archibald Campbell and Cornelia Frances Pearson Campbell. In January, 1887, James A. Campbell founded Buies Creek Academy, which grew into what is today Campbell College.

Leslie attended elementary and high school at the academy conducted by his parents. He was graduated in 1908. While in school at Buies Creek he participated in the work of the literary society and played on the baseball team as catcher.

In the fall of 1908 he entered Wake Forest College from which he was graduated three years later. At the same time he received his A.B. degree, so did his father and brother. His father had studied at Wake Forest two years before he started the academy at Buies Creek, but being unable to return had been allowed to work in absentia and thus qualify for his degree. Leslie's younger brother had entered Wake Forest at the same time he did and also finished in three years. During the summers Leslie attended summer schools and thus completed the requirements for a master's degree from Wake Forest.

After the commencement exercises at Wake Forest in 1911, Leslie returned to Buies Creek to join his father and brother. The financial status of the school was such that he did not receive a set salary, but simply told his father when he was in need of some money.

After teaching for several years Leslie decided to open a mercantile business in the community. He operated this until 1920, when he returned to the academy and teaching.

Leslie's father sold the educational institution he had founded to the Baptist State Convention for $28,000 in 1925. It was his feeling that this would be the best way to insure the continuation of the school. The following year the school was changed from an academy to Buie's Creek Junior College and Leslie was made dean of the college and his father became its president. Later in the year the school's name was changed again, to Campbell College. James A. Campbell remained president of the college until his death in 1934.

After the death of his father, Leslie Campbell was elected by the board of trustees of the school as its new head. His tenure as president began during the depression, and the college, like individuals, faced hard times. From his first year as president until 1937 the Baptist State Convention was unable to render any financial support to the institution. The college officials often allowed students to pay their fees with farm produce. At one point during the depression Campbell had to call the faculty together and explain that the school could no longer pay their regular salaries. Instead they would receive a percentage of whatever money the college received.

After the depression the financial condition of the college improved, but World War II shortly brought new problems for Campbell. As most of the younger men of college age were inducted into the armed forces, the student body of the college was made up mostly of girls. Then when the war ended, and many young men wanted to continue their education, the college did not have room for them to enroll.

Under Leslie Campbell's administration Campbell College grew from a small junior college with an enrollment of 312 to a fully accredited senior college with an enrollment of over 2,200. Its physical facilities increased to a value of $7,000,000 and its operating budget rose to over $2,700,000 annually. Campbell College changed from a junior college to a four-year institution in 1961. Five years later, in November of 1966, it received full regional accreditation. This was perhaps the greatest achievement in the college's history under the leadership of Leslie Campbell.

In 1967 Campbell gave up the reins as head of the school and shortly thereafter was named president emeritus by the board of trustees. The trustees also named a new science building on the campus in his honor.

Campbell served as vice president of the Baptist State Convention, as moderator of the Little River Baptist Association, as trustee of Pittman Hospital, and president of the Harnett County Centennial Association. He was also a member of the Harnett County Historical Society. His political affiliation was with the Democratic party and his religious affiliation was with the Baptist Church.

He was married in 1914 to Viola Haire and one son was born to this marriage: Arthur Hartwell. His first wife died in 1920 and in 1925 he married Ora Green. Four children were born to this marriage: Catherine McLean, Elizabeth Pearson, Ora Green, and James Archibald.

Leslie Campbell died on November 25, 1970.

A portrait of Leslie Campbell is owned by Campbell College and hangs on the campus at Buies Creek.

For additional information concerning Leslie Campbell, see: the *News and Observer*, Raleigh, North Carolina, September 12, 1954.

James W. Cannon

James William Cannon was born in Mecklenburg County, North Carolina, on April 25, 1852. He was the son of Joseph Allison Cannon and Eliza Long. His father was a farmer and as a young boy James worked on the family farm. He acquired the fundamentals of an education in a private school which was conducted in the Session House of Sugaw Creek Presbyterian Church in Mecklenburg County.

When the Civil War ended Cannon was thirteen years of age. He went to Charlotte where he found employment in a general store. The first six months he worked he received only bed and board for his labors, but after that he was given four dollars per month in addition to bed and board. At about the age of sixteen he moved to Concord, North Carolina, where he accepted a position as clerk in a general store which operated under the name of Cannon, Fetzer, and Wadsworth, of which his brother, D. F. Cannon, was one of the partners. Before he was twenty-one he was a member of the firm which did a large mercantile business and also engaged in cotton buying and banking.

During the two decades after the war the majority of the cotton manufacturing was conducted in the New England states. J. W. Cannon reasoned that the manufacturing should be carried on where the raw material was produced and so

in 1887, after becoming a very successful merchant, he
ventured into a new career. He went to New York, Philadelphia, and Boston and convinced businessmen there of
the soundness of his idea and soon had $75,000 to begin
construction of a mill. In 1888 the Cannon Manufacturing
Company's first mill began operation in Concord with 4,000
spindles producing cotton yarn. J. M. O'Dell was president
and J. W. Cannon was the secretary and treasurer.

From the beginning his textile business proved a success
and he soon started expanding, opening mills in Salisbury,
Albemarle, China Grove, and Mt. Pleasant. Later he moved
into other states—South Carolina, Georgia, and Alabama.

In 1898 Cannon made a survey of the textile industry
and observed that more people were beginning to use towels.
Previous to this time the wealthy used linen towels, but the
majority of the people used some type of cheap cloth or
flour sacks. In 1898 one of the Cannon Mills produced the
first towel ever finished in the South. In 1906 Cannon
decided to build a mill to manufacture towels exclusively
and purchased a 600-acre tract of land seven miles from
Concord on which to construct this new plant. This tract
of land became the site of Kannapolis. The decision to
manufacture towels proved to be a very wise one, and by
1914 his mills were turning out over 300,000 towels daily.
Six freight cars left his mills loaded with towels each night.

The decision to build a mill for the manufacture of towels
led to the creation of Kannapolis, one of the largest unin-
corporated towns in the world. Cannon built the town into
a model mill town. It was his desire that those dependent
upon his mills for their living should have access to religious,
educational, and recreational facilities. To achieve this
goal he built schools, churches, parks, dormitories for single
women workers, and other facilities for those employed by
him. In Kannapolis he founded the Y.M.C.A., which after

his death grew to be the largest Y.M.C.A. south of Washington, D. C.

At the time of Mr. Cannon's death, the Cannon Manufacturing Company and its affiliates were operating twelve mills, employing 15,000 persons, and had gross sales of over $40,000,000. This network of textile mills controlled 600,-000 spindles and 10,000 looms.

J. B. Sherill, publisher of the *Concord Tribune*, said this of J. W. Cannon:

"Truly it may be said of him that he had built up the waste places and had raised the foundations for many to dwell upon through the ages."

Cannon was a member of the Masonic order. In political matters he was an independent. His religious affiliation was with the First Presbyterian Church of Concord to which he donated a pipe organ.

He was married on November 24, 1875, to Mary Ella Bost, daughter of Martin Luther Bost. Ten children were born to this marriage: Joseph Franklin, Adelaide, Margaret, James William, Mary, Martin Luther, Eugene Thomas, James Ross, Charles Albert, and Laura.

He died December 19, 1921, and is buried in Oakwood Cemetery in Concord, North Carolina.

In 1926 Mr. Cannon's children endowed a chair in Biblical Literature at Davidson College in his honor. In 1935 a new high school in Kannapolis was named the J. W. Cannon High School.

A portrait of J. W. Cannon is owned by his youngest son, C. A. Cannon.

For additional information concerning James W. Cannon, see: *The National Cyclopaedia of American Biography*, volume XXXIII.

Julian S. Carr

Julian Shakespeare Carr was born in Chapel Hill, North Carolina, on October 12, 1845. He was the son of John Wesley Carr and Elizabeth Pannill Bullock.

Carr completed his elementary education at an Orange County boarding school. In 1862 he entered the University of North Carolina in his home town. Two years later he put aside his school books for the uniform of a private in the Confederate Army. When peace was restored, Carr returned to the University and completed his formal education.

In 1868 "Jule" left North Carolina and went to Little Rock, Arkansas, where he went into business with his uncle. Two years later, due to the urging of his father, he returned to his native state. His father had invested $4,000 into one-third interest of the tobacco enterprise of W. T. Blackwell and Company. Young Carr associated himself with the business and immediately assumed responsibility for the marketing and financial departments. When the company was incorporated, Carr became its president. Later he acquired Blackwell's interest in the company. In 1898 the Blackwell Durham Tobacco Company was acquired by the American Tobacco Company for nearly four million dollars.

As head of the marketing department of the W. T. Blackwell Company, Carr became one of the nation's first mass advertisers. The "Durham Bull" was in use before he became associated with Blackwell and his tobacco venture; but it was Julian Carr who made the symbol known throughout the world.

In addition to tobacco manufacturing, Julian Carr had interests in other areas of the business world. He organized Durham's first textile mill, the Durham Cotton Manufacturing Company. He started the Golden Belt Manufacturing Company which made the tobacco pouches for nearly all of the tobacco companies in the country. He built the Durham Hosiery Mills which had plants in five North Carolina towns. In 1887 he opened the First National Bank in Durham and later helped organize several other banks. He built the Claiborne and Carolina hotels in Durham. In cooperation with others he helped build the Durham-Roxboro Railroad. Together with George W. Watts and Eugene Morehead he organized the Durham Electric Lighting Company. Carr also had interests in several other concerns.

Business endeavors did not consume all of Julian Carr's time. He was a benefactor of many worthwhile causes, especially in the fields of education and religion. When Trinity College (now Duke University) was experiencing financial difficulty, Carr, in cooperation with J. W. Alspaugh and James A. Gray, came forward and undertook the operation of the college for three years without cost to the Methodist Church. At the end of this period, Carr further aided the finances of the college with a large donation. When Trinity moved from Randolph County to Durham, Julian Carr donated the grounds upon which the school located. Trinity College was not alone in receiving aid from Carr. The University of North Carolina, Wake Forest College, Davidson College, Elon College, St. Mary's Junior College, and the Baptist University for Women all looked upon Carr as a benefactor.

The Confederate veterans always received special attention from Carr, himself a veteran. He was elected president of the Confederate Veterans' Association of North Carolina. Upon the formation of the United Veterans' Association of the Confederate States, he was elected the major-general of the North Carolina Division and for this reason he was often referred to as General Carr.

General Carr took a Chinese youth, Charlie Soong, into his home and financed his education at Trinity College and Vanderbilt University. After the completion of his education, Charlie returned to China where he later became the head of one of the most powerful families. His three sons attained high positions and his three daughters became the wives of H. H. Kung, Sun Yat-sen, and Chiang Kai-shek.

Carr was a Mason of high degree. He served on the boards of trustees of the University of North Carolina, Trinity College and the North Carolina Colored Normal School. He was a delegate to the National Democratic Convention of 1900 and received thirteen votes for vice president of the United States. He was a member of the Methodist Church.

Julian Carr and Nannie Graham Parrish, the daughter of Colonel D. C. Parrish, were married on February 19, 1873. Six children were born to the couple: Eliza Morehead, wife of Henry Corwin Flower; Lallah Rooke, wife of William F. Patton; Julian S., Jr.; Albert Marvin; Claiborne McDowell; and Austin Heaton.

Carr died in May, 1924. He is buried in Maplewood Cemetery in Durham, North Carolina.

A portrait of Carr is owned by the University of North Carolina and hangs on the Chapel Hill campus.

For additional information concerning Julian Shakespeare Carr, see: *General Julian S. Carr—Greathearted Citizen*, edited by C. Sylvester Green; and *Biographical History of North Carolina*, volume 2, by Samuel A. Ashe.

Thurmond Chatham

Richard Thurmond Chatham was born in Elkin, North
Carolina, on August 16, 1896. He was the son of Hugh
Gwyn Chatham and Martha Thurmond. He was the grandson of Alexander Chatham, the founder of Chatham Manufacturing Company.

Thurmond attended the public schools and then entered
Woodberry Forest in Orange, Virginia. In 1915 he entered
the University of North Carolina, and the following year
attended Yale University. He left college to enter the Navy
as a seaman, second class, in 1917, upon the entrance of
the United States into World War I. He was honorably
discharged as an ensign in 1919.

After the war he began work in his father's textile mill
in Elkin. He held various positions, starting as worker and
advancing upward. In 1929 he took over the reins from
his father and became president of the business. Under his
guidance the enterprise grew into one of national prominence. The company had long had a reputation as a blanket
manufacturer. When his grandfather began the company,
in cooperation with his father-in-law, Thomas Lythe Gwyn,
they began the manufacture of woolen blankets on a part-
of-the-crop agreement with sheep farmers from the western
part of the state who had no market for their wool. This

continued to be and remains their number one product. They
have manufactured millions of these for the United States
government to be used by military personnel. Thurmond
saw the advantage of going into other areas and under his
supervision the company began the manufacture of a complete line of fabrics for the interiors of automobiles. With
his approval they also began the manufacture of a line of
material for men's suits. These expansions brought problems as well as advantages. Chatham was in large part
responsible for solving these. In 1945 he resigned as president of the company and was made chairman of the board
of directors. In 1955 he resigned from the latter position
and retired from active management of the company.

During World War II he again joined the Navy. An
office job in Washington was not to his liking and he volun-
tarily took a reduction in rank in order to get sea duty. He
served as damage control officer aboard the U.S.S. *Phoenix*
and saw action first in the European Theater at Casablanca
and later in the Pacific Theater from Guadalcanal to Leyte
Gulf. Before the war's end he attained the rank of Commander in the United States Naval Reserve, and after the
war remained in the Reserve and was promoted to Captain
in 1954. During the war he was awarded a number of
medals including: the Bronze Star Medal, the Secretary of
the Navy's Commendation Medal, the American, European,
and Asiatic Theater Ribbons with three battle stars, and
the Royal Order of Nassau with Swords from the Dutch
Government. His interest in the military continued and he
founded a magazine, *Army and Navy Bulletin* (later
Armed Forces), and operated it at a loss for five years.

In 1946 Chatham decided to seek a seat in the United
States House of Representatives. He entered the race for
the Fifth Congressional District seat against incumbent John
Folger. Chatham led Folger in the first primary election

for the Democratic nomination, but lost in a second primary. Two years later he received the nomination and won election to the position.

In addition to his other pursuits, Chatham developed Klondike Farm near Elkin where he built up a herd of about 200 purebred Guernseys. In connection with his interest in agriculture he served as president of the North Carolina Dairymen's Association and was a member of the National Grange and the Farm Bureau.

He contributed to a number of charities, but his two favorites were the Hugh Chatham Memorial Hospital at Elkin and the North Carolina Archaeological Society. The hospital is named for his father.

He was a member of the State Board of Conservation and Development, the board of trustees of the University of North Carolina, the National Association of Manufacturers, the National Association of Wool Manufacturers, the American Legion, and the Veterans of Foreign War. His political affiliation was with the Democratic party and his religious affiliation was with the Methodist Church.

Chatham was married on October 28, 1919, to Lucy Hodgin Hanes. Two sons were born to this marriage: Hugh Gwyn II and Richard Thurmond, Jr. After his first wife's death he married Mrs. Patricia Firestone Coyner, on November 16, 1950. One son was born to this marriage: Walter Firestone.

He died February 5, 1957, and is buried in Salem Cemetery in Winston-Salem, North Carolina.

For additional information concerning Thurmond Chatham, see: *Chatham Blanketeer*, February 11, 1957, and the *News and Observer*, Raleigh, North Carolina, January 14, 1951.

R. Gregg Cherry

Robert Gregg Cherry was born at Catawba Junction, York County, South Carolina, October 17, 1891. He was the son of Chancellor Lafayette Cherry and Harriet Davis Cherry. Gregg's parents died while he was still a child and he was taken to the home of his uncle, Henry M. Lineberger. Shortly after Gregg Cherry began living with the Lineberger family, they moved to Gastonia and Gregg continued to live with them until adulthood.

Gregg attended the public schools of Gastonia and was graduated from high school there in 1908. In this same year he entered Trinity College (now Duke University) and thus began his six years of college education.

While he was at Trinity, he was an outstanding basketball player and was captain of the team.

Cherry completed the regular undergraduate program at Trinity in 1912 and remained for two more years to take a law degree. He returned to Gastonia, where he had grown up, to begin his practice of law.

In 1917, before Cherry was even well established in his law practice, war was declared and the United States entered World War I. A group of Gaston County men, later designated as Company A, 113th Field Artillery, Thirtieth Division, was organized by Gregg Cherry. He continued his interest in military affairs and served as Major in the state National Guard.

While Cherry was still in Europe during World War I, some of the citizens of Gastonia, without his knowledge, placed his name on the ballot as a candidate for mayor of that city. He returned home about a month before he was elected to that position and was re-elected in 1921 to a second term. This was the beginning of Cherry's political career.

In 1931, 1933, 1935, 1937, and 1939, Gregg Cherry served Gaston County as its representative in the General Assembly. In 1937 he was elected Speaker of the House of Representatives. It was while serving as Speaker that Cherry received the nickname the "Iron Major." In 1941 and 1943 Cherry served in the State Senate. From 1937 to 1940 he served as chairman of the State Democratic Executive Committee.

When the 1944 Democratic Primary was over, Robert Gregg Cherry had received his party's nomination for governor of North Carolina. In November the Republicans offered little opposition, and R. Gregg Cherry was elected governor of North Carolina. At the time of his election he was fifty-three years old and the first governor to be elected from Gaston County. He was inaugurated January 4, 1945.

Cherry's administration was carried out during a most difficult period in the state's history. It was begun while the United States was still engaged in World War II and ended before the country had completely readjusted to a peacetime economy. Because of these difficulties there was a shortage in machinery, materials, and personnel. In spite of these hardships Governor Cherry had a long list of achievements by the end of his administration. Among the more important are: the mental hospitals of the state were expanded; a pay increase for state employees (including teachers) was granted; expenditures for the public schools were increased; and a road improvement program was carried out. In the mental health field the most important single step was the acquisition of Camp Butner and the establishment of a mental hospital. This allowed over one thousand patients not previously cared for to receive treatment. In education expenditures were increased from $38 million in 1945 to $60 million in 1948. Four thousand miles of hard surface roads were added to the eleven thousand built in the previous twenty-four years.

After his term as governor, Cherry returned to Gastonia and his law practice.

Gregg Cherry was a member of the Masons, the Elks, Knights of Pythias, Red Men, Odd Fellows, Junior Order, and of the American Legion. He served as State Chancellor of the Knights of Pythias and as State Commander of the North Carolina Department of the American Legion. He was a member of the Board of Stewards of Main Street Methodist Church of Gastonia.

In 1921 Gregg Cherry married Mildred Stafford. She was the daughter of E. J. Stafford, the mayor of Greensboro. They had no children.

R. Gregg Cherry died June 25, 1957. He is buried in his hometown of Gastonia, North Carolina. A portrait of Governor Cherry was presented to the State of North Carolina in December, 1959, by some of his relatives.

For additional information concerning Robert Gregg Cherry, see: *Addresses and Papers of Governor Robert Gregg Cherry, 1945-1949*, edited by David Leroy Corbitt; his private papers can be found in the North Carolina Department of Archives and History.

Joseph B. Cheshire

Joseph Blount Cheshire was born in Tarboro, North Carolina, March 27, 1850, the son of Joseph Blount and Elizabeth Parker Cheshire.

Joseph Cheshire began attending the Tarboro Male Academy at the age of nine. Early in 1866 he left his native state and went to Hartford, Connecticut, where he entered Trinity College. He studied at Trinity for three and one half years, graduating in June, 1869.

In the fall of 1869 Cheshire took a position teaching Latin and Greek at St. Clement's Hall in Ellicott City, Maryland. He remained here until June, 1871, when he returned to North Carolina and began reading law in Hillsboro under William K. Ruffin. He was licensed to practice law in January, 1872.

After practicing law about four years, in 1876 Cheshire took a step he had been contemplating for some time, and presented himself and was accepted as a candidate for Holy Orders. He took and passed his examinations for the diaconate in September of 1877. The following April he was ordained deacon.

Cheshire served his diaconate in Chapel Hill. While serving here he established the church of St. Phillip the Deacon in Durham. On May 30, 1880, he was ordained priest and the next year was called to St. Peter's Church in Charlotte, which call he accepted at the direction of his Bishop.

While serving as rector of St. Peter's, Cheshire did not confine his activities to that church alone. He found many worthwhile projects had been begun by the previous rector, but not carried to conclusion. One of these was the St. Peter's Home and Hospital. Through the direction of Cheshire, this institution was strengthened and elevated to a level of usefulness to the community. In addition he helped establish the Good Samaritan Hospital for Negroes and the Thompson Orphanage. Seeing the need for a place of worship in the Negro community, he started St. Michael and All Angels Mission. He also developed three other missions: St. Martin's at Charlotte, St. Paul's at Monroe, and St. Mark's in Long Creek Township in Mecklenburg County. In the diocesan convention of 1883, held at St. Peter's, the question of dividing the state into two dioceses was raised. Cheshire supported this motion and was instrumental in seeing it through.

In 1893 Cheshire was chosen Bishop Co-adjutor to aid Bishop Theodore Lyman who was in poor health. A few months later he became Bishop upon the death of Lyman. He continued in this position until his death. He was the first bishop of the Diocese of North Carolina who was a native of the state.

Perhaps the most outstanding acquisition of the church during Cheshire's period as Bishop was that of St. Mary's School in Raleigh. The school had been founded in 1842 by Dr. Aldert Smedes and had been maintained by him and his son. In 1896 he announced that he could not continue to maintain the school. The church took the school into its custody and saw it grow into the largest Protestant Episcopal school for girls in America.

As he had done as rector at St. Peter's, Bishop Cheshire

continued his interest in missionary work in the rural areas of the state and his interest in the welfare of the Negro race. The mission efforts in the mountain area of the state were so successful that a missionary jurisdiction was established and in 1898 a bishop was elected. Churches, hospitals and schools were built and strengthened among the Negroes.

Bishop Cheshire had a great interest in the history of his state and was noted as a historian. He wrote numerous pamphlets and articles for periodicals in addition to several books. His two better known books are: *The Church in the Confederate States: A History of the Protestant Episcopal Church in the Confederate States* and *Nonnulla: Memories, Stories, and Traditions, More or Less Authentic, About North Carolina.*

He was a member of the North Carolina Literary and Historical Association, the Society of the Cincinnati, and the board of trustees of the University of the South.

On December 17, 1874, Cheshire married Annie Huske Webb of Hillsboro. Six children were born to them: Elizabeth, Sarah, Joseph Blount, Annie, Godfrey, and James Webb. Mrs. Cheshire died in 1897, and the Bishop married Elizabeth Lansdale Mitchell of Beltsville, Maryland, two years later. They had no children.

Bishop Cheshire died in Charlotte, December 27, 1932. He is buried in the cemetery of Calvary Episcopal Church in Tarboro.

A life-size portrait of Cheshire is owned by St. Mary's School in Raleigh.

For additional information concerning Joseph Blount Cheshire, see: *Bishop Joseph Blount Cheshire—His Life and Work,* by Lawrence Foushee London. His private papers are located in the North Carolina Department of Archives and History.

Walter McK. Clark

Walter McKenzie Clark was born in Halifax County, North Carolina, on August 19, 1846. He was the son of David Clark, who served as a brigadier-general in the North Carolina militia during the Civil War, and his wife, Anna M. Thorne.

Clark received his first formal education at a school in Granville County taught by Ralph Graves. In the fall of 1860 he entered Tew's Military Academy in Hillsboro where he was enrolled when the fighting between the North and South began. Upon the request of Governor Ellis that a cadet be chosen from the academy to drill troops near Raleigh, young Clark, only fourteen years of age, was chosen. When the troops left to join the Army of Northern Virginia, their young drill-master went with them. He resigned from the army in 1863 and entered the University of North Carolina that autumn. Taking both the junior and senior courses in one year, he was graduated in 1864 at the head of his class. In spite of his heavy course load, he managed to undertake some law study under Judge William H. Battle. The day after he left the University he reentered the military and three months later was elected Lieutenant Colonel of the 70th North Carolina Regiment, and being only seventeen years of age he was the youngest officer of that rank in either the Confederate or Union armies.

After the war he went to New York City and continued his law study in a law office there. He did further work in the field of law at Columbian University (now George Washington University) Law School. In 1868 he was admitted to the bar and returned to Halifax County to begin practice. In November of 1873 he moved to Raleigh.

In 1885 Clark was appointed to the Superior Court bench and the following year was elected to the same position. In 1889 a vacancy was created on the Supreme Court bench and Governor Fowle appointed Clark to the state's highest court. The next year he was elected to fill out the unexpired term. Unanimously, he won election to a full eight-year term in 1894 after receiving the nomination of the Democratic party and the endorsement of both the Populist and Republican parties. In 1902 Clark was elected Chief Justice of the Supreme Court and was re-elected to this post twice, serving the state in this capacity until his death. During his thirty-five years on the Supreme Court, he wrote over 3,200 opinions.

Judge Clark was not only an outstanding Supreme Court Justice, but an outstanding legal scholar. He annotated 164 volumes of the North Carolina Reports. He published an *Annotated Code of Civil Procedure*, which went through three editions.

Legal matters were not the sole concern of Clark; he also possessed a keen interest in the history of his native state. In 1892 Governor Carr requested him to undertake the monumental task of compiling the *State Records*. He accepted and prepared sixteen volumes of this standard North Carolina historical work. At the request of the Confederate Veterans' Association he compiled a five-volume work entitled, *Histories of the Several Regiments and Battalions From North Carolina in the Great War 1861-'65*. In the process of obtaining the data for the latter work he wrote over 4,000 letters. It took over twelve years to complete these two works and Clark received no compensation for the time and effort which he put into them. He translated Constant's *Life of Napoleon* from French into English, a three-volume work. He was also the author of a number of articles of an historical nature in scholarly journals and magazines.

Until 1893 North Carolina was the only one of the thirteen original states which did not have a motto. In that year Judge Clark selected "Esse Quam Videri," and drew the bill which was passed in the Legislature adopting this as the official motto of North Carolina.

Clark was a very active member of the Methodist Church. In 1881 he represented the church as a lay delegate from the North Carolina Conference to the Methodist Ecumenical Council in London. In 1890 he was a delegate to the Methodist General Conference in St. Louis and in 1894 represented the state at the General Conference at Memphis. His political affiliation was with the Democratic party.

He was married on January 28, 1875, to Susan Washington Graham, the daughter of William A. Graham, governor of North Carolina, United States Senator and Secretary of the Navy. Eight children were born to this marriage.

He died May 20, 1924, and is buried in Raleigh.

A portrait of Judge Clark is owned by the State of North Carolina and hangs in the Supreme Court Building in Raleigh.

For additional information concerning Walter Clark, see: *Walter Clark—Fighting Judge*, by Aubrey Lee Brooks and *The Papers of Walter Clark*, 3 volumes, edited by Aubrey Lee Brooks and Hugh Talmage Lefler.

Albert Coates

Albert Coates was born in Johnston County, North Carolina, on August 25, 1896. He was one of nine children born to Daniel Miller Coates and his wife, Nancy Lassiter.

After graduating from Smithfield High School in 1913, he went to work in the Bank of Smithfield. The president of the bank offered him annual unsecured loans of $100 to help finance a college education, an offer which he accepted. He entered the University of North Carolina in 1914 and received his A.B. degree in 1918. While at the University he undertook a number of jobs, such as establishing his own pressing club, serving as secretary to President Edward K. Graham, and working in the dining hall to help meet his expenses. He also participated in student affairs, being elected president of the junior class and of the Athletic Association and winning many of the oratorical contests.

Upon graduation he enlisted in the Army and was commissioned a second lieutenant. At the end of World War I he returned to Chapel Hill and worked with alumni for two years raising funds to build the student union building, Graham Memorial.

In 1920 he entered the Harvard Law School, and received his degree in 1923. Coates had planned to return to Smithfield and practice law, but an offer to teach law at the University of North Carolina changed this. He thus assumed the duties of assistant professor of law in 1923, was made an associate professor in 1925, and a full professor in 1927.

Shortly after Coates began his career as a criminal law teacher, he realized that the law contained in the textbooks and the law practiced in the real arena were vastly different. With this awareness he joined a police force and began learning how the law actually operated. He went from town to town and county to county learning the procedures they used in the administration of justice. From this experience was born the idea of a school for public officials and law enforcement officers: a school where the most efficient methods, based on experience, could be taught. Thus came the idea for the Institute of Government.

The first "institute" was a three-day conference of law enforcement officers from across the state. It consisted of panel discussions and speakers from the National Police Academy and the F.B.I. This grew to a ten-day training school and began to draw attention outside North Carolina. The Institute expanded and clerks of court, firemen, judges, coroners, city councilmen, county commissioners, and other public officials came to the Institute for special sessions. State Highway Patrolmen and Wildlife Protectors began receiving their training here. The location for these activities was Chapel Hill where Coates was teaching law at the University. Business leaders in the state saw the value of the Institute and in the 1930's began making donations for its support. The University of North Carolina finally, in 1942, recognized it as one of its divisions and began contributing to its support. An adequate building had been a constant problem until the early 1950's when the Knapp Foundation gave a half-million dollars which was matched by the General Assembly for construction of the Joseph Palmer Knapp building. Albert Coates resigned as director of the Institute in 1962, but the work he started goes forward at a fast pace. In addition to training public officials, it publishes numerous handbooks and pamphlets for the guidance of these officials.

The establishment of the Institute of Government was accomplished through the personal sacrifices of Coates and his wife. He used his income derived from teaching to meet the expenses of the Institute. During the depression they moved from a house and lived in a rented room for three years. Their telephone and lights were cut off because of their inability to pay the bills. After their grocery bill got too high, two friends in the restaurant business allowed them to eat on a credit which never ran out. These privations kept the Institute alive.

In 1967 Coates received a North Carolina Award. In the presentation of this award it was said: "Today the work [of the Institute] goes on apace, under dedicated men trained by the founder, not only in county and city government, but at the state capital. . . . There is nothing like it in the history of American government, and the ideas and ideals and dreams of Albert Coates are among the foremost of precious gifts that North Carolina has been able to offer her emulating sister states in the American union."

Coates was the recipient of the O. Max Gardner Award in 1952. He is a member of the North Carolina Bar Association and the Order of the Coif. His political affiliation is with the Democratic party and his religious affiliation is with the Methodist Church.

He was married June 23, 1928, to Gladys J. Hall, the daughter of William A. Hall of Portsmouth, Virginia. Dr. Coates makes his home in Chapel Hill, N. C.

For additional information concerning Albert Coates, see: *The Chapel Hill Weekly*, September 2, 1962.

7

Norman Atwater Cocke

Norman Atwater Cocke was born on November 20, 1884, in Prince George County, Virginia. His parents were John J. and Sara Atwater Cocke.

He was educated in the local schools of Prince George County and completed his preparatory studies at Petersburg Academy, in Petersburg, Virginia. In 1905 he was graduated from New York Law School in New York City. In 1906 he was admitted to the bars for the practice of law in New York, South Carolina and North Carolina.

Cocke began private practice in New York but quickly left that state to join the fledgling utility industry in North Carolina as an attorney with Duke Power Company.

At that time, the utility was known as the Southern Power Company, and it was just beginning to become a factor in the growth of the Piedmont area of the Carolinas. Cocke served the company for more than fifty years and had a profound influence on the social and economic welfare of the region.

He quickly became closely associated with James B. Duke, whose name the company bears, and shared Duke's dream of extensive industrial development along the Catawba River Valley in central North Carolina.

When Cocke joined the power company, the Catawba River

Valley was predominately agricultural. As a student of agriculture and of land management and conservation, he conceived and directed the company's extensive forestry and land management program. In little more than thirty years, Duke Power Company and its wholly-owned subsidiary, Crescent Land and Timber Corporation, planted more than thirty-eight million trees on the company's watershed lands. Furthermore, the company now has more than two hundred and seventy thousand acres of timberland under scientific forest management.

In 1927, Cocke became vice president of Duke Power Company and on October 27, 1949, he was selected to succeed E. C. Marshall to its presidency, a position he held until his retirement from active service on January 1, 1959. Under his direction, Duke Power Company grew enormously; and it was largely through his efforts that the company has become one of the nation's leading producers of electric power.

Besides sharing Duke's dream of extensive industrial development of the Catawba River Valley and the Piedmont region of the Carolinas, Cocke also secured the confidence and respect of James B. Duke. In 1925, Duke appointed Cocke as one of the original trustees of the Duke Endowment. As a trustee and later as vice chairman and chairman of the board of trustees of the Endowment, he played a large role in the work of the Endowment, which has meant so much to educational institutions, hospitals, orphanages and churches of the region. He is today the sole surviving member of the original board, and serves as its honorary chairman.

Despite his necessary preoccupation with the management of a large, far-flung business and many smaller ones, Cocke found time to become a champion of education in both Carolinas. He served Duke University in many capacities, including that of chairman of the board of trustees for six years. He also served as trustee of Converse College and as trustee and later chairman of the John Motley Morehead Foundation, which is largely interested in academic scholarships.

When the four major power companies in the two Carolinas and Virginia organized the Carolinas-Virginia Nuclear Power Associates in 1956 for the purpose of constructing the first nuclear fuel generating plant in the Southeast, Cooke became its first president as well as a member of its board of directors. About the same time he was elected to the board of directors of the Edison Electric Institute.

Cocke has been a director of Duke Power Company and of the Piedmont and Northern Railway since 1927. Widely recognized for his contributions to textile and other industrial development in the Piedmont Carolinas, he served as officer or director of seventeen companies affiliated with the Duke system, as well as other enterprises, during his active career.

In 1951 he received the degree of Doctor of Industry from Clemson University. In addition, he has been honored with doctorate degrees from Davidson College, Furman University and Duke University.

In 1959 he was selected "Citizen of the Year" by the North Carolina Citizens Association, the highest civic honor in the Tar Heel State. Duke Power Company's largest power impoundment, Lake Norman, near Charlotte, North Carolina, is named in his honor.

He was married on November 28, 1911, to Mary Sommers Booth of Petersburg, Virginia. Their children are Norman Atwater, Jr., William Booth and John.

Norman Atwater Cocke, Sr. resides at 816 Harvard Place, Charlotte, North Carolina.

William C. Coker

William Chambers Coker was born in Hartsville, South Carolina, on October 24, 1872. He was the son of Major James Lide Coker and Susan Armstrong Stout. His father was founder of Coker College in Hartsville.

Coker received his first formal education in his home town and then entered South Carolina College (now the University of South Carolina) from which he was graduated in 1894. During his undergraduate days he was a member of the varsity tennis team and actively participated in the Euphradian Literary Society.

After graduation, Coker left his native state and moved to Wilmington, North Carolina, where he took a position in the Atlantic National Bank. Two years later he was made a vice-president, but next year he decided to abandon his banking career and entered Johns Hopkins University where he began a graduate program in botany. He was graduated with the Ph.D. degree in 1901 and his dissertation, "On the Gametophytes and Embryo of Taxodium," is considered a classic in the area of seed development. He completed a semester of further study in Strasburger's laboratory at Bonn-am Rhine, Germany.

In 1902 Dr. Coker accepted a position on the faculty of the University of North Carolina as Associate Professor of

Botany. He rendered active service to the University for forty-two years, thirty-six of which he was head of the Botany Department, retiring in 1945 as Kenan Research Professor of Botany, Emeritus. He was at one time the oldest member of the faculty. Under his leadership the Botany Department of the University acquired one of the largest and best herbaria in the South and one of the best botanical libraries in the nation.

As a scholar Dr. Coker was very productive, publishing several books and over one hundred articles on botanical subjects. His monograph on Saprolegniaceae appeared in 1923 as the first book published by the University of North Carolina Press. *The Trees of the Southeastern States,* written by Dr. Coker and H. R. Totten, proved to be a very popular book and went through several printings. He continued research on fungi over nearly a half century and the publication of his studies established for him the reputation as the foremost authority on the taxonomy of many groups of fungi and as the leading botanist in the South.

Dr. Coker served as editor of the *Journal of the Elisha Mitchell Scientific Society* for forty-one years. During this time he built it into one of the leading journals of its type and developed a world-wide circulation.

The beauty for which the Chapel Hill campus is so well known is due in large part to the foresight and work of Dr. Coker. He served as chairman of the University Buildings and Grounds Committee from its beginning in 1913 until 1942. In spite of the growth in the number of buildings of the University during these years, under his direction they remained uncrowded and were not by him considered completed until landscaped.

The eastern edge of the campus was a low, swampy cow pasture for over the first century of the University's history. Only a short time after Dr. Coker assumed his duties as associate professor, he had a vision of turning this area into a naturalistic garden. After gaining the permission of University authorities, he began work on what finally became known as the Coker Arboretum. In this arboretum are about 500 varieties of native and exotic trees, plants, and shrubs.

Dr. Coker had been on the faculty of the University about one year when he was invited to serve as chief of the botany staff on an expedition to the Bahamas for the Geographical Society of Baltimore. In 1927 he was honored by being elected chairman of the Mycological Section of the Botanical Society of America. He presented a paper on aquatic fungi before the Sixth International Plant Congress in 1935 in Amsterdam, Holland. He served as vice-president of the Mycological Section of the International Plant Congress in Stockholm, Sweden, in 1950. He also served from January, 1939, to December, 1941, as the first chairman of the Southeastern Section of the Botanical Society of America.

He was a member of the American Society of Naturalists and the Elisha Mitchell Scientific Society. He was a Fellow in the American Association for the Advancement of Science. His political affiliation was with the Democratic party.

He was married on October 28, 1934 to Louise Manning Venable, the daughter of University president, Francis P. Venable. Mrs. Coker gave $25,000 to double a fellowship fund set up by her husband and thus established the William Chambers Coker Fellowship in botany at the University of North Carolina. They had no children.

Coker College named their new science building, erected in 1951, in his honor.

Dr. Coker died June 27, 1953, and is buried in the Chapel Hill Cemetery. There is a portrait of Dr. Coker in Coker Hall, named for him, on the campus of the University.

For additional information concerning William Chambers Coker, see: *The Kenan Professorships*, by A. C. Howell.

Ceasar Cone

Ceasar Cone was born in Jonesboro, Tennessee, in 1859, the son of Herman Cone and his wife, Helen Guggenheimer. Ceasar attended the public schools until he reached the age of fourteen, at which age his formal education ceased.

Ceasar and his older brother, Moses, were connected with the family grocery business until it dissolved in 1890. It was through the business connections associated with this enterprise that they learned of the resources and opportunities which were to be found in the South. In the early 1890's these two brothers established the Cone Export and Commission Company, a business venture which put them in touch with the cotton manufacturing mills in North Carolina. Many of the largest textile mills in the South sold their products through the Cone Commission House. The Cones not only sold the products produced by the textile mills, but on many occasions also financed their operations and prevented many from going into bankruptcy during difficult times.

Ceasar Cone was quick to realize the advantages of setting up a manufacturing establishment in North Carolina. He chose Greensboro, North Carolina, as the best location because the cotton fields were nearby and the land was relatively inexpensive. He, with his brother, Moses, who

was associated with him in all his business dealings until
his death in 1908, purchased several hundred acres of land
near the city limits. In 1895 and 1896 they erected the
cotton mills of Proximity Manufacturing Company. Their
idea was to manufacture a type of cotton goods not manufactured in the South before—denim. They began with 240
looms and within ten years constructed another mill, White
Oak, which was many times larger than their first one. In
fact, White Oak was the largest cotton mill in the South
and the largest denim plant in the world. The two mills contained 3,600 looms, employed about 4,000 persons, used
over 30,000,000 pounds of cotton, and produced over 60,-
000,000 yards of cloth per year. They also acquired interests in a number of other textile manufacturing plants
and other type businesses.

As the fortune of Ceasar Cone increased, so did his feeling of responsibility toward those who made it possible—
his workers. Around the mills he built villages where the
workers could rent homes at a rental below comparable
housing elsewhere. He began a program of offering prizes
to those who excelled in keeping their homes neat and
improving them. Sanitation was a major concern and he
provided facilities for the villages not found in many towns
of that day. The mill graded the streets of the village and
planted trees and shrubs and took other steps to make the
surroundings of the employees more enjoyable. At the company's expense, Cone established a system of schools for
the children of his employees which ran from kindergarten
through high school. At this time the public schools of
the state often operated less than six months, but the schools
for the Cone mill operatives' children were open nine months.
Cone also employed trained nurses to take care of the sick
in the villages and built a model dairy to provide milk for
the workers and their families.

Ceasar Cone consulted with Charles D. McIver, president of the North Carolina State Normal and Industrial College (now the University of North Carolina at Greensboro), about what could be done to make the lives of his employees fuller and happier. After this consultation, Cone hired a graduate of the State Normal who had received special training in home economics to come to the mill villages and undertake a program of social welfare. She began an extensive program at Proximity aimed at bettering the lives of the residents. Cooking and sewing classes were begun for the women and girls and gardening clubs for boys and girls. The social life of the workers was promoted through parties and celebrations held on holidays such as Valentine, Easter, and Independence Day. Picnics, camp suppers and Mother-Daughter banquets were held. The social workers also promoted the establishment of community clubs whose aim was the undertaking of projects which would better the villages.

Mr. Cone served as president of the Greensboro Chamber of Commerce, president of the Central Carolina Fair Association, as vice president of the American Cotton Manufacturer's Association, and in leadership capacities in a number of other civic and professional organizations. His religious affiliation was Jewish.

He was married in 1894 to Jeanette Siegal and to this union were born three sons: Herman, Benjamin and Ceasar.

He died March 1, 1917, and is buried near White Oak mill in Greensboro, North Carolina.

For additional information concerning Ceasar Cone, see: *Biographical History of North Carolina*, Vol. 8, edited by S. A. Ashe and a special issue of the *American Wool and Cotton Reporter*, published shortly after his death.

R. D. W. Connor

Robert Digges Wimberly Connor was born in Wilson, North Carolina, on September 26, 1878, the son of Henry Groves Connor and Kate Whitfield.

Bob Connor was prepared for college in the public schools of Wilson and then entered the University of North Carolina from which he was graduated in 1899. He studied at Columbia University during the 1920-21 school year.

Upon leaving the University he had wanted to attend Johns Hopkins graduate school, but lack of financial resources prevented this. Instead, he took a teaching position in Winston, where he taught two years. The next two years he divided between serving as school superintendent in Oxford and principal of the Wilmington High School.

In 1904 he gained employment in the State Department of Public Instruction as secretary of the Educational Campaign Commission. In this position he was thrown in the midst of the struggle for better schools in North Carolina, a fight being led by Governor Charles B. Aycock. He wrote letters and newspaper articles, and made speeches seeking the support of the people for the cause of education

Partially as a result of his efforts, the State Literary and Historical Association in 1903 requested the legislature to establish a State Historical Commission for the purpose of collecting valuable documents pertaining to the history of the state. The request was granted and the commission appointed, with Connor as secretary. The General Assembly of 1907 revised the act creating the commission. The revision permitted the appointment of a full-time secretary, provided an annual appropriation of $5,000, and enlarged the powers and duties of the commisison. Connor was again chosen secretary, and served in that capacity until 1921. As head of the commission he built it into one of the most outstanding archival programs in the nation. At the time of his resignation the commission had saved thousands of documents of the Executive and Legislative Departments dating from the colonial period to the twentieth century, it had collected over 100,000 objects dealing with North Carolina's part in World War I, it had secured many private manuscript collections for the state, it had published eighteen books and twenty-seven bulletins, it had maintained the Hall of History, and it had encouraged the study of North Carolina history in the public schools.

Connor resigned his position with the commission in 1921 in order to accept a Kenan Professorship in history and government at the University of North Carolina. His capabilities as a teacher are demonstrated by the fact that he was repeatedly chosen by the students as one of their favorite professors. He succeeded Dr. J. G. deR. Hamilton as head of the Department of History and Government in 1928 and University President Frank P. Graham cited him as one of the co-builders of the department. He served until 1934.

The United States Congress passed a bill in 1932 establishing the National Archives. On the recommendation of leading historians and the Executive Committee of the American Historical Association, President Franklin D. Roosevelt appointed Connor the first Archivist of the U. S.

Connor left Washington in 1941 and returned to Chapel

Hill where he filled the position of Craige Professor of Jurisprudence and History until his retirement in 1949. His love for his alma mater is evidenced by his statement that he left "the world's greatest bughouse" so that he could return to "the world's greatest intellectual center."

The major portion of Connor's writings dealt with North Carolina history. Perhaps his most outstanding contribution in this field is his two-volume history of the state, *North Carolina, Rebuilding an Ancient Commonwealth, 1584-1925*, which was published in 1929. Other notable works are: *Cornelious Harnett, An Essay in North Carolina History; Race Elements in the White Population of North Carolina; Revolutionary Leaders of North Carolina; Ante-Bellum Builders of North Carolina;* and *The Life and Speeches of Charles Brantley Aycock,* compiled and written with Clarence Poe.

He was a member of the Board of Trustees of the University of North Carolina (1913-20), the North Carolina Teachers Assembly, the North Carolina Literary and Historical Association, General Alumni Association of the University of North Carolina, National Board for Historical Service, the American Historical Association, Society of American Archivists, and the Southern Political Science Association. His political affiliation was with the Democratic party and he was an Episcopalian.

He was married December 23, 1902, to Sadie Hanes, a fellow teacher he met while teaching in Winston. They had no children.

R. D. W. Conner died February 25, 1950. He is buried in the Chapel Hill Cemetery.

A portrait of R. D. W. Connor hangs in the National Archives in Washington, D. C.

For additional information concerning Robert D. W. Connor, see: *Keepers of the Past,* edited by Clifford L. Lord.

8

Josephus Daniels

Josephus Daniels was born in Washington, North Carolina, May 18, 1862. He was the son of Josephus and Mary Cleaves Seabrook Daniels.

Josephus acquired his first formal education, as did most other boys of that day, in a one-room schoolhouse. He later attended the Wilson Collegiate Institute, which had a nine-month school term. In 1885 he attended the Summer Law School at the University of North Carolina and was admitted to the Bar that same year, but never practiced.

It was while a student in Wilson, that Josephus entered into a field of endeavor which he would follow for most of the remainder of his life—journalism. At the age of sixteen, he and his younger brother, Charles, began an amateur newspaper, *The Cornucopia*. They published issues of their paper on a somewhat irrregular schedule. Also during his school days he was correspondent and subscription agent for the *Observer* and *Hale's Weekly*, both Raleigh newspapers. Young Daniels left school at eighteen and became local editor of the Wilson *Advance*. He purchased an interest in the paper and later became sole owner. In 1882 he and Charles established the Kinston *Free Press* and he became part owner of the Rocky Mount *Reporter*. Daniels purchased a controlling interest in the Raleigh *State Chroni-*

cle in October of 1885, and soon converted the then weekly paper into a daily. In spite of the fact that he was state printer from 1887-1893, the *Chronicle* continued to lose money.

In 1893 Josephus went to Washington, D. C., to serve as Chief of the Appointment Division of the Interior Department. He was soon promoted to Chief Clerk of the Department. While serving in this position in 1894 with the financial assistance of Julian S. Carr, he purchased the *News and Observer*, a Raleigh daily. When Daniels assumed management of the paper, it was a losing enterprise, but he breathed new life into it and made it the leading paper in the state. At the time he acquired the paper it had a circulation of only 2,500; before his death the circulation had grown to over 98,000. He continued in active management of the paper until his death.

Daniels was a lifelong Democrat and used his papers to support the candidates and platforms of his party. The *News and Observer* became a more potent Democratic organ under his management than under its previous editor. Because of his support of the party, he acquired a high standing in Democratic circles. From 1896 to 1916 he was a member of the Democratic National Committee from North Carolina. At the Democratic National Convention at Baltimore in 1912, Daniels played a key role in the nomination of Woodrow Wilson for president. As a result, he became Wilson's Secretary of the Navy, a position he filled during both of Wilson's terms in office.

The position of Secretary of the Navy proved to be a very important one, especially after the United States became engaged in World War I. Daniels had the Navy in a high degree of preparedness before war was officially declared, and on that occasion it took only five hours for complete mobilization. He compiled a distinguished list of achievements as head of the Navy. In 1921, at the end of Wilson's administration, Daniels returned to Raleigh and his duties as editor of the *News and Observer*.

Franklin D. Roosevelt was assistant Secretary of the Navy during most of the time that Daniels served as Secretary. When Roosevelt became President, he appointed Daniels to the post of Ambassador to Mexico. He served in this capacity from 1933 until 1941, when he resigned because of the failing health of his wife. He returned to Raleigh.

Daniels was the author of *The Life of Worth Bagley, The Navy and the Nation, Our Navy at War*, and the *Life of Woodrow Wilson*. In addition, he wrote a five-volume autobiography under the titles of *Tar Heel Editor, The Editor in Politics, The Wilson Era: Years of Peace, 1910-1917, The Wilson Era: Years of War and After, 1917-1923*, and *Shirt Sleeve Diplomat*.

He was a member of the North Carolina Press Association and the National Editorial Association. He served for many years on the Board of Trustees of the University of North Carolina. From his youth he was a Methodist.

On May 2, 1888, Josephus Daniels married Addie Worth Bagley, the daughter of William Henry Bagley, clerk of the state supreme court. Six children were born to the couple: Adelaide, Josephus, Worth Bagley, Jonathan Worth, Frank Arthur, and Addie.

Daniels died January 15, 1948, in Raleigh, North Carolina, and is buried in that city.

For additional information concerning Josephus Daniels, see: *The End of Innocence*, by Jonathan Worth Daniels; *Josephus Daniels says . . . An Editor's Political Odyssey from Bryan to Wilson to F. D. R., 1849-1913*, by Joseph L. Morrison; *Josephus Daniels . . . the Small-d Democrat*, by Joseph L. Morrison; *Josephus Daniels in Mexico*, by David Cronon; and his five-volume autobiography.

Wilburt C. Davison

Wilburt Cornell Davison was born on April 28, 1892 in
Grand Rapids, Michigan, the son of a Methodist minister,
William L. Davison. His mother was Mattie E. Cornell.

Davison received the Bachelor of Arts degree from Princeton in 1913, followed by study at Oxford University, England, as a Rhodes Scholar where he received three degrees:
A.B., 1915, B.Sc., 1916, and M.A., 1919. In 1915 he was
elected to a Senior Demyship at Magdalen College, Oxford,
which he held for two years. Returning to America, he was
given advanced standing in the medical school at Johns Hopkins where he was awarded the M.D. degree in 1917. Later
he was awarded a Doctor of Science degree from Wake
Forest College in 1932, and the Doctor of Laws degree from
the University of North Carolina in 1944 and from Duke
University in 1961.

During 1914, he served with the American Red Cross in
France and Serbia. From 1917 to 1919 he served with the
Army Medical Corps in the American Expeditionary Forces
in France and was discharged a captain.

Davison interned at Radcliffe Infirmary, Oxford, before
returning to Johns Hopkins, where he finished medical
school. He was a resident physician at Johns Hopkins Hos-

pital, Maryland, from 1919 to 1921, after which, he was associate professor, acting head of the department of pediatrics and assistant dean of Johns Hopkins University Medical School until 1927.

On January 21, 1927, Dr. Davison was chosen to head the School of Medicine at Duke University. Coming to Durham in September of 1927, he at once assumed the responsibility of organizing and building the new Duke University School of Medicine and Medical Center. As Dean of the Medical School, Chairman of the Duke University Medical Center, and James B. Duke professor of pediatrics until 1961, Dr. Davison established a medical school of international renown.

Sensitive to the public and hospital problem of financing hospital care, Dr. Davison was a proponent of methods of prepayment of such medical care, as early as 1928. As a result of his efforts, two of the earliest Blue Cross plans in the nation were established in North Carolina: one in 1932 and one in 1935. Moreover, his pioneer work contributed significantly to the development of the National Blue Cross program.

A man of tremendous energy, Davison has held a host of public service jobs including vice chairman of the National Research Council's Division of Medical Sciences and membership on the National Health Council. He has been a consultant to the United States Army Surgeon General, a member of the executive committee of the Association of American Medical Colleges, and a member of the Executive Reserve in the office of the Assistant Secretary of Defense.

He was named to Governor Luther Hodge's Nuclear Energy Advisory Committee to represent North Carolina in atomic energy development in the South.

He was a member of the Medical Advisory Committee of the North Carolina Hospital Board of Control, and of the Advisory Council of the North Carolina Board of Mental Health, vice president and a member of the board of directors of the Doris Duke Foundation, trustee for the Educational Council of Foreign Medical Graduates, and a member of the national advisory commission on Chronic Diseases and Health of the Aged.

Following his retirement as Dean of the Duke University Medical School in 1961, Davison was named a trustee of the Duke Endowment.

On top of these, and dozens of other activities at the national and state levels, Dr. Davison found time to write many scientific papers for professional journals, and his book, *The Complete Pediatrician,* is now in its eighth edition.

He was married on June 2, 1917 to Atala Thayer Scudder, and to them were born three children: William Townsend, Atala Jane Scudder, and Alexander Thayer.

Dr. Davison makes his home in Roaring Gap, North Carolina.

For additional information on Wilburt C. Davison, see: *North Carolina Lives,* by William Stevens Powell.

B. B. Dougherty

Blanford Barnard Dougherty was born in a log cabin on a small farm near Boone, North Carolina, on October 21, 1870. He was the son of Daniel Baker Dougherty, a blacksmith, and Ellen Bartlett, who died when he was about five years old.

Dougherty was reared in a section of the state that was known for a long time as the "Lost Provinces" of North Carolina. Opportunities for education in this area were few. He had reached his sixteenth birthday before he finished the sixth grade, and he had only eleven months of high school training, which were divided among three schools. He entered Wake Forest College in 1892, but remained only one year. The next year he attended Holly Springs College and the next two years he studied at Carson-Newman, both in Tennessee. He was graduated from Carson-Newman in 1896. In 1899 he entered the University of North Carolina and received the Ph.B. degree that same year. As a student Dougherty found it necessary to work to meet his expenses and served as principal of Globe Academy from 1893 to 1895 and as professor of Latin and Psychology at Holly Springs for the 1896-97 school year.

Upon leaving the University, Dougherty returned to his home county, Watauga, and took the position of superintendent of schools which he held for seventeen years. That same year he and his brother, D. D. Dougherty, built a two-room school, Watauga Academy, at Boone. Since the public schools operated only four months in the fall, closing at Christmas, the Dougherty school opened the first of the year and operated for the four months before early summer. They taught the first three grades.

The brothers soon realized that the money from tuition alone was inadequate for the support of the school, so in 1903 Blan Dougherty went to Raleigh to seek state aid for their school. A bill for this purpose passed the house, but the senate education committee returned an adverse report. When the bill came to the senate floor for approval or disapproval, the vote was a tie. Future governor and U. S. Senator Clyde R. Hoey was presiding and it was he who broke the tie in favor of state support for the school. In addition to a $2,000 a year appropriation the name of the school was changed to Appalachian Training School. Until 1921 it was the only state supported high school in northwestern North Carolina.

By 1925 the school had grown to include seven grades and its name was changed to Appalachian State Normal School. Four years later it became a four-year college and underwent another name change, this time to Appalachian State Teachers College, and Blan Dougherty became a college president.

The college continued to grow and in 1942 a graduate school was established. Before Dougherty's death around 5,000 degrees had been granted by the institution. The physical facilities were greatly increased and the faculty was approaching one hundred. A dream had come true.

While Appalachian was Dougherty's main interest, it was by no means his only interest. One of his most revolutionary ideas was the creation of a state equalization fund through which part of the tax money collected in the wealthier counties would be spent in the schools of the poorer counties. After a bitter struggle this idea won approval and each session of the legislature after 1927 increased the appropriation to the fund until the state undertook support of the public schools in 1933.

Dougherty was also a leader in demanding that the state issue teaching certificates which would be recognized throughout the state. Up until this time the county superintendents certified the teachers within their county and it took a major legislative battle to wrest this power from them.

Along with his belief that money spent on education in the state should not be disproportionate because of the wealth of the county, was a belief that teachers' salaries should be equalized. To this end he, as a member of the State Board of Education, shaped the teacher salary schedule to give the Negro teachers equal salary.

Although never acquiring great wealth, Dougherty was recognized as an outstanding businessman. He helped to establish a formula for the reopening and sustaining of failing banks during the depression years. In the late 1940's he became president of the Northwestern Bank, the seventh largest bank chain in the State.

He served on the State Board of Education, the State Textile Commission, the State Board of Equalization, and the State School Commission. His religious affiliation was with the Baptist church.

He never married.

Blan Dougherty died May 27, 1957, and is buried in the town cemetery of Boone, North Carolina.

For additional information concerning Dougherty, see: *Blanford Barnard Dougherty, A Man to Match His Mountains*, by O. Lester Brown.

Rufus A. Doughton

Rufus Alexander Doughton was born in Laurel Springs, Alleghany County, North Carolina, on January 10, 1857. He was the son of J. Horton Doughton, who served on the board of county commissioners and as chairman of the Inferior Court of Alleghany, and Rebecca Jones. He was the brother of Congressman Robert L. Doughton, for many years chairman of the House Ways and Means Committee.

Doughton's boyhood was spent on a farm. He attended the local schools and Independence Academy in Virginia. He decided to pursue law as a profession and entered the University of North Carolina for his preparation and was graduated in 1880 with the LL.B. degree. That same year he received his license and began practice in Sparta, the county seat of his native county.

In 1887 he received the Democratic nomination as a candidate for the State House of Representatives from his county. The county was about evenly divided between Democrats and Republicans and a vigorous campaign ensued from which he emerged the winner. He was re-elected in 1889 and 1891 without opposition. His influence in the House increased during his first two terms to the point that he was elected speaker of the 1891 session. The next year he received his party's nomination for the office of lieutenant-governor and won election to that office. It was because of this office that he was later known as "Governor Rufe." He returned to the General Assembly in 1903 and served a number of additional terms, the last being in 1933. His many years of service to the people of the western part of the state earned him the title, North Carolina's "Grand Old Man of the Mountains."

Of his more than a quarter of a century in the General Assembly, perhaps the most important piece of legislation with which he was connected was the Doughton-Connor-Bowie Highway Law of 1921. It was this act which created the State Highway Commission and started the state on a program of constructing a modern, paved network of roads.

The act authorized the state to issue up to $50,000,000 in bonds for highway construction. These were to be financed by a one cent increase in gasoline taxes and an increase in motor vehicle licenses. Governor Morrison had campaigned on a platform of good roads and now the state was in the road building business in a big way.

Morrison appointed Doughton to the Highway Commission in 1921, and he served until 1923 when the governor appointed him State Commissioner of Revenue. He won election to this position in 1924 and was re-elected in 1928. Doughton was perhaps the best qualified man in the state to assume the responsibilities of Revenue Commissioner. He had for many years been chairman of the House Finance Committee and was therefore well acquainted with the financial resources of the state and the ways to go about tapping these. He also was connected with a number of banks in the state and from this experience had firsthand knowledge of the general economy of the region. The high degree of respect he commanded throughout the state also qualified him for the job at this time, for the Revenue Department had just been the object of scandal and needed a man with his reputation to restore the confidence of the people in this area of their government. He resigned the Revenue office in 1929 upon his appointment as chairman of the State Highway Commission by Governor O. Max Gardner.

Doughton was also highly qualified for the post of chairman of the State Highway Commission. His leadership in the passage of the 1921 Highway Act gave him personal knowledge of desirable goals for the Commission. His previous two years experience on the Commission also acquainted him with its operation.

In addition to law and politics, Doughton was interested in business affairs, primarily banking and farming. He was a member of the Masonic Order and the Kiwanis Club. He served on the board of trustees of the University of North Carolina for fifty-seven years. His political affiliation was with the Democratic party, of course, and his religious affiliation was with the Methodist Church.

He was married on January 10, 1883, to Sue B. Parks. Two children were born of this union: Kemp Doughton and Annie Doughton, who married Sidney Thomas.

He died August 17, 1945, and is buried in Shiloh Cemetery at Sparta, North Carolina.

For additional information concerning Rufus A. Doughton, see: *Biographical History of North Carolina*, edited by S. A. Ashe, and *Here In Carolina*, by R. C. Lawrence.

James B. Duke

James Buchanan Duke, named for President James Buchanan, was born near Durham, North Carolina, on December 23, 1856. He was the son of Washington Duke and Artelia Roney. His father was later the founder of W. Duke, Sons and Company, which grew into the world's largest tobacco manufacturing company. His mother died while he was yet a very young child.

Buck, as he was usually called, acquired little formal education. He did at times attend the Durham Academy, but when his father wanted to send him to college, he declined the opportunity.

Washington Duke left his children with kin in 1863 and went to fight in the Confederate Army. When he returned in 1865, he and his sons began the manufacture of tobacco in a log factory. Their business prospered and soon larger quarters were needed. In 1876 they moved from their farm to Durham, where Buck's brother Brodie already had a tobacco factory. A short time later the business was expanded by taking Brodie and George L. Watts into the partnership. In 1881 they began the manufacture of cigarettes. By this time they were big business.

The business had grown to such an extent that in 1884 it was decided to build a branch in New York City and Buck was sent to make such arrangements. By this time his salary from the business was considerable, yet he stayed in a $2 a week room and ate his meals in a Bowery restaurant in order to have every possible dollar to invest in the business.

Competition in the tobacco industry was very keen; firms often spent twice as much in advertising as they made in profits. In 1889 the five leading firms decided to stop cutting each others' throats and combine their businesses, so in 1890 the American Tobacco Company, or as it was often referred to, the American Tobacco Trust, was formed. W. Duke, Sons and Company was the center of this organization and James B. Duke was its president. The combination controlled 90 per cent of the market for their products. Buck Duke continued as president until 1912, leaving the company with a capitalization of $316,000,000.

Duke's tobacco empire helped the farmers of the state by giving them a market for their product. He also helped the growth of industry in North Carolina by providing a system of electric power for operating plants. Duke saw the need for this source of power in his home state and harnessed the Catawba River to furnish it. The Southern Power Company (now Duke Power Company) was the source of power for many of the early cotton mills in the piedmont region of the state.

Throughout his life Duke gave generously to charitable organizations and educational institutions, but his greatest gift was a $40,000,000 trust fund to finance an educational institution in Durham to be known as Duke University. The main corpus of the fund consisted of three-fourths of his holdings in the Southern Power Company. The trustees were directed to give $6,000,000 to Trinity College if its trustees would change the name to Duke University, which they did. After this, twenty per cent of the income was to be added to the fund until it totaled $80,000,000. The income was to be divided as follows: thirty-two per cent to Duke University, thirty-two per cent for maintaining and establishing hospitals primarily in North and South Carolina, ten per cent for the benefit of orphans, both white and Negro in North and South Carolina, six per cent for building Methodist Episcopal churches in North Carolina, four per cent for maintaining Methodist Episcopal churches in North Carolina, two per cent pensions for retired ministers, their widows and orphans, who served in the North Carolina Conference, five per cent for Davidson College, five per cent for Furman University, and four per cent for Johnson C. Smith University.

When Duke made the announcement of the trust, he made the following statements as indicative of his motives:

"I have selected Duke University as one of the principal objects of this trust because I recognize that education, when conducted along sane and practical, as opposed to dogmatic and theoretical lines, is next to religion, the greatest civilizing influence. . . ."

In politics Mr. Duke was affiliated with the Republican party and in religion with the Methodist Church.

He was married on November 29, 1904, to Mrs. Lillian McCredy of New Jersey; they were divorced after about one year. He was married a second time on July 23, 1907, to Mrs. Adeline Lee Molt Inman of Atlanta. One child, Doris, was born of this union.

Mr. Duke died October 10, 1925. He is entombed in the Duke Chapel on the campus of Duke University.

For additional information concerning James B. Duke, see: *Tobacco Tycoon, The Story of James Buchanan Duke*, by John Kennedy Winkler, and *James B. Duke, Master Builder*, by John Wilbur Jenkins.

Washington Duke

Washington Duke was born in Orange (now Durham) County, North Carolina, on December 20, 1820. He was one of ten children of Taylor Duke and Dicie Jones. The size of the family and the difficulties of the times made it impossible for the children to receive any education beyond what could be taught at home.

At the age of twenty-one Washington Duke rented land and began farming on his own, and in the course of four years he saved enough money to buy a farm. He continued this process of saving money and buying land so that at the outbreak of the Civil War he had acquired a farm of 300 acres. In 1863 he enlisted in the Confederate Army and served until he was captured in the retreat at Appomattox. At the war's end the government sent him to New Bern, North Carolina, and from there he walked the 135 miles home. His assets at this time in his life consisted of a neglected farm, two blind army mules, and fifty cents.

He immediately began the task of rebuilding his farm and also began to manufacture tobacco. His first tobacco factory was constructed on his farm and consisted of a log building sixteen feet by eighteen feet. The business prospered and soon larger quarters were needed. In 1874 a factory was built in the town of Durham, where one of his sons, Brodie, already had a tobacco factory. Shortly thereafter the operations were combined and the W. Duke, Sons & Company became big business. The firm continued to grow. In 1881 the manufacture of cigarettes was added to the operations, and three years later a branch factory was built in New York City. In the 1890's the firm became part of the American Tobacco Company, and was then doing an annual business of over $4,500,000. The Duke firm was the center of the American Tobacco Company and was always the largest branch of it.

The contributions made by Washington Duke to Trinity College (now Duke University) established for him the reputation as one of the South's greatest philanthropists. When a decision was reached in 1890 to move Trinity from Randolph County, Mr. Duke offered the school $85,000 if it would locate in Durham. The offer was accepted and three years later when the institution began operations in its new location it was disclosed that he had exceeded his promised amount and given $110,000. Seeing the great need for adequate educational opportunities for women, he gave $100,000 to the Trinity endowment in 1896 on the condition that women be admitted to their school. In 1898 and 1900 he made additional gifts of $100,000 to Trinity. Duke made other significant contributions to Trinity, many of which were never publicized. For example, on one occasion the lawn was graded at considerable expense and Mr. Duke quietly paid the bill himself.

Trinity was not the only college to receive aid from Washington Duke. Louisburg Female College in Louisburg, North Carolina, was constantly plagued by financial crises after the Civil War and was finally put on the market for sale. In 1891 Duke purchased the college and put its operation in the hands of the North Carolina Conference of the Methodist Church. At his death the ownership of the school was passed to his son, B. N. Duke, who in 1907 deeded the property to the Conference.

The establishment of the Southern Conservatory of Music in Durham was another notable enterprise undertaken by Mr. Duke. To this project in 1898 he gave the land and building required for its operation.

His generosity knew no color bounds. He and two of his sons provided the funds to establish the Lincoln Hospital, which was to be used exclusively for citizens of the Negro race.

Mr. Duke was politically affiliated with the Democratic party until shortly after the Civil War when he became a Republican. By way of explaining this change he said that he believed the program for internal improvements endorsed by the Republicans would do more good to advance the interests of the South. His religious affiliation was with the Methodist Episcopal Church, South, and he gave generously of his wealth to its administration and support.

He was married in 1844 to Mary C. Clinton of Orange County, North Carolina. Two children were born of this union: Samuel T. Duke and Brodie L. Duke. His first wife died in 1847 and in 1852 he was married to Artelia Roney of Alamance County, North Carolina. Three children were born of this union: Mary Elizabeth Duke, Benjamin Newton Duke, and James Buchanan Duke.

Washington Duke died on May 8, 1905, and was buried in Maplewood Cemetery in Durham. His body was later moved to the Memorial Chapel in Duke University Chapel.

For additional information concerning Washington Duke, see: *Biographical History of North Carolina,* edited by A. S. Ashe.

J. C. B. Ehringhaus

John Christoph Blucher Ehringhaus was born in Elizabeth City, North Carolina, February 5, 1882, the son of Erskine and Catherine Colville Matthews Ehringhaus.

As a boy Ehringhaus attended the Elizabeth City Public Schools. In 1898 he was graduated from Atlantic Collegiate Institute and in the same year entered the University of North Carolina. He started his college education before reaching his sixteenth birthday. Through diligent study and hard work Ehringhaus completed the regular four-year program leading to a bachelor's degree in three years and he graduated with Phi Beta Kappa honors. After receiving his Bachelor of Arts degree, he entered the Law School of the University of North Carolina. While a law student, Ehringhaus was also an instructor of English. He received his Bachelor of Laws degree in 1903 and was admitted to the bar in the same year.

Upon admission to the bar, Ehringhaus began practice in his home town of Elizabeth City. The Pasquotank County Democratic Convention nominated him, in 1905, as a candidate for the State House of Representatives. He won the election and served two terms in the General Assmbly. As a member of the House of Representatives, Ehringhaus was co-author of two bills which marked him as a friend of education in North Carolina. One was the bill to create East Carolina Teachers College and the other was a bill setting up a system of high schools for the state.

At the age of twenty-eight, Ehringhaus was elected solicitor of the First Judicial District. He served in this capacity for three terms or a total of twelve years. With his third term as solicitor completed, Ehringhaus returned to the private practice of law in Elizabeth City.

The name of J. C. B. Ehringhaus became known throughout the state during the campaigns of 1928. In this election year he canvassed the state for the Democratic candidates. There was division within the ranks of the Democratic party because their nominee for President, Alfred E. Smith, was a Roman Catholic. Ehringhaus supported Smith and won votes for the national ticket everywhere he campaigned.

The stock market crash of 1929 brought on the Great Depression of the thirties. Nearly 130 banks in the state closed their doors. Farmers were losing their farms due to the foreclosure of mortgages. Both the state and nation were in economic ruin. It was in this setting that J. C. B. Ehringhaus decided to seek his party's nomination for the office of governor. He had the endorsement and support for his campaign of the incumbent governor, O. Max Gardner. The Republicans offered little opposition and the Democrats easily put their man in office in the November general election. Ehringhaus was inaugurated January 5, 1933.

When Ehringhaus took up residency at the Governor's Mansion, the state had a deficit of approximately $15,000,-000. When he left, the state had a surplus of over $5,000,000. In spite of the trying depression years, he ran his administration without borrowing any money whatsoever. During his administration the state undertook a number of programs in cooperation with the federal government aimed at bringing the nation out of the depression. Even in the face of the shortages of financial resources, the state undertook many programs for the advancement of the state and the benefit of its citizens. Some of the more important of these were: the establishment of the eight-month school term in every school in the state, the establishment of a rental system for school textbooks, the expansion of the transportation system for rural schools to embrace all students living over one mile from the school, the enlargement and modernization of the parole system, the laying of plans for a women's prison, the abatement of all tolls on state bridges and highways, and the setting up of a state rural electrification program before the federal government entered this area.

After his term as governor, Ehringhaus engaged in the private practice of law in Raleigh.

Ehringhaus was a Mason, Shriner, Odd Fellow, Elk, and a member of Delta Kappa Epsilon. He also was a member of the North Carolina Judicial Conference. He was an active communicant of the Episcopal Church.

In 1912 Matilda Bradford Haughton became the wife of J. C. B. Ehringhaus. She was the daughter of the Reverend Thomas Benbury Haughton, an Episcopal minister and chaplain in the Confederate Army, and Susan Lamb Haughton. Three children were born to them. They are J. C. B. Ehringhaus, Jr., Haughton Ehringhaus, and Matilda Ehringhaus, who married James Telfair Cordon. Haughton and Matilda are twins.

Governor Ehringhaus died in Raleigh, July 31, 1949, after a heart attack. He is buried in Elizabeth City.

A portrait of Ehringhaus is owned by the state of North Carolina and hangs in Raleigh.

For additional information concerning J. C. B. Ehringhaus, see: *Addresses and Papers of Governor John Christoph Blucher Ehringhaus, 1933-1937*, edited by David Leroy Corbitt.

William P. Few

William Preston Few was born in Greenville County, South Carolina, December 29, 1867. He was the son of Franklin Few and his wife, Rachel Kendrick Few.

Few's elementary education was gained through the guidance of private tutors and at the public schools. In 1889 he received his A.B. degree from Wofford College in Spartanburg, South Carolina. The next three years were spent teaching at St. John's Academy and Wofford College, both in his home state. He received his Masters degree in 1893 from Harvard and was awarded a Ph.D. in 1896 from the same institution.

Upon completion of his formal education, Few came to Durham, North Carolina, to fill the appointment of professor of English literature at Trinity College. Few was not only an able teacher, but also an able administrator. For this reason he was made the first dean of the college in 1902 and eight years later was elected the fifth president of Trinity.

When Few first began teaching at Trinity, it was intended to be only a temporary appointment. The college did not have the income to hire another professor in the English department. However, Dr. John Kilgo, then president of Trinity, approached Benjamin Duke about the matter and he provided the funds to enable the college to continue the services of the young Harvard graduate. Few taught English literature with his specialty being Shakespeare.

James B. Duke in 1924 established, for the purpose of furthering and for charitable causes in North and South Carolina, a trust fund with a principal of about $40,000,000. A large portion of the trust was to go toward establishing an educational institution at Durham to be called Duke University. Trinity College was to become the nucleus of this university. With the founding of the new institution, Few became its president and continued to serve in that capacity until his death in 1940.

The trustees of the new institution immediately embarked upon a building program. The sum of $6,000,000 was set aside from the endowment for this purpose. The next year $2,000,000 was added to this building fund by Duke. Twenty per cent of the trust fund was set aside for investment purposes with the aim of increasing the total of the endowment to $80,000,000. When the income of the fund was divided, it was decided that thirty-two per cent would go to the university. The additional sum of $17,000,00 was provided for the buildings and the trust fund in James Duke's will. Of this bequest $4,000,000 was to be used to provide a medical school within the university.

Through the financial aid of the Duke endowment and the careful guidance of Dr. Few, a small college grew into a great university. Within the total complex of the institution, a hospital, medical school, divinity school, college of engineering, school of forestry, graduate school, and liberal arts college were created. According to Dr. Robert Woody this transformation took place within a shorter period of time than had ever occurred in the South.

The establishment of the co-ordinate college for women at Duke is one example of the broad development which took place there under William Few. There had been some women graduated from the institution, even as early as 1878 when it was still called Trinity College, but the school was still primarily a men's school. Dr. Kilgo had considered the idea of a co-ordinate woman's college, but no real steps had been taken to bring the idea to reality. In 1921 the citizens of Durham donated Southgate building to the college and it was made available to women students. Finally in 1930, the Woman's College was opened with Dr. Alice M. Baldwin as its dean.

William Few was a trustee of Jeanes Foundation for the assistance of Negro rural schools and he served as joint editor to the *South Atlantic Quarterly* from 1909 to 1919. He was a member of the North Carolina Education Association, the North Carolina Literary and Historical Association, the Association of Colleges and Secondary Schools of the Southern States, and Chi Phi. He was devoted to the Methodist Episcopal Church, South. In this connection he served as lay leader of the North Carolina Conference, chairman of the general board of lay activities, member of the General Sunday School Board, the General Board of Christian Education, and the commission of 1939 which unified this church with other branches to form the Methodist Church.

In 1911 he was married to Mary Reamey Thomas. Five sons were born of this union: William, Lyne Starling, Kendrick Sheffield, Randolph Reamey, and Yancey Preston.

Dr. Few died at the Duke Hospital in Durham, North Carolina, October 16, 1940. His body was placed in the crypt of the Duke University Chapel, the first ever to be so placed.

For additional information concerning William Preston Few, see: *Papers and Addresses of William Preston Few,* edited, with a biographical appreciation by Robert H. Woody.

Adelaide L. Fries

Adelaide Lisetta Fries was born in Salem, North Carolina, on November 12, 1871. She was the daughter of John W. Fries and Agnes Sophia de Schweinitz Fries.

She received her formal education at Salem Academy and College, receiving her Bachelor of Arts degree in 1890 and her Master of Arts degree in 1916. She went twice to Herrnhut, Germany, with her father who was attending international gatherings of the Moravian Church, and there studied in the archives of the town where the renewed Moravian Church was born. She found the original records of the Moravians as they had been kept by ministers of the church.

The Moravians of Wachovia, as elsewhere, kept detailed reports of their activities as was required by a church edict passed in the early days of the founding of the church. The Wachovia records date back to 1752. Adelaide Fries' interest in these began when she was yet a child and continued throughout her life. With her interest in the records grew a desire to tell what was in them and in 1892-93 when she published "A Sketch of Salem History" and "History of the Salem Female Academy," these two interests received a coordination which lasted until her death. The records for the first 100 to 150 years are in German and the task of translating them was made more difficult by changes in the language since they were written.

On September 26, 1911, she was appointed archivist for the Southern Province of the Moravian Church, the first person so appointed. She immediately began to gather the old records which were in many forms—diaries, business records, and letters—and were scattered in many places. These she brought to a single location, which after several moves came to be the old Moravian Land Office on Bank and Main streets in Salem.

By 1918 she had completed this initial phase of getting these early records into a form that could be used. Now the job was to translate them from German into English. The North Carolina Historical Commission agreed to publish these if Miss Fries would undertake the task of translating the early manuscripts. This she agreed to do, without any promise of monetary reward. Two years later, in 1920, the first volume was printed. Before her death she completed six additional volumes and was working on an eighth. The work was continued after her death by others so that the *Records of the Moravians in North Carolina* is a ten-volume set.

The first book written by Miss Fries was a history of Forsyth County (1898). She wrote many other books and articles, usually using the material she had gathered in the Moravian archives as sources. The most outstanding of these is *The Road to Salem*, an historical novel. In this book Miss Fries translated the autobiography of Anna Catharina and then added to it to present a complete picture of what frontier life was really like. For this work she was awarded the Mayflower Cup, as the North Carolinian who had written the best book of 1944. Some other works she produced were: *The Moravians in Georgia, 1735-1740* (1905), *The Town Builders* (1915), *Moravian Customs—Our Inheritance* (1936), *Some*

Moravian Heroes (1936), *Forsyth, a County on the March* (1949), and *The Moravian Church: Yesterday and Today* (1926), written with J. Kenneth Pfohl.

Miss Fries found time in her busy schedule to participate in club work and was very active in the North Carolina Federation of Women's Clubs, an organization with which she was associated from the time of its founding in 1902. In 1907 she was instrumental in getting the Federation to establish a scholarship at Salem Academy in honor of Mrs. Stonewall Jackson, an alumna of the school. She also helped establish a department of literature within the Federation and served as its chairman. She was elected president of the State Federation in 1913 and served in this capacity for two years. After her term as president, she was elected to the board of trustees of the State Federation.

She was a member of the Salem College Alumnae Association (president 1905-1934), North Carolina Literary and Historical Association, North Carolina Historical Society, the American Association for State and Local History, North Carolina Folklore Society, the North Carolina Society for the Preservation of Antiquities, the National Genealogical Society, the Institute of American Genealogy, the board of directors of the Wachovia Historical Society, and the executive board of the State Department of Archives and History. Her religious affiliation was naturally with the Moravian Church.

Miss Fries died November 29, 1949, and is buried in the Moravian Graveyard, Salem.

For additional information concerning Alelaide Lisetta Fries, see: "Dr. Adelaide L. Fries" by Geraldine B. Eggleston, unpublished master's thesis, University of North Carolina and "Adelaide Lisetta Fries" by Douglas LeTell Rights, *The North Carolina Historical Review*, XXIX (January, 1952), 1-7.

Francis Henry Fries

Francis Henry Fries was born on February 1, 1855, in Salem, North Carolina. He was the son of Francis Levin Fries and Lisetta Vogler Fries.

Amidst the hardships of the Reconstruction period, Fries completed his elementary and high school education in Salem. He had prepared himself to go to the University of North Carolina, but finding it closed by the aftermath of the war, chose instead to go to Davidson College. He was graduated in 1874 with a Bachelor of Science degree.

Returning to Salem, he joined the family-owned mills, starting in the blacksmith and machine shops. At age twenty-one, he was taken into the firm with his uncle, Henry, and brother, John. In 1878, Fries was named superintendent of the family's Arista Mill in Salem, managing it until 1887.

On the election of Alfred M. Scales as governor of North Carolina in 1884, Fries was called on to take a position on his military staff. He accepted this honorary position, serving with the rank of colonel during the years 1885 to 1889.

Having acquired as complete a knowledge of the manufacture of textile goods as the state of the art then afforded, Colonel Fries turned his support to a railroad for the towns of Winston and Salem. At the appeal of his fellow citizens, Fries accepted the responsibility of financing and building this road. He was elected president and general manager of the Roanoke and Southern Railway Company, and for the next four years, supervised the construction of the southern half of the 122-mile railroad. With a subscribed capital of only forty thousand dollars, he played a leading role in financing the more than two million dollar project which was completed in 1892.

In February, 1891, John and Henry Fries and other local citizens had obtained a charter for organization of a trust company. John continued working in the mills, so Francis Fries, assisted only by his nephew, Henry Shaffner, organized the company. Moving a small iron safe into what had been a Chinese laundry, the two opened for business on June 15, 1893. From these humble beginnings and two hundred thousand dollars in capital, the Wachovia Loan and Trust Company began to grow.

In the beginning, Colonel Fries, as president, served as chief executive officer, made the loans, and was head of the trust business, while Mr. Shaffner handled the administrative and banking duties. By 1898 the company had made tremendous strides and had banking resources totaling seven hundred and fifty thousand dollars.

Having laid a sound local foundation for the company, Fries started adding Wachovia offices in other towns, and by 1903 had branches in Asheville, Salisbury, Spencer, and High Point, as well as in Winston-Salem.

Eager to learn more about the fields of banking and trust, Fries early became active in the North Carolina Bankers Association and in 1899 attended his first meeting of the new Trust Company Section of the American Bankers Association. His leadership was quickly recognized by both organizations. He was elected president of the North Carolina association in 1904 and president of the trust company section of the American Association in 1912.

On January 1, 1911, the Wachovia Loan and Trust Company and the Wachovia National Bank merged under the name of the Wachovia Bank and Trust Company. By 1912 the trust phase of the business had increased to such an extent that Fries felt it necessary to divorce himself from direct administration of trust affairs and turn these responsibilities over to A. H. Eller, who was elected trust officer in charge of the department. In 1918 Wachovia joined the Federal Reserve System and during the 1920's continued to expand and grow, adding another office in Raleigh.

In the thirty-eight years that Fries was president of Wachovia it grew from the humblest of beginnings into the largest bank in the Southeast.

Though best known for his banking genius, Fries continued to follow the textile manufacturing business. In 1896 he and W. C. Ruffin established the Mayo Cotton Mills at Mayodan, and in 1902 he helped establish the Washington Mills at Fries, Virginia, which later merged with the Mayo Mills. In addition, he was instrumental in the building of the Winston-Salem Southbound Railroad.

At the time of his death, Fries was vice-president of the Mayo Sales Corporation, and president of Wachovia Bank and Trust Company, Washington Mills and Oakdale Cotton Mills of Jamestown. He was a director of Indera Mills, Arista Mills, and the North Carolina Granite Corporation at Mount Airy.

Fries was married in 1881 to Letitia Walker Patterson, daughter of the Hon. Rufus L. Patterson and granddaughter of Governor John M. Morehead. She, together with their infant daughter, died on May 28, 1884. In 1886 he married Anna de Schweinitz, daughter of Bishop E. A. de Schweinitz, One daughter was born of this marriage.

Francis Henry Fries died on June 5, 1931, and is buried in God's Acre, the Moravian cemetery in Winston-Salem, N. C.

O. Max Gardner

Oliver Max Gardner was born in Shelby, North Carolina, March 22, 1882, the youngest child of Dr. Oliver Perry Gardner and Margaret Young Gardner.

Young Gardner attended Shelby High School and while there won a scholarship to A. & M. College, now North Carolina State University. He entered in January, 1900, and received the Bachelor of Science degree three and a half years later. After graduation he accepted an appointment as instructor in chemistry at his alma mater which he served for two years. In 1905 he became a student of law at the University of North Carolina.

After law school Gardner returned to Shelby to practice, and he formed a partnership with J. A. Anthony, his brother-in-law. He continued his Shelby practice until 1928, but this was not his only source of income. In addition to other interests, Gardner and O. M. Mull were the organizers and owners of the Cleveland Cloth Mill, a large rayon weaving plant.

Gardner was not long out of college when he became active in politics. When Gardner was twenty-six years old, Josephus Daniels, the National Committeeman of the Democratic party from North Carolina, selected him to organize the Young Men's Democratic Clubs in the state. Two years later, in 1910, he was elected to the state senate. In 1914 he was re-elected to the senate, and when the General Assembly convened in 1915 he became president *pro tempore* of the Senate. In 1916 Gardner moved further up the political ladder when he received the unanimous nomination of the Democratic party for the office of lieutenant governor of North Carolina. He won election easily, and when his term as lieutenant governor ended, Gardner filed as a candidate for the Democratic nomination for governor. It was then that he lost his first and only political election. In 1921 he was appointed by Governor Morrison to the State Board of Agriculture, a post which he filled for eight years. In 1924 Gardner was chairman of the North Carolina delegation to the National Democratic Convention.

In 1928 Gardner again made a bid for the gubernatorial nomination. This time he received it without opposition— the only man to win nomination without a primary since the adoption of the primary system. Gardner won the governorship overwhelmingly. Oliver Max Gardner was inaugurated Governor of North Carolina on January 11, 1929.

Before he had completed his first year in office, the stock market had crashed and the Great Depression was a reality. Most if not all of his programs were aimed at helping the state and its citizens recover from this economic collapse. North Carolina's governor was the first in the nation to cut his own salary. He reduced the state budget by over ten million dollars during his four years in office. Many state departments were reorganized. The state assumed full responsibility for roads and schools since county governments were no longer financially able to do so. Gardner's live-at-home program encouraged farmers to grow all the food they needed to survive. A workmen's compensation act was passed, and a bill was adopted to provide secret ballots for elections. Gardner, however, considered the most significant achievement of his administration to be the consolidation of the University of North Carolina, North Carolina State College, and the North Carolina College for Women into the greater University of North Carolina. Under this plan the three institutions had one board of trustees, one executive head, and for a time coordinated programs.

After his term as governor, Gardner moved to Washington, D. C., where he practiced law. In 1942 he became a director of the Sperry Corporation. In 1944 he was appointed by President Franklin D. Roosevelt to be chairman of the advisory board of the Office of War Mobilization and Reconversion. He served as Undersecretary of the Treasury during part of the Truman administration. President Truman also appointed him to be ambassador to the Court of St. James', but Gardner died about eight hours before sailing time of his ship.

Gardner endowed fifty scholarships at the struggling junior college at Boiling Springs in his native county. In appreciation of this, the institution was renamed Gardner-Webb Junior College. He was an active member of the First Baptist Church of Shelby.

In November, 1907, Fay Lamar Webb became the wife of Max Gardner. Mrs. Gardner was the daughter of Judge James L. Webb and Kansas Andrews Webb. Four children were born to them: Margaret Love Gardner, who married N. E. Burgess; James Webb Gardner; Ralph Webb Gardner; and O. Max Gardner, Jr.

O. Max Gardner died on February 6, 1947, and is buried in his hometown of Shelby. The State of North Carolina owns a portrait of Governor Gardner.

For additional information concerning Oliver Max Gardner, see: *Papers and Letters of Governor Oliver Max Gardner, 1929-1933*, edited by David Leroy Corbitt, and *O. Max Gardner, A Power in North Carolina and New Deal Washington* by Joseph L. Morrison.

Carl Goerch

Carl Goerch was born on June 10, 1891, in Tarrytown, New York, the son of Mr. and Mrs. Herman Goerch. His father was for many years in the landscape gardening business there, working on one of the big estates along the Hudson River.

Goerch attended the public schools of Tarrytown, graduating from its Washington Irving High School.

Having completed his formal education, he went into newspaper work in his hometown. After several years he decided that he would like to see some of the country, so in the fall of 1912, he placed an advertisement in a newspaper trade journal for a job as a reporter or city editor. He got two replies, one from a paper in Orange, Texas, and the other from one in Washington, North Carolina.

Texas had a somewhat romantic appeal, so he accepted the job of city editor on the Orange paper. After six months there he decided it was time to make a change. Consequently, he wrote the editor of the *Daily News* in Washington, North Carolina, and inquired as to whether or not the job was still available. Receiving an affirmative answer, he packed up and moved to Washington.

Having been there only six months, he received a letter from the editor in Orange, saying that a new oil field was being developed near the town, that prospects for the future looked bright, and that the paper could use him; so back to Orange he went, remaining there over a year. When the oil field fizzled and things began to look dim, Goerch recalled what a nice town Washington had been; so he wrote Jim Mayo, publisher of the *Daily News,* and hinted strongly that he would like to return to North Carolina. Mayo told him to come ahead, and he has been here ever since.

He worked on the *Washington Daily News* for four years until the paper was sold in 1920. Finding himself without a job, Goerch went to New Bern where he found newspaper work. Moving to Wilson, he was offered the opportunity to manage a recently-begun morning newspaper. He accepted, but the proposition did not work out, and at the end of two years the paper ceased publication.

In 1925, he moved back to Washington and bought the *Progress,* a weekly newspaper, and ran it until 1933. In that year he sold the *Progress,* moved to Raleigh, and went with the Durham Life Insurance Company, broadcasting for them over radio station WPTF a series of programs, "Doings of the Legislature." He covered fourteen regular sessions and three extra sessions.

Also in 1933, Goerch started publication of *The State* magazine. Although he became its editor and publisher in the depth of the depression, he never put out a single issue that did not realize a profit. He summed up his magazine's policy very nicely when he declared, "The policy of the magazine has never been to try to tear down things, but to boost worthwhile things: industry, tourist attractions and the natural resources of the state." He operated the magazine until 1951 when he sold control of it to Bill Sharpe and Bill Wright. He still maintains an office in the magazine's headquarters and contributes regular feature articles to its issues.

In June of 1933, Goerch started a series of Sunday night broadcasts entitled "Carolina Chats." The program ran on

WPTF for some twenty-eight years until its last broadcast on September 10, 1961.

In 1937 he began a "man-on-the-street" program. Broadcasting from the front of the Wake County courthouse every Saturday morning, he would give money to persons who answered his questions correctly. The popular program usually found several hundred people standing around. In addition, he has broadcast many special programs, interviews and reports of special events on WPTF. Goerch has also had regular television programs.

Besides his radio and television work, which he carried on for more than thirty years, Goerch has done a considerable amount of public speaking to various civic organizations and other groups. In addition to talks made in one hundred and ninety-six communities in North Carolina, he has spoken in thirty-one different states. An avid traveler, he has visited some fifty-two foreign countries.

Goerch has had numbers of feature articles published in national magazines and various newspapers, and he is a noted author of some half-dozen books on North Carolina subjects, including: *Ocracoke, Carolina Chats, Down Home, Just For the Fun of It*, and *Characters . . . Always Characters*.

Goerch's only real hobby is flying, and he has been at it since 1933, when he talked barnstorming pilot Warren Pennington into letting him "steal" his plane. Never having taken off or landed a plane before, Goerch "flew" Pennington's plane from New Bern to Washington. Since then and until 1969, when, at seventy-eight years of age, he was the oldest pilot in North Carolina, he was still flying.

In 1916 Goerch married Sibyl Wallace, a teacher in the Orange, Texas, school system. They have two daughters: Doris and Sibyl. The Goerches reside at 1610 Iredell Drive in Raleigh, North Carolina.

11

Frank P. Graham

Frank Porter Graham was born in Fayetteville, North Carolina, on October 14, 1886. He was the son of Alexander Graham and his wife, Katherine Sloan.

Frank Graham was graduated from high school in Charlotte and then attended the University of North Carolina from which he received his A.B. degree in 1909. The quality of his academic work at the University earned him a Phi Beta Kappa key, but studies occupied only part of his time as he was head cheerleader, president of the campus Y.M.C.A., and a member of the student legislature. The next year he studied law at the University and received his license to practice. Instead of practicing law, however, he took a position teaching English in a Raleigh high school where he remained until he returned to Chapel Hill as secretary of the Y.M.C.A. and in 1914 received an appointment as instructor in history at the University. He was awarded a masters degree from Columbia University in 1916.

At the beginning of World War I he enlisted in the Marine Corps as a private. By the time of his discharge in 1919 he had risen to the rank of first lieutenant. After the war he returned to the University of North Carolina as assistant professor of history. He served one year as dean of students and in 1921 was promoted to an associate professorship.

The next year he spent doing graduate work at the University of Chicago where he was awarded the two-year Amherst Memorial Fellowship. He spent one year in Washington, D. C., where he studied at Brookings Institute and the Library of Congress. He spent the next year doing research at the British Museum and the London School of Economics and also attended sessions of the League of Nations in Geneva. He returned to his home state and the University in 1925 and was elevated to full professor two years later. He was elected president of the University of North Carolina in June 1930.

Frank Graham took over the reins of the University at a difficult time, for the depression was just beginning. He also had a larger area of responsibility as the University at Chapel Hill, State College at Raleigh, and Woman's College at Greensboro were consolidated into the greater University of North Carolina with Graham as president. In spite of these difficulties all three branches of the University experienced an increase in student enrollment, in number of buildings, and in the number of faculty members. For his contributions to education, *Time* magazine named him the outstanding state university president in the nation.

In 1949 Governor W. Kerr Scott appointed Graham to fill the United States Senate seat left vacant by the death of J. Melville Broughton. Graham ran for re-election in 1950, but was defeated by Willis Smith.

Graham's services to the nation are illustrated by the number of boards and agencies on which he has served. Some are as follows: Vice-chairman of the Consumer Board of the National Recovery Administration, chairman of the National Advisory Council to the Cabinet Committee on Economic Security, member of the President's Committee on Education, member of the U. S. Commission to study the University of Puerto Rico as a possible inter-American University, member of the U. S. Commission to commemorate the 300th anniversary of the founding of Harvard University, president of the National Association of College Writing Groups, chairman of the Industries Committee of American Railroads, member of the National Defense Mediation Board, member of the National War Labor Board, chairman of Public Hearing Committee of the President's Labor-Management Conference, chairman of the Oil Panel, president of the Oak Ridge Institute of Nuclear Studies, and chairman of National Sharecroppers Fund.

Graham twice served as president of the North Carolina Conference of Social Service, which drafted and sponsored the first workmen's compensation act in this state. In 1920-21 he headed a successful campaign to raise $20,000,000 for a state institutions building program. He was given the responsibility by the board of trustees to write a plan of consolidation for the establishment of the greater University of North Carolina. Graham has also served as president of the North Carolina Literary and Historical Association.

Graham has rendered service on an international scale through his work with the United Nations. He has served as a U.N. representative in the India-Pakistan dispute and represented the U.N. in the Dutch-Indonesian dispute. After his defeat for Senator, he served as a U.N. mediator.

His religious affiliation is with the Presbyterian Church and his political affiliation is with the Democratic party.

He was married on July 21, 1932 to Marian Drane, daughter of Robert Brent Drane of Edenton.

A portrait of Frank Graham is owned by the University of North Carolina and hangs on the Chapel Hill campus.

For additional information concerning Frank P. Graham, see: *Carolina Magazine*, October, 1946, and *The New Republic*, August 10, 1942. His papers are in the Southern Historical Collection, Chapel Hill.

Paul Green

Paul Eliot Green was born in Harnett County, North Carolina, March 17, 1894, the son of William Archibald Green, and his wife, Betty Byrd.

With his brothers and sisters, he attended a one-room country school for six months each year.

After finishing at the little country school, Green entered Buie's Creek Academy (now Campbell College) and there came under the influence of its founder, James Archibald Campbell. He graduated from the Academy in 1914 and wanted to attend the University of North Carolina. Because of the financial burdens of a large family, however, his father was unable to send him. In the fall of 1916 he became a student at Chapel Hill.

Military service in World War I interrupted Green's college education. Before he had completed his first year, he left for the trenches of France. Yet one very important event occurred during this brief stay at Carolina: he wrote his first play. The Senior Class decided to do a play as part of the Commencement exercises and held a contest for an original manuscript. Green won with his play, "Surrender to the Enemy," and it was produced in the Forest Theater.

Paul Green returned to the University in 1919 and continued his education. His major field of study was philosophy, and he spent two years in this area beyond the undergraduate level. It was during this period that he came under the influence of Professor Frederick H. Koch, who aroused his interest in writing plays, instead of short stories and poems in which he had previously been interested. He wrote several plays for the Carolina Playmakers which was established by Koch in 1918. In the fall of 1922 Green went to Cornell University for a year of study in philosophy, after which he returned to Chapel Hill to become a member of the faculty.

During the time he was teaching philosophy at the University, Green was also writing plays. In the six years after graduation, he wrote twenty-one plays. On December 30, 1926, one of his plays, *In Abraham's Bosom*, was produced at the Provincetown Playhouse in Greenwich Village. The play ran for just over two months and then moved uptown where it ran for another two months. In May 1927 *In Abraham's Bosom* was hailed as the best American play of the year and Green received the Pulitzer Prize for his drama.

A Guggenheim Fellowship was awarded to Green in 1928 for a year in Europe to study the theater. At the end of the year his fellowship was extended for another six months; after which Green returned to Chapel Hill and resumed his position as a member of the faculty at the University.

A contract to write for Warner Brothers took Green to Hollywood in 1932. He wrote scripts for twenty-five or thirty movies, but the experience was a disappointing and disillusioning one. His scripts were edited to give them mass appeal, often destroying the feeling and meaning which he wanted his work to have. After a few years he returned to Chapel Hill and this time devoted full time to writing instead of resuming his position on the faculty.

In the summer of 1937 *The Lost Colony* was produced

at Manteo, the first of the outdoor dramas to be written by Paul Green and for which he is now famous. They are "symphonic dramas," combining music, dance, and history with a fictitious plot, a formula invented by Green. Some of the other better known of these are: *The Common Glory* (1948) at Williamsburg; *Wilderness Road* (1953) at Berea, Kentucky; and *The Founders* (1957) also at Williamsburg.

Besides plays, Green has written many short stories as well as two novels—*The Laughing Pioneer* and *This Body the Earth*. Some of the other major plays he has written include: *The House of Connelly* (1931), *Roll, Sweet Chariot* (1935), *Shroud My Body Down* (1935), *Johnny Johnson* (1937), *Salvation on a String* (1946), *The Confederacy* (1958), *Cross and Sword* (1964), and *Texas* (1966).

Green became a member of the National Institute of Arts and Letters in 1941; he has represented the United States as a "cultural ambassador" in both Europe and Asia; and in 1952 he was the recipient of the first Sir Walter Raleigh Award for outstanding creative writing by a North Carolinian.

While working with the Carolina Playmakers, Green met Elizabeth Lay, who became his wife in July, 1922. She was the daughter of the Reverend George Lay, an Episcopal minister. She has participated in all phases of the Playmakers' work: acting, writing plays, and helping design and build scenery. The Greens have four children: Paul Eliot, Nancy Byrd, Betsy McAllister, and Janet McNeill.

The Greens continue to make their home in Chapel Hill, where the author devotes all his time to literature. He can often be found in the University library doing research that will become part of a new play.

For additional information concerning Paul Eliot Green, see: *Paul Green of Chapel Hill*, written by Agatha Boyd Adams.

J. G. de R. Hamilton

Joseph Gregoire de Roulhac Hamilton was born in Hillsboro, North Carolina, on August 6, 1878. He was the son of Daniel Heyward Hamilton and Frances Gray de Roulhac.

As a youth Hamilton was taught the fundamentals of education by his mother and later entered the University of the South at Sewanee, Tennessee. During his first two years he seriously considered studying medicine, but in his junior year switched to history and received his masters degree in 1900. Upon leaving college he took a position teaching at Horner Military Academy at Oxford, where he remained one year. From 1904 to 1906 he was principal of Wilmington High School. During this period he also studied at Columbia University and was granted a Ph.D. degree from that institution in 1906. In this year he went to the University of North Carolina where he remained until his retirement.

Dr. Hamilton had been at the University only one year when he was made acting head of the history department; the next year he was promoted to Alumni Professor and made head of the department. In 1920 he was elected a Kenan Professor.

While teaching history Hamilton began collecting documents of historical value and depositing them in the University Library. He even pleaded with students to search their attics for old papers which might be worth keeping. By 1930 this collection had grown to such proportions that the Southern Historical Collection was established as a separate division of the University Library and Dr. Hamilton was made its first director. In accepting the director's position, Hamilton gave up the headship of the History Department, but retained his Kenan Professorship.

Before he gave up direction of the collection in 1948, it grew to contain millions of items which tell the story of the history of North and South Carolina and other southern states. Scholars and writers from all over the nation come to Chapel Hill to do research in this collection.

In spite of the time required by this position with the Southern Historical Collection and his teaching duties, Hamilton found time to do extensive writing, the main emphasis dealing with North Carolina and the Civil War and Reconstruction. He published almost fifty articles in leading historical journals such as *Agricultural History, American Historical Review, Journal of Southern History,* and the *North Carolina Historical Review.* He also had articles published in more general magazines such as *The Reviewer, South Atlantic Quarterly, Scribner's,* and *Current History.* He wrote more than one hundred biographical sketches which were published, most of these in either the *Dictionary of American Biography* or *Biographical History of North Carolina.* In 1921 he established the Book Review Page in the Greensboro *Daily News.* He served until 1924 as Book Review Editor of this paper. In this capacity he contributed a number of the reviews himself and the section became so popular that one year after it was started the *Book Review Digest* listed the Greensboro paper as one of five regular contributors. He also wrote a number of books, either alone or in conjunction with others; some of these were: *Reconstruction in North Carolina* (1914), *Our Republic* (1910), *Party Politics in North Caro-*

lina, 1835-1860 (1916), *North Carolina Since 1860* (1919), *Making of Citizens* (1922), and *Henry Ford* (1926). He edited a number of volumes of papers among which were: *The Correspondence of Jonathan Worth*, 2 volumes (1909), *The Papers of Thomas Ruffin*, 4 volumes (1918-1921), *Selections From the Writings of Abraham Lincoln* (1921), *The Best Letters of Thomas Jefferson* (1926), and the *Papers of Randolph Abbott Shotwell*, 3 volumes (1929-1936). Hamilton also served as editor of the *James Sprunt Historical Publications* from 1908 to 1924.

During World War I Dr. Hamilton served as an AEF lecturer in France, as a director of military education courses, and as a consultant to the War Plans Division, U. S. General Staff on general education. He was a member of the American and Southern Historical Associations, the North Carolina Literary and Historical Association, and the Historical Society of North Carolina. He was a member of Kappa Alpha and Phi Beta Kappa fraternities. In 1932 he was the recipient of the Columbia University Distinguished Alumni Medal. His political affiliation was with the Democratic party and his religious affiliation was with the Episcopal Church.

He was married on December 22, 1908, to Mary Cornelia Thompson, daughter of Alfred and Laura Thompson of Raleigh. Two children were born of this union: J. C. de Roulhac, Jr. and Alfred Thompson.

Dr. Hamilton died November 11, 1961, and is buried in the old Chapel Hill Cemetery.

A portrait of Dr. Hamilton is owned by the University of North Carolina and hangs in the Southern Historical Collection.

For additional information concerning Joseph G. de Roulhac Hamilton, see: *The Kenan Professorships* by A. G. Howell.

Robert M. Hanes

Robert March Hanes was born on September 22, 1890, at Winston-Salem, North Carolina. He was the son of John Wesley Hanes and his wife, Anna Hodgin.

Hanes attended the Winston-Salem public schools and Woodberry Forest School in Virginia. He was graduated from the University of North Carolina in 1912, where he received the Bachelor of Arts degree. He was a student of the Harvard University School of Business Administration in 1912 and 1913. In 1945 the University of North Carolina awarded him a Doctor of Laws degree.

In 1917 Hanes enlisted in the army, and after training at Fort Oglethorpe, Georgia, went to France as a captain in the 113th Field Artillery. He saw action at St. Mihiel, the Argonne, and with the First and Second Armies. He was a major at the time of his discharge.

In December of 1919, Hanes returned from France and joined the Wachovia Bank organization. In January, 1920, he was elected a vice president. Throughout the period of the 'twenties, he served as loan officer at the Winston-Salem office. He worked closely with Colonel Francis H. Fries, the president of Wachovia, in the over-all administration of the institution, and, in 1930, he was elected administrative vice president. In 1931, following the death of Colonel Fries, Hanes was elected president of Wachovia.

He was elected to the North Carolina House of Representatives in 1929 and 1931, and to the State Senate in 1933. He was a leader in the fight for a general sales tax which was adopted in 1933, and he helped ward off efforts to adopt a luxury tax, which would have taxed, among other things, cigarettes.

Even before his service in the legislature, Hanes had become prominent in the affairs of the North Carolina Bankers Association. In 1928 he was named third vice president and was elected president in 1931. In order to aid banks in North Carolina which were struggling to combat the forces of depression, he led in developing the National Credit Association that aided many banks prior to the establishment of the Reconstruction Finance Corporation.

During the period of the 'thirties, Hanes served the American Bankers Association in many capacities. He was a member of its executive council, a member of its policy-making Administrative Committee, and in 1936 and 1937, he served as chairman of the Federal Legislative Committee. In 1937 the American Bankers Association elected him second vice president and in 1939 he was named president of this nationwide organization.

In 1945, he was elected president of the Association of Reserve City Bankers. The result of all this national recognition was, among other things, an offer of the presidency of the Chase National Bank of New York, now the Chase Manhattan Bank. At that time it was the world's largest financial institution. Hanes turned it down.

Hanes also served on the board of the North Carolina State Sanatoriums. In 1946 and 1947 he helped organize the Business Foundation of the University of North Carolina and served two years as its president. In 1948 he was appointed to the State Education Commission. He was chairman of the Commerce and Industry Division of the North Carolina Department of Conservation and Development, district chairman of the federal Committee for Economic Development, advisor to the finance section of the Navy Department's office of procurement and material, and chairman of the finance department committee of the United States Chamber of Commerce. He served on national committees of Community Chests of America. He was a trustee for the University of North Carolina, the Morehead Foundation, Salem College and Winston-Salem Teachers College.

His directorships include the Southern Railway, P. H. Hanes Knitting Company, Colonial Stores, Borden Manufacturing Company, Carolina Power and Light, Thomasville Chair, Chatham Manufacturing Company and R. J. Reynolds Tobacco Company, and a number of other companies.

The peak of his career as a citizen and statesman came in April, 1949, when the United States appointed him chief of the Belgium-Luxembourg Mission of the Economic Cooperation Administration with headquarters in Brussels. Six months later he was named economic advisor to the High Commissioner of West Germany and chief of the Economic Cooperation Administration Mission.

On July 3, 1917, Hanes married Mildred Borden of Goldsboro, North Carolina. They had two children, Anne and Frank Borden.

Robert March Hanes died on March 10, 1959, and is buried in Salem Cemetery.

12

Archibald Henderson

Archibald Henderson was born in Salisbury, North Carolina, June 17, 1877. He was one of four children born to John Steele and Elizabeth Brownrigg Cain Henderson.

Before beginning his college education at the University of North Carolina, Henderson attended private and Episcopal Church schools, where he excelled in mathematics and showed a love for literature. He entered the University in 1894 and was graduated at the head of his class in 1898. That same year he was appointed instructor in mathematics and one year later he received his M.A. degree from the Chapel Hill institution. He continued teaching and doing graduate work and in 1902 he was awarded a Ph.D. degree by his alma mater. Further research and study in the field of mathematics at the University of Chicago earned him a second doctorate in 1915. He spent 1910-1911 abroad where he undertook more research and study in his field at Cambridge, the University of Berlin, and the Sorbonne. In 1923-1924 he returned to Cambridge and the University of Berlin to do research in relativity and astrophysics and during this time studied with Albert Einstein.

Henderson succeeded his uncle, Dr. William Cain, as head of the Mathematics Department of the University of North Carolina in 1920, and in 1925 was made a Kenan professor.

Because of his innovations in the mathematics program, he became known as the "Father of Modern Mathematics Curriculum"at the University. Dr. Henderson retired from his position on the faculty in 1948, after half a century as a member of the faculty.

While in Chicago in 1903, Henderson saw George Bernard Shaw's play, "You Never Can Tell." He immediately recognized the genius of Shaw and decided to tell the world about it. As the result of a series of letters between the two men, he became Shaw's authorized biographer. He wrote hundreds of articles on Shaw in addition to three full biographies—*George Bernard Shaw: His Life and Works*, (1911); *Bernard Shaw: Playboy and Prophet*, (1932); and *George Bernard Shaw: Man of the Century*, (1956). It is as Shaw's biographer that Henderson is best known in this country and abroad.

In addition to his reputation as a biographer and mathematician, Henderson was a noted and respected historian. Because of the hundreds of articles published in newspapers and magazines and the many books he wrote in this area, he was considered a leading authority on the westward expansionist movement in this country. His leading book on this subject was *Conquest of the Old Southwest*. North Carolina received constant attention by Henderson, and he continuously sought to point out her greatness to her people. Perhaps his best known books dealing with this state are: *North Carolina: The Old North State and the New*, a history of the state, and *The Campus of the First State University*, a history of the University of North Carolina.

In the field of drama, Henderson was respected as an able critic. His rank as a critic was mainly based on three of his books: *Interpreters of Life and the Modern Spirit, European Dramatists*, and *The Changing Drama*. Even in this area Henderson sought to point out to the people of North Carolina that strides were being made in the theater of their state. This was done through editing a book entitled *Pioneering a People's Theatre*, telling of the work of the Carolina Playmakers at Chapel Hill.

Dr. Henderson was also known through the eastern part of the United States for his speaking ability. Because of his almost unlimited vocabulary, his polished style, and the wide range of subjects on which he could speak with authority, he was in great demand as a guest lecturer and speaker for special occasions.

Dr. Henderson was made a Fellow of the Royal Society of Literature of the United Kingdom, one of the few men in this country to ever have gained this honor. He was affiliated with many organizations and associations in the fields of literature, history, science, poetry, and drama. He was a member of the Episcopal Church.

In 1903 Dr. Henderson was married to Minna Curtis Bynum, daughter of William Shipp Bynum, an Episcopal minister, and his wife, Mary Curtis Bynum. Five children were born to Archibald and Minna Henderson. They are: Mary Curtis, Elizabeth Brownrigg, Barbara Gray, Archibald, and John Steele. After the death of his first wife, Henderson married Lucile Kelling, dean of the School of Library Science at the University of North Carolina.

Dr. Henderson died December 6, 1963, at his home, "Fordell," in Chapel Hill. He is buried in the old Salisbury Cemetery at Salisbury, North Carolina. The University owns two portraits of Dr. Henderson.

For additional information concerning Archibald Henderson, see: *Archibald Henderson, the New Crichton,* edited by Samuel Stevens Hood.

D. H. Hill, Jr.

Daniel Harvey Hill was born at Davidson College, North Carolina on January 15, 1859. He was the son of Daniel Harvey Hill and Isabella Morrison.

Hill received his elementary education at Horner's School and the North Carolina Military Institute, after which he entered Davidson College. He was graduated from Davidson in 1880 and almost immediately took a position as professor of English at the Military and Agricultural College of Georgia, in Milledgeville, where he taught for nine years. In 1886 he had received his masters degree from Davidson.

In 1889 he returned to his home state and assumed the position of professor of English at the North Carolina College of Agriculture and Mechanical Arts, now North Carolina State University. Through the years his reputation as an educator grew, and in 1905 he was elected by the Board of Trustees as vice president of the college. Three years later, upon the retirement of Dr. George T. Winston, he was elected president of the school.

Having served in the college for a number of years before becoming president, Hill knew its problems firsthand and during the eight years he was head of the school it experienced great expansion. Some of the buildings which were constructed or begun during his administration are: an Electric

Laboratory was erected for use by the junior and senior classes; a large dormitory was built in 1909 and added to in 1911; two barns and silos were constructed; Winston Hall was erected as an engineering building; the Animal Industry Building was constructed; the Dining Hall was completed; the Y.M.C.A. Building was completed; and the Shop and Laboratory Building was opened. The size of the campus was also enlarged by the purchase of two tracts of land near the entrance to the college.

The faculty was increased significantly during Hill's eight years as president. When he assumed the position, the college had a staff of nine. At the date of his resignation, there were twenty full professors, six associate professors, eight assistant professors and twenty-eight instructors.

The Department of Agricultural Extension was organized on July 1, 1909, under the supervision of Professor I. O. Schaub, at the college. Funds for the department were supplied by the General Education Board and the work of the new department was to act as a connecting link between the school and the rural citizens of the state.

The student body during this period nearly doubled, climbing from 446 to 723. The number of students was less than the number attending the University at Chapel Hill, but well exceeded the student bodies of the other educational institutions in the state.

In 1916 Hill resigned his position as president of A. and M., thus severing his relationship with the school after twenty-six years of service. He left the institution to accept the job of writing a history of the North Carolina troops in the Civil War. Hill had plans for four volumes in which to cover the subject, but illness and death intervened and only two of those planned were completed. In these two he records the story of the Tar Heel troops in the battles from Bethel to Sharpsburg and the efforts at home to keep them supplied. The volumes were printed in 1926 by Edwards & Broughton Company of Raleigh.

Before the undertaking of Civil War history, Hill had written a number of other books in the field of North Carolina history. The more important of these are: *Confederate Military History*, volume on North Carolina in a twelve-volume set (1889), *Young People's History of North Carolina* (1907), and a number of textbooks.

Hill was a member of the North Carolina Historical Commission, serving as secretary of the commission, 1921-1924; was chairman of the state council of defense during World War I, and served as president of the North Carolina Teachers Assembly, the North Carolina Folklore Society, and the North Carolina Literary and Historical Association. He was also a member of the North Carolina Society of the Sons of the Revolution and the United Sons of Confederate Veterans. In religion he was a member of the Presbyterian Church and in politics was affiliated with the Democratic party.

He was married to Pauline White on July 22, 1885, the daughter of Dr. Samuel G. White, a surgeon in the United States Navy. Five children were born of this union: Pauline, Daniel Harvey, Elizabeth, Samuel White, and Randolph Isabel.

D. H. Hill, Jr. died July 31, 1924, in Blowing Rock, North Carolina, where he had gone in hopes that the mountain air would help restore his health. As a memorial to him, State College named their library, completed in 1926, the D. H. Hill Library.

For additional information concerning Daniel Harvey Hill, Jr., see: *History of North Carolina State College*, by David A. Lockmiller.

John Sprunt Hill

John Sprunt Hill was born near Faison, North Carolina, on March 17, 1869. He was the son of William E. Hill, a Duplin County attorney, and his wife, Frances Diana Faison.

By the age of twelve Hill had completed the high school course at Faison. Four years later, in the fall of 1885, he entered the University of North Carolina and was graduated in 1889 with the degree of Ph.B. Upon leaving Chapel Hill he returned to Duplin County where he taught school for two years after which he studied law at his alma mater for one year. Hill then went to New York City where he attended Columbia University Law School on a scholarship. He was graduated from this institution in 1894.

He passed the New York bar examination and immediately became associated with the firm of Pechham and Tyler. The following year he went into practice on his own and established the firm of Hill, Sturcke, and Andrews, which soon grew into a successful New York firm. During the war with Spain he served with Troop A of the New York Calvary in the Puerto Rican campaign. In 1900 he received the Democratic nomination as a congressional candidate from the Fourteenth District, but though he lost the election, his personal popularity allowed him to run some four thousand votes ahead of the Democratic ticket.

In the autumn of 1903 Hill gave up his New York law practice and returned to his native state, making his home in Durham. This same year he began a business career which was to amass for him great wealth. He undertook the establishment of the Home Saving Bank and the Durham Bank and Trust Company. He also headed a group which financed the building of a five-story office building in the downtown area of Durham. Two of Mr. Hill's other business endeavors were as director and vice president of Ervin Mills and as director of Home Security Life Insurance Company of Durham, a company he had helped to form.

Hill is known as the "Father of Rural Credits in North Carolina." With little help Hill drafted the Credit Union Act which was passed by the North Carolina General Assembly in 1915, providing a plan whereby the small farmers of the state could receive short-term loans at low interest rates. The act was first implemented under his personal direction by the establishment of the state's first credit union at Lowe's Grove, Durham County.

Politics interested Hill and he served his home area and the state in this field. He served on the North Carolina State Highway Commission for eleven years beginning in 1920; and he was elected to the State Senate for three two-year terms beginning in 1933.

Education was a cause to which Hill was devoted, and the University of North Carolina especially benefited from this. In 1906 he provided an endowment for the North Carolina Collection of the University Library, to which he and his family made subsequent gifts. He financed the building of the Carolina Inn in 1924 and turned it over to the University in 1935, the income derived to be used for the maintenance of the hotel and in support of the library. He was a member of the Board of Trustees from 1905 until his death, being made an honorary lifetime member by the legislature in

1959. He was chairman of the Trustee Committee on University Buildings from 1923 to 1931, the period when the South Campus was developed. Hill and his wife were responsible for the conversion of the Carnegie Library building into Hill Music Hall, which is named for them. His gifts to the University Library totaled over $1,000,000.

Recognizing the need for recreational areas for children in a city, Hill donated several tracts of land in Durham to be used as parks. He also made substantial contributions to Watts Hospital, founded by his father-in-law, George Watts. He was a leader of many other civic activities.

He was a member in the American Institute of Genealogy, a Fellow in the American Geographical Society, a member of the American and North Carolina Forestry Associations, a member of the Sons of the American Revolution, and a member of the Phi Beta Kappa scholastic fraternity. His religious affiliation was with the Presbyterian Church and his political affiliation was with the Democratic party. He served on the Boards of Trustees of the University of North Carolina and Union Theological Seminary.

He was married November 29, 1899, to Annie Louise Watts, daughter of George W. Watts. Three children were born of this union: George Watts Hill, Laura Valinda Du-Bose, and Frances Faison Fox.

John S. Hill died July 29, 1961, and is buried in Maplewood Cemetery, Durham, North Carolina.

Three portraits of Hill are owned by the University of North Carolina at Chapel Hill; one hangs in the North Carolina Collection, one in the Carolina Inn, and another in Hill Hall.

For additional information concerning John Sprunt Hill, see: *John Sprunt Hill, a Biographical Sketch*, by Archibald Henderson, and *Biographical History of North Carolina*, volume 8, edited by Samuel Ashe.

Luther H. Hodges

Luther Hartwell Hodges was born in Pittsylvania County, Virginia, March 9, 1898, the son of John James and Lovicia Gammon Hodges.

Hodges received his elementary and high school education in the public schools of Leaksville and Spray. He entered the University of North Carolina in the fall of 1915, after having been graduated from Leaksville High School that spring. Financial difficulties faced young Hodges as a college student, and he worked at a number of jobs at the University to meet these needs, as well as working summers between terms. He was held in high esteem by his classmates and was voted best all-around man in his class.

After he was graduated from the University, Hodges was undecided whether to take a position offered to him with the Y.M.C.A. in Alabama or one offered by the Marshall Field mills in which he had worked as a boy. His decision was to return to Leaksville and the textile mills. His first position was secretary to the general manager of the Marshall Field mills in the Leaksville-Spray area. In 1938 he rose to general manager, in charge of sales and production, of all the Marshall Field mills in this country and abroad. He was named a vice president of the company in 1943 and remained in this position until his retirement in 1950.

Hodges decided to seek the nomination of the Democratic party for the office of lieutenant governor in the primary of 1952. Prior to this time he had never run for public office. When the votes were counted, Hodges led his three opponents by a considerable margin, but not a majority. A second primary was averted, however, when his nearest rival, Roy Rowe, failed to call for a run off. He had little opposition in the general election and thus took office in January, 1953.

Upon the death of Governor William Bradley Umstead on November 7, 1954, Luther Hartwell Hodges succeeded to the office of governor. He took the oath of office on November 9, 1954. At the end of this term, he was elected, with little opposition, to a full four-year term of his own. Luther Hodges served longer in the office of governor than anyone since North Carolina became a state.

Some of the major accomplishments of the Hodges' administration were: a revision of the revenue allocation formula for the domestic corporations to encourage new industry to come to North Carolina, re-organization of the State Highway Commission, establishment of the Department of Administration to bring together several fiscal agencies, the enactment of a state minimum wage, and compulsory polio vaccination for children. The growth and importance of the Research Triangle came directly as a result of Governor Hodges' undying efforts. Hodges sought to bring more efficiency to government by applying sound business methods to its problems.

Shortly after his term as governor ended, Hodges went to Washington, D. C., where he served in the cabinet of President John F. Kennedy as the Secretary of Commerce. After the death of President Kennedy in 1963, Hodges continued to serve in this position until his resignation was accepted by President Lyndon B. Johnson in 1965.

Hodges is the author of two books: *Businessman in the*

Statehouse (1962) and *The Business Conscience* (1963).

Luther Hodges is, or has been, a member of the American Legion, the Board of Trustees of the University of North Carolina, and the Board of Trustees of George Peabody College. He has been active in the Y.M.C.A. on many different levels. He is a member of the Rotary Club and in 1967 served as president of Rotary International. He has also been interested in and worked with a number of other civic organizations and campaigns. He is a Mason and a member of the Methodist Church, in which he has been very active.

In 1922 Hodges married Martha Blakeney, who was at that time teaching in the Leaksville schools. She was a native of Monroe, North Carolina, and a graduate of the North Carolina College for Women (now the University of North Carolina at Greensboro). Their three children are Betsy Blakeney, Nancy Houston, and Luther Hartwell Hodges, Jr. In 1969 Mrs. Hodges perished in a fire at the home in Chapel Hill. Hodges was remarried in 1970 to Mrs. Louise Butler Finlayson.

A portrait of Hodges hangs in the Commerce Department in Washington, D. C., and the State of North Carolina also has one in Raleigh.

Today former Governor and Mrs. Hodges make their home in Raleigh. He spends part of his time as chairman of the board of the Research Triangle Foundation at an annual salary of one dollar.

For additional information concerning Luther Hartwell Hodges, see: *Addresses and Papers of Governor Luther Hartwell Hodges* (3 volumes), edited by James W. Patton; *The Kennedy Circle*, edited by Lester Tanzer; and *Luther H. Hodges, Practical Idealist*, by A. G. (Pete) Ivey.

13

Clyde R. Hoey

Clyde Roark Hoey was born in Shelby, North Carolina, December 11, 1877, the son of Samuel Alberta Hoey and his wife, Mary Charlotte Roark.

Because of the poor health of his father, Clyde Hoey laid his school books aside and went to work at the age of twelve. His first job was as a "printer's devil" in the office of a home town newspaper, the Shelby *Aurora*. He worked here only a short time and then went to work for the *Charlotte Observer* as a full printer.

While working in Charlotte, young Hoey learned that the Shelby *Review* was having financial troubles and was about to collapse. With this information, he returned to Shelby and made arrangements to purchase the paper. The price of the paper was Clyde's acceptance of its debts as his personal obligations. So, at the age of sixteen, Clyde Hoey began publication of his own newspaper, which he named the *Cleveland Star*.

When only twenty years of age, Hoey made his first political race. He was nominated by the Democratic party of Cleveland County to run for the General Assembly. One fact which the young political aspirant kept secret during his campaign was the fact that he would not be able to vote for himself—he became of legal voting age about five weeks after the election. The campaign was a hard one, perhaps his hardest, but young Hoey came out the victor.

In spite of the time required by his paper and his political career, Clyde Hoey found time to read law. After attending one summer session studying law at the University of North Carolina, his only formal education since he was forced to quit school at the age of twelve, he took the State Bar examination and in 1899 was licensed to practice law. His practice quickly grew to the point that he was forced to give up his newspaper and devote full time to the law.

Clyde Hoey was active in politics most of his life. In 1899 and 1901 he was the Representative from Cleveland County in the State House of Representatives, and in 1903 he was the State Senator from his district. From 1903 to 1909 Hoey was the chairman of the Cleveland County Democratic Executive Committee, and from 1913 to 1919 he was Assistant United States Attorney for the Western District of North Carolina. In 1919 he was elected to the United States House of Representatives to fill the vacancy left by the resignation of Edwin Y. Webb. At the end of this term he declined renomination and returned to his law practice. For the next sixteen years Hoey did not seek political office for himself, but he did campaign for other Democratic candidates in both this state and others.

It was during the primary campaign of 1936 that Clyde Hoey decided to enter politics again as an active candidate. On May 15, 1935, Hoey became a candidate for governor. The Republicans offered little opposition in November and Clyde Roark Hoey was inaugurated governor of North Carolina in January, 1937.

During Governor Hoey's administration the state began furnishing free textbooks to the elementary schools; a teacher pay increase was approved; graduate courses were offered in Negro colleges; the state highway system was expanded;

an advertising program to attract tourists was approved; a modern parole system was developed; child labor laws were passed by the General Assembly; and the Alcoholic Beverage Board of Control and the State Bureau of Investigation were established.

After his term as governor, Hoey again returned to his law practice which he pursued until 1945 when he was elected to the United States Senate. He served the state of North Carolina in this capacity until his death.

Hoey was a member of the Masons, the Odd Fellows, Woodmen of the World, and the Junior Order. He belonged to the Knights of Pythias, as well as Omicron Delta Kappa and Sigma Chi fraternities. He was also a very active Methodist layman and while governor taught the Men's Bible class at Edenton Street Methodist Church where his lessons were broadcast.

On March 22, 1900, Clyde Hoey and Bess Gardner, the sister of O. Max Gardner, were married. Three children were born to Clyde and Bess Hoey. They are Clyde R. Hoey, Jr., Charles A. Hoey, and Isabel Y. Hoey.

Senator Hoey died of a stroke, May 12, 1954, while sitting at his desk in his Senate office. He is buried in his home town of Shelby, North Carolina. The State of North Carolina owns a portrait of Governor Hoey.

For additional information concerning Clyde Roark Hoey, see: *Addresses, Letters and Papers of Clyde Roark Hoey, Governor of North Carolina, 1937-1941,* edited by David Leroy Corbitt.

George A. Holderness

George Allan Holderness was born on June 15, 1867, in Caswell County, North Carolina, near the town of Milton. He was the son of William H. and Sarah Foreman Holderness.

He started to work early, securing a job as a traveling salesman of dry goods operating out of Baltimore, Maryland, and Philadelphia, Pennsylvania. In the fall of 1888, Holderness moved to Tarboro, North Carolina.

From Tarboro, Holderness continued his job as a salesman, traveling the whole state of North Carolina. It was in Greensboro, Charlotte, and other larger towns in the state that he came in contact with telephone service; for at that time none of the towns in North Carolina, with the exception of the larger ones, had telephone service.

In 1895, Holderness and W. H. Powell decided to try to raise twenty-five hundred dollars to build a telephone exchange in Tarboro. In October of 1895, the Tarboro Telephone Company was incorporated with a capital stock of twenty-five hundred dollars. Since both men had traveling jobs, they did not take an active part in the early management of the company; although later Powell became its president and Holderness the secretary-treasurer and general manager.

The first switchboard that was installed had a maximum of seventy-five stations. However, the exchange grew rapidly and a year or two later the board was junked and equipment for one hundred and twenty-five stations was installed. The exchange proved to be a success from the time it was put into service, and before very long, the 125-line board gave way to a 150-line board, which in turn was replaced by a multiple switchboard of two hundred lines.

The continued growth of the company resulted in the demand for new capital and at various times the capital stock of the company was increased until on May 24, 1897, the Tarboro Telephone and Telegraph Company was formed with a paid-in capital of ten thousand dollars.

Shortly after it became evident that the Tarboro enterprise was a success, Holderness and others built exchanges at Washington and Kinston; and soon thereafter purchased the Fayetteville exchange. The exchanges at Tarboro, Washington, Kinston, Fayetteville and Scotland Neck were merged into one ownership in 1900, forming the Carolina Telephone and Telegraph Company, with a paid-in capital of fifty thousand dollars. When the Wilson, Elm City, Smithfield, Dunn, Benson, Maxton, Red Springs, and Lillington exchanges were purchased by the company, Holderness, as general manager, found himself the leader of a considerable telephone company in the eastern part of North Carolina.

In October of 1903 a contract for connection with the long-distance lines of the Southern Bell Telephone and Telegraph Company was made. This necessitated the expenditure of considerable sums of money and the securing of new sources of capital. By 1904 the capital stock of the company had been increased to one hundred and fifty thousand dollars.

In 1915 the business of the company had grown to such proportions that it was necessary to have a competent engineer in charge of the operating department, so Holderness offered his resignation as general manager and retained his job as secretary-treasurer. C. P. McCluer was secured from the Bell

Company and elected the general manager of the company.

In 1918 Holderness purchased six small automatic exchange switchboards against the advice of the Bell Company. The installation of this group of exchanges was possibly the first installation of a group of automatic exchanges in the United States. In 1926, eighteen more were purchased and placed in operation in very small towns, providing satisfactory automatic service at relatively low rates to their rural subscribers.

In 1926 the properties of the Carolina Telephone and Telegraph Company and those of the Home Telephone and Telegraph Company, located at Henderson, North Carolina, were merged under the present name of the Carolina Telephone and Telegraph Company. Tarboro became the location of the general offices of the new firm.

Today the company owns eighty-five exchanges, including the largest group of automatic exchanges of any telephone company in the United States. This enables nearly every village and farm in Eastern North Carolina to have telephone service. Carolina Telephone and Telegraph Company operates in thirty-five Eastern North Carolina counties with more than thirty-five thousand telephones.

In 1926, after he had seen the merger of the two telephone companies through to completion, Holderness moved to Richmond, Virginia, where he became associated with the Virginia-Carolina Chemical Company as its vice-president and treasurer. He subsequently became president of the company. Upon his retirement, he returned to Tarboro, where he remained for the rest of his life.

Holderness was married to Harriet Howard of Tarboro. They had seven children: George Allan, Jr., Howard, William Henry, Thomas Thurston, Haywood Dial, Anna Stamps, and Harriet Howard.

George Allan Holderness died on December 23, 1947.

Robert P. Holding

Robert Powell Holding was born on December 31, 1896, in Wake Forest, North Carolina. He was one of seven children of Thomas Elford Holding and Minta Royall.

Holding attended the local public schools during his elementary and high school years, and entered Wake Forest College in the fall of 1912. He was graduated in 1916 with the degree of Bachelor of Arts. Immediately entering the Wake Forest Law School, he earned the Bachelor of Laws degree in 1917.

He passed the North Carolina Supreme Court examination for a license to practice law on February 5, 1917; however, Holding was six months too young to receive his license.

He applied for and was accepted for the position of bookkeeper-teller in the Bank of Morehead City. He undertook his banking responsibilities enthusiastically and was elected an assistant cashier later in the year.

In January of 1918, Holding joined the First National Bank of Smithfield in Johnston County, North Carolina, as assistant cashier and bookkeeper-teller. The First National Bank was an outgrowth of the Bank of Smithfield which was begun in 1898 with paid-in capital of $10,000. In 1916 the bank purchased the Smithfield Savings Bank, and in 1919 when Holding was elected cashier, total resources amounted to $500,000. In 1921 First-Citizens merged with Citizens National Bank and became First and Citizens National Bank. Holding was elected vice president of this growing firm in 1926, and at thirty years of age had established himself as a hard-working, far-seeing, aggressive leader. Adopting a state charter in 1929, the bank changed its name for the last time to First-Citizens Bank & Trust Company.

During the ensuing depression years a great many banks failed, but not First-Citizens. From 1929 through 1934, First-Citizens, under Holding's dynamic leadership, opened banks in fifteen towns throughout Eastern North Carolina.

In 1932, when the Federal Government established the Regional Agricultural Credit Corporation, to serve the two Carolinas, Georgia, and Florida, Holding was made its president. With all the millions of dollars loaned out by the Corporation, 99.9 per cent of principle and interest was collected.

In 1934, the Board of First-Citizens elected him its president and chairman, positions he maintained until his death.

During the depression years, he was a financial advisor to President Franklin D. Roosevelt. By 1938, when a wrecked national economy had spawned a rash of defunct banks throughout the country, First-Citizens paid its eightieth consecutive semi-annual dividend.

In addition to his countless hours in the service of First-Citizens, Holding was a true public servant. In 1939, he was appointed to the newly-created State Banking Commission by Governor Clyde R. Hoey. He retained his seat on this body until his death. As president of the North Carolina Bankers Association during 1942 and 1943, he began an illustrious career of service to numerous professional organizations, including a period on the executive committee of the American Bankers Association.

He was named one of the original members of the North

Carolina Securities Advisory Commission and became widely recognized in the national bond market as a securities expert. He personally handled the investment portfolio for First-Citizens.

Holding served on the Board of Trustees of Wake Forest College, and in 1957, was awarded, by his alma mater, the honorary degree of Doctor of Laws. He also served actively as a trustee for Campbell College.

He was a director of State Capital Life Insurance Company, Carolina Telephone and Telegraph Company, and Textron, Inc.; and was president of Seashore Transportation Company.

In addition to his work in the Baptist Church and the Kiwanis Club, Holding was an extremely generous and totally unassuming philanthropist, making countless contributions to individuals and educational institutions.

The First-Citizens Bank & Trust Company continued to grow and prosper under his direction, adding four more offices in the 1940's and additional branches in communities already served. By the end of 1949 the bank's total resources amounted to more than $132,000,000. Under his supervision, the bank established the first installment loan or time payment department of a bank in North Carolina. At the time of Holding's death in 1957, the bank was operating in thirty-two communities through forty-five separate offices. Its resources totaled more than $200,000,000.

Holding was married on January 11, 1922, to Maggie Brown of Bethel, North Carolina. They had three children: Robert Powell, Jr., Lewis Royall, and Frank Brown.

Robert Powell Holding died on August 26, 1957.

Robert Lee Humber

Robert Lee Humber was born in Greenville, North Carolina, on May 30, 1898, the son of R. L. and Lena Davis Humber. At the age of fifteen Robert was graduated from Winterville High School and soon afterward entered Wake Forest College, from which he received both a Bachelor of Arts and a law degree. While at Wake Forest he participated in a number of extracurricular activities. He edited both *Old Gold and Black* and *The Student,* was president of the senior class, played on the varsity football team, was a manager for the baseball team, and was active in many other facets of student life.

He volunteered for military service during World War I and received a commission as second lieutenant. After the war he entered Harward and was awarded an M.A. degree in 1920. At Harvard he also served as a faculty tutor in history, political science, and government. Leaving Harvard he went to New College, at Oxford, England, as a Rhodes Scholar. He also studied at the University of Paris and while not receiving a degree, he did considerable research into the history of law.

Paris appealed to Humber and it was there he began the practice of law and soon acquired a reputation as an outstanding international lawyer. He became counselor for an American oil company and was later promoted to its chief executive officer in France.

Hitler's invading troops forced Humber to leave Paris; he and his family fled the city only fifty-five hours ahead of the German invasion. He returned to North Carolina and his native Greenville. At this time he had a determination to seek to do something which would prevent another war such as the world was then experiencing.

On December 28, 1940, Humber formally began his campaign for a world government as the only method by which world peace could be obtained. On that day he met with thirty-nine friends on Smith Island, in Core Sound, and laid before them his theory for world peace. He also read to them a resolution he had prepared which embodied his beliefs and which he hoped to have passed by the legislatures of the states in hopes of gaining Congressional action in the area. In 1941, North Carolina became the first state in the Union to endorse Humber's resolution. Since that time nearly half the states have done so and some have gone further and called for a national convention to amend the Constitution to give the United States authority to participate in such a federation.

This personal crusade continued and Humber took it outside the United States and sought the support of other nations. He was joined by other individuals and organizations in his efforts to see his dream come true. To this end he founded the Movements for World Federation and co-founded the United World Federalists. At the San Francisco Conference which formulated the United Nations charter, he represented the Southern Council on International Relations.

Humber had many other interests from which the public has received benefit. One of these was art. It was largely due to his efforts that the North Carolina Museum of Art was established. For his work in this field the State Art Society adopted a resolution which expressed to Humber their appreciation for:

" . . . His long and untiring service to our State. . . .

" . . . His magnificent accomplishment aimed toward securing for this State the gift of $1,000,000 in paintings from the Kress Foundation. . . .

"For his astute and successful presentation of the interests of this Society to the General Assembly . . . to the end that the Society became the beneficiary of an appropriation of an additional $1,000,000 for the purchase of pictures for the State's Art Gallery at Raleigh. . . ."

Humber had led a campaign which resulted in an appropriation of $1,000,000 by the General Assembly in 1947 for the purchase of works of art. The appropriation had a provision that $1,000,000 from private sources would have to be raised before the money would be available. When the 1951 Assembly met, the money still had not been raised and many legislators thought of using the appropriation for other purposes. However, Humber came forward with a letter from the Samuel H. Kress Foundation agreeing to match the funds. Shortly thereafter the North Carolina Museum of Art became a reality.

His political affiliation was with the Democratic party and his religious affiliation was with the Baptist denomination.

He was married in October 1929, to Lucie Berthier of Paris, France. Three children were born of this union: Marcel B., John Leslie, and Eileen Genevieve, deceased.

He died November 10, 1970, and is buried in Greenville, North Carolina.

For additional information concerning R. L. Humber, see: *North Carolina Lives*, by William S. Powell, and "Tar Heel of the Week," Raleigh *News and Observer*, February 5, 1950.

14

Thomas J. Jarvis

Thomas Jordan Jarvis was born at Jarvisburg, in Currituck County, North Carolina, on January 18, 1836. He was the son of Bannister Hardy Jarvis and his wife, Elizabeth Daly. He attended the country schools and at the age of nineteen entered Randolph-Macon College, then located at Boydton, Virginia. He completed his undergraduate course in 1860 and continued his studies for an additional year to receive his A.M. degree.

Leaving his college days behind, Jarvis went to Pasquotank County where he was teaching school at the outbreak of the Civil War. He volunteered his services to the cause of the South and soon after enlistment was commissioned first lieutenant of Company B, Eighth North Carolina Regiment and about two years later was raised to the rank of captain.

After the war Jarvis opened a store in Tyrrell County. Having no capital he purchased his stock on credit and even had to borrow the money to pay freight on it. In his spare time he read law and in June, 1867, he received his license and began practice.

Jarvis' public career began in 1865 when a state convention was called after President Johnson had declared North Carolina restored to the Union. He had been elected to represent Currituck County in that body. Johnson's plans for reconstruction were nullified by the Reconstruction Acts of 1867 and the following year a new state constitution was adopted. The same year Jarvis was elected to the legislature from Tyrrell County. He was one of a few Democrats in the General Assembly and voiced strong opposition to the proposals of the carpetbag majority. This leadership in opposition accounts for his election as Speaker of the House in 1870. At the end of this legislature he moved to Pitt County.

In 1875 he was elected as a delegate from Pitt to the Constitutional Convention. He exerted great influence at the convention and it was largely through his efforts that an amendment was adopted which freed the white population of eastern North Carolina from Negro rule.

In 1876 Zebulon B. Vance was nominated as a candidate for governor and Jarvis as a candidate for lieutenant governor. Both were elected. Two years later Jarvis succeeded to the governor's chair when Vance was elected to the United States Senate. In 1880 he was elected to a full term.

During the Jarvis administration North Carolina was still feeling the economic effects of the war and reconstruction, yet many constructive and progressive programs were undertaken. D. H. Hill says this of his contribution to education: "During his six years in office the amount set aside for public schools was nearly doubled. The sum rose from three hundred and twenty-six thousand dollars in 1879 to six hundred and fifty-two thousand dollars in 1885. This increase led to the lengthening of the school term, the payment of better salaries to teachers, and the opening of schools within the reach of many more children."

The State debt, which was in the millions of dollars, was settled during the Jarvis administration, thus enabling North Carolina to build up her credit. The Western North Carolina Railroad was completed. Plans were made and construction begun on the Governor's Mansion while he was in office. Through his urging the Western Asylum at Morganton and the Eastern Asylum at Goldsboro were constructed. Other measures for the benefit of the state were also undertaken.

When his term as governor expired, Jarvis was appointed by President Cleveland as United States Minister to Brazil. He served in this position four years and then returned to North Carolina and again practiced law in Greenville in partnership with Judge Frank Wooten. On the death of Senator Vance in 1894, he was appointed by Governor Carr to fill his unexpired term. He served less than a year, for that fall the Republicans and Populists fused and elected members of their party to the Senate. The remainder of his life he spent as a lawyer and private citizen, but he often took part in political campaigns. He played an active role in the establishment of East Carolina Teachers Training School (now East Carolina University) at Greenville. He and William H. Ragsdale wrote the bill which was passed in 1907 establishing the school. During his latter years, he was often referred to as North Carolina's "Grand Old Man."

He was a member of the Odd Fellows and the Knights of Pythias. He served on the board of trustees of Trinity College. His religious affiliation was with the Methodist Church.

Jarvis was married to Mary Woodson, daughter of Judge John Woodson of Virginia, in 1874.

He died June 17, 1915, and is buried in Cherry Hill Cemetery in Greenville, North Carolina.

Portraits of Thomas Jarvis are owned by the State of North Carolina and by East Carolina University and can be found in Raleigh and Greenville, respectively.

For additional information concerning Thomas J. Jarvis, see: *Biographical History of North Carolina*, volume 1, by Samuel A. Ashe, and W. Buck Yearns, editor, *The Papers of Thomas Jordan Jarvis*.

Kate Burr Johnson

Kate Burr was born in Morganton, North Carolina, on February 14, 1881. She was the daughter of Frederick Hill Burr and Lillian (Walton) Burr.

She received her early educational training in the public schools of Morganton and then attended Queen's College in Charlotte, North Carolina, but only for a short period. In addition to her work at Queen's, Mrs. Johnson, as her jobs demanded specialized knowledge, attended summer sessions at the New York School of Social Work and at the University of North Carolina.

By 1915, Mrs. Johnson's interest in the area of public welfare had led to work with the North Carolina Conference for Social Service. Having served on its executive committee, she was elected vice-president of the organization for the 1915-1916 term.

The old North Carolina State Board of Charities, which was established by the Constitution of 1868, had the duty of supervising all charitable and penal institutions in the state, which meant inspecting them and reporting to the governor on their condition.

In 1917 the Board's activities were greatly expanded. The words "and Public Welfare" were added to the Board's name, a system of county superintendents of public welfare was set up under its supervision, and R. F. Beasley was appointed as its first state commissioner. In 1919 Mrs. Johnson began working for the reorganized Board of Charities and Public Welfare as director of the Division of Child Welfare. Two years later, Beasley resigned, and Mrs. Johnson was appointed to that office. She was the first woman to head a major state department in North Carolina, and the first woman in the United States to be a state commissioner of public welfare.

On the positive side of developments by Mrs. Johnson's administration and the Board of Public Welfare is the establishment of a mothers' aid program, a forerunner of the present aid to dependent children programs. Another is the Board's successful support of enactment of a sterilization law. While she was commissioner, the sensational trial of a chain gang boss, indicted by a grand jury at the instigation of the State Board of Public Welfare for cruelty to prisoners, helped to clean up chain gangs in North Carolina. Although he was freed, the trial resulted in improvement of conditions generally, both on the road gangs and in the prisons as well. There was constant development and growth in the public welfare program. There were important changes in the law and the formation of new and needed institutions. The staff of the Board was enlarged and the work was more fully organized into specialized departments.

Mrs. Johnson's finest contribution to public welfare in North Carolina was in her role as a pioneer. She kept it out of politics as much as possible and put it on a solid foundation, breaking ground for its later expansion. Additionally, she proved beyond doubt the ability of a woman to hold a high administrative office in state government.

When she was asked to become superintendent of New Jersey's State Home for Girls at Trenton, she took the job. Beginning in 1930, she spent some nineteen years administering the home for delinquents, and with that work, was instrumental in developing a state-wide program of classification work for and among the women prisoners of the state of New Jersey. In 1948, Mrs. Johnson retired and returned to Raleigh.

After her retirement, she served on the Prison Advisory Commission in North Carolina under Governor Kerr Scott.

She served in numerous other capacities as a public servant. During World War I, she was a member of the state committee charged with selling Liberty Bonds. She was elected a member of the American Academy of Political and Social Sciences and of the National Probation Association. She was a member of the executive committee on the Child Welfare League of America and was chairman of a committee on state and local organizations for the handicapped. In addition she was a member of the American Association of Social Workers, the National Conference of Juvenile Agencies, and the American Prison Association.

In 1951 she was awarded the honorary degree of Doctor of Humane Letters by Woman's College of the University of North Carolina at Greensboro. In 1954 she was the recipient of the North Carolina Distinguished Service Award for Women, presented annually by the Chi Omega Sorority.

On April 14, 1903, Kate Burr was married to Clarence A. Johnson, who died on September 9, 1922. The Johnsons had two children: Clarence A. and Frederick Burr.

Kate Burr Johnson died on August 22, 1968 and is buried in Oakwood Cemetery in Raleigh, North Carolina.

James Y. Joyner

James Yadkin Joyner was born in Davidson County, North Carolina, on August 7, 1862. He was the son of John Joyner and his wife, Sallie Wooten.

Joyner acquired the fundamentals of education at La Grange Academy. In 1878 he entered the University of North Carolina and was graduated three years later with the degree of Bachelor of Philosophy.

Upon leaving the University he returned to Lenoir County and took a position teaching at La Grange Academy and the next year was made principal of the school. During this same time Joyner served as superintendent of Lenoir County schools. In 1884 he left the eastern part of the state and took a position as superintendent of Winston (now Winston-Salem) schools.

In the winter of 1885 Joyner began to study law under the supervision of the firm of Dick and Dillard in Greensboro. He was admitted to the Bar in the summer of 1886 and went to Goldsboro to begin practice.

Even though the legal profession was momentarily rewarding to Joyner, he was happier in the field of education. In 1889 he was offered the position of superintendent of the Goldsboro city schools and accepted. He continued in this position four years and gained a state-wide reputation as an enlightened school leader. Charles D. McIver, then president of the State Normal and Industrial College (now the University of North Carolina at Greensboro), prevailed upon Joyner to come to the college in the capacity of professor of English literature and dean of the Normal School. During this time the college became the first state institution to begin the training of women for positions as classroom teachers. He spent his summers during the nine years he was associated with the college conducting teachers' institutes. These had been begun by McIver and Alderman and consisted of five-day workshops.

Thomas F. Toon was elected State Superintendent of Public Instruction in 1901, but died the next year leaving Governor Charles B. Aycock the task of appointing a successor. Aycock appointed Joyner to the position. Joyner filled the superintendent's office, by continuous re-election, until he chose to retire after seventeen years service.

When Joyner assumed the responsibility as administrative head of North Carolina's school system, public education was at a low ebb. The state had only thirty high schools and these were not supported by the state, but by the citizens of some of the larger towns. There were over 5,000 one-teacher schools in North Carolina and these teachers received an average of only twenty-four dollars per month. Libraries in the schools were almost non-existent. School terms ran for only three or four months. These and many other problems faced the new superintendent as he began his efforts to provide educational facilities for North Carolina children.

When Joyner left office in 1919, he could look back on many accomplishments. Teachers' salaries had been raised, total school expenditures were tripled in the first ten years he was in office, over 3,000 new school buildings were erected during his first decade in office, many additional teachers were employed, libraries were provided for most of the schools, the Public High School Act was passed which provided partial funds for communities desiring a high school, many of the one-teacher schools were consolidated into larger units, and many other advancements were made in the cause of public education.

Upon his retirement Joyner returned to his farm in Lenoir County. In 1922 he returned to Raleigh as an organizer and director of the Tobacco Growers Co-operative Association. Leaving the "Co-op" in 1926, he worked with Prudential Life Insurance Company until 1932, then returned to his La Grange farm, where he lived until his death.

Joyner was elected president of the National Education Association in 1910. He served on the boards of trustees of East Carolina College, the University of North Carolina at Greensboro, the University of North Carolina at Chapel Hill, the Agricultural and Technical College at Greensboro, and Meredith College. He was also a member of the Rotary. In politics he was a Democrat and in religion was affiliated with the Baptist Church.

He was married on December 14, 1887, to Effie Rouse. Two sons were born of this union: James N. Joyner and William T. Joyner.

Joyner died January 24, 1954, and is buried in Oakwood Cemetery in Raleigh.

A portrait of J. Y. Joyner is owned by the State of North Carolina and hangs in Raleigh.

For additional information concerning James Y. Joyner, see: Gilbert Allen Tripp, "James Yadkin Joyner's Contributions to Education in North Carolina as State Superintendent," master's thesis, University of North Carolina, 1939, and "James Yadkin Joyner, Education Statesman" by Elmer D. Johnson in *North Carolina Historical Review*, XXXIII (July, 1956), 359-383.

William R. Kenan, Jr.

William Rand Kenan, Jr., was born in Wilmington, North Carolina, on April 30, 1872. He was the son of William R. Kenan, a wholesale grocer, and his wife, Mary Hargrave of Chapel Hill.

Kenan received his first formal education at Tileston High School in Wilmington. He later attended Horner's Military Academy at Oxford before entering the University of North Carolina in 1890. At the University he played on the varsity baseball team for two years and managed the team for two years. In 1893 he tried out for the football team and, although weighing less than 150 pounds, he made the right halfback position. Kenan was also a member of the SAE fraternity and the Order of the Gimghouls. He was graduated in 1894.

The summer after graduation Kenan spent time making water analyses for the North Carolina Geological Survey. When the school term began in 1894, he took a position as teacher of mathematics at St. Albans School in Radford, Virginia. The next year he returned to his alma mater as a chemistry instructor.

It was while working at the University that Kenan made a discovery which would change the direction of his life. He and Dr. F. P. Venable engaged in chemical research which eventually led to a formula for carbide and acetylene gas. Kenan later remarked that the discovery of carbide was really an accident, a by-product of experiments on a method of producing graphite paint.

Money did not come to Kenan directly from the manufacture of carbide, but rather through his supervision of the manufacture of the product for others. He left the University in 1896 and assumed the responsibility of designing and supervising construction of a plant for the Carbide Manufacturing Company at Niagara Falls, New York. Over the next several years he performed these same services in many countries.

At the beginning of the century he became associated with Henry Flagler, one time partner of John D. Rockefeller, who hired him to construct the first power plant in Miami, Florida. This led to other projects and the accumulation of a financial empire which ran into the millions of dollars. Kenan built hotels, railroads, and utility plants during the Florida boom. In addition to these business undertakings, he had interests in paper mills and was president of the Western Block Company.

As Kenan's wealth increased, so did his generosity towards the University of North Carolina. In 1926 he made a gift to his alma mater of $275,000 for the construction of a football stadium to be named in memory of his parents. Before the completion of the stadium he gave an additional $28,000 for the construction of a field house. The stadium was dedicated on Thanksgiving Day, 1927, and Kenan was present to watch the Tar Heels defeat Virginia. In 1944 he made a donation of $5,000 for repairs to the stadium and five years later donated $75,000 toward the construction of enlarged press and visitors boxes. In 1962 he made still another gift, this time for $750,000, which was used to increase the capacity of the football amphitheater from 24,000 to 44,000.

Kenan made other gifts to the University during his lifetime. Among these were books to the University chemistry library, and monetary donations to both the University Press and WUNC-TV.

With his sisters, Kenan provided the funds for the chapel and spire of the First Presbyterian Church in Wilmington. He also made a number of contributions out of North Carolina. Some of these are: a summer camp for boys at Lockport, New York, the Y.M.C.A. building in Lockport, a radiation laboratory to the University of California.

At W. R. Kenan's death, the bulk of his estate was left in trust to be used for charitable and educational purposes. One such fund, valued at $2,000,000, and Randleigh Farm, a model dairy farm operated by Kenan, were left to North Carolina State University at Raleigh. In 1966 the trustees of William R. Kenan, Jr. Charitable Trust of New York announced a gift of $5,000,000 to be given to the University at Chapel Hill over a five-year period for the purpose of establishing William R. Kenan, Jr. Professorships.

He was a charter member of the American Chemical Society and was a recipient of the American Jersey Cattle Association's Master Breeder Award in 1945. In religion he was affiliated with the Presbyterian church.

He was married in 1904 to Alice Pomrey of Lockport, New York. They had no children.

W. R. Kenan, Jr. died on July 28, 1965. He is buried in Glenwood Cemetery, in Lockport, New York, the city in which he had lived for a number of years.

For additional information concerning William Rand Kenan, Jr., see: *Incidents By the Way*, an autobiography in five volumes.

Thurmond Kitchin

Thurmond Delna Kitchin was born in Scotland Neck, North Carolina, on October 17, 1885, the son of William E. Hodge Kitchin and his wife, Marie Figus Arrington.

He received his preparatory education at Vine Hill Academy in his home community and before entering Wake Forest College from which he was graduated in 1905. He then attended the University of North Carolina for a year before entering Jefferson Medical College in Philadelphia. He received his M.D. from this institution in 1908.

Leaving college, he went to Lumberton to become a practicing physician. He stayed there only two years before returning home to Scotland Neck where he practiced for the next seven years.

In 1917 Dr. Kitchin went to Wake Forest College to fill the position of professor of physiology and pharmacology. Two years later he was made Dean of the School of Medicine. He continued in this position for thirteen years.

In 1930 Dr. Kitchin was elected to the presidency of Wake Forest College. He served in this capacity for twenty years.

Perhaps the greatest crisis in the life of the college while he served as president was a series of fires which destroyed two major buildings on the campus, partially destroyed two others, and razed two smaller wooden structures. These occurred in 1933-34, but Kitchin, in spite of the depression, refused to allow these misfortunes to hinder the growth of the school. A major building program was conducted during his administration which saw the following buildings constructed: Wait Hall (replacing the building by the same name which was destroyed by fire), the William Amos Johnson Building, the Religion and Music Building, Simmons Hall, the Lois Johnson Dormitory for Women, South Dormitory, Gore Gymnasium, Groves Stadium, and the Chapel.

During the 1930's there was a movement to close two-year medical colleges and Dr. Kitchin played a key role in keeping these open. In 1939 he completed negotiations which resulted in the establishing of the Bowman Gray School of Medicine of Wake Forest College at Winston-Salem.

Enrollment was a problem in all colleges during the depression. During Kitchin's first year as president, Wake Forest's student body numbered 698. Due to a vigorous recruitment policy, the enrollment was almost doubled within five years. At his retirement, the school enjoyed its largest student body—2,249. World War II presented an even more serious crisis than the depression in maintaining student enrollment. Shortly after Pearl Harbor the number declined to 310 and the college was faced with the possibility of having to close; however, Dr. Kitchin secured a contract from the government setting up an Army Finance School at the college. This brought 1,200 additional students to the college and ensured that it remain open for the duration.

In 1942 the college and the State Baptist Convention voted to allow women students of junior and senior standing to enter Wake Forest. Two years later the decision was made to admit freshman and sophomore girls.

President Kitchin's administration also saw the school's accreditation strengthened. The college was accepted as an unconditional member of the Southern Association of Colleges and Secondary Schools, received the approval of the Association of American Universities, became a member of the Association of American Colleges, and gained a chapter of the Phi Beta Kappa.

In 1946 the most drastic decision since the founding of the college was made, the decision to move from Wake Forest to Winston-Salem. The move was prompted by an offer from the Z. Smith Reynolds Foundation of $350,000 annual income if the college would come to Winston-Salem.

Other accomplishments during the presidency of Kitchin were: the standardization of the Law School, addition of the department of music, addition of the School of Business Administration, and the adoption of a retirement system for faculty and other employees.

Illness forced Dr. Kitchin to leave the presidency in 1950.

Dr. Kitchin was the author of the three books: *Lectures on Pharmacology*, *The Doctor and Citizenship*, and *Doctors in Others Fields*.

In politics his affiliation was with the Democratic party and his religious affiliation was Baptist. He was also a Mason.

He was married November 3, 1908, to Reba Calvert Clark of Scotland Neck. Three children were born of this union: Thurmond D. Kitchin, Jr., Irving Clark Kitchin, and William Walton Kitchin.

Dr. Kitchin died August 28, 1955, and is buried in Scotland Neck.

A portrait of Dr. Kitchin is owned by Wake Forest College.

For additional information concerning Thurmond D. Kitchin, see: *The Wake Forest Magazine*, October, 1955.

W. W. Kitchin

William Walton Kitchin was born at Scotland Neck, North Carolina, on October 9, 1866, the son of W. H. Kitchin and his wife, Marie Figus Arrington.

Kitchin received his first formal education at Vine Hill Academy in his home community and then entered Wake Forest College from which he was graduated in 1884 at the age of eighteen.

After graduation he spent a very short period in Texas, returning to his home county to edit the *Scotland Neck Democrat*. During the year he served as editor of the paper, its circulation increased 300 per cent.

The study of law next attracted young Kitchin and he studied at the direction of his father and later at the University of North Carolina under John Manning. In 1888, after he had received his license, he went to Roxboro, in Person County, and there began the practice of law.

As a young attorney he was quick to enter politics and in 1890 he became the chairman of the Democratic Executive Committee for Person County. Under his leadership the county voted Democratic for the first time in a number of years. Two years later he made a race for the State Senate, but was defeated. In 1896 his party put him up as a candidate for the United States House of Representatives against Thomas Settle, the Republican incumbent. His chances of winning were considered slim, but in a year when all other Democratic Congressional candidates in the state lost, Kitchin won. He continued to represent his district, the fifth, for twelve years.

During most of his Congressional career, Kitchin was a minority party member; however, his influence was felt in that body. He was the first Democrat to become a member of the Committee of Naval Affairs and during most of his twelve years in Congress served on the Congressional Campaign Committee for the Democratic party. During the White Supremacy and Suffrage Admendment campaigns in North Carolina, the suffrage amendment became an issue in Congress and Kitchin defended it in a speech before that body.

When the Democratic Convention met in Charlotte in 1908, there were three candidates in the running for the gubernatorial nomination: Locke Craig, Ashley Horne, and Kitchin. Each candidate had strong support, but after sixty-one rounds of balloting, Kitchin emerged with the nomination. In the general election he easily won over his Republican opponent, J. Elwood Cox, and was inaugurated governor on January 12, 1909.

During the Kitchin administration the state made progress on almost every front. Expenditures for public education were increased $750,000; expenditures for public health were increased from $4,000 to $26,500 per year; 1,300 miles of roads were built; a state-supported school for the feeble-minded was established at Kinston; and 604,000 acres of swamp land came under the state's drainage laws. The economic condition of the state was strengthened with the laying of 250 additional miles of railway and an increase in bank capital by $1,800,000.

Kitchin made sweeping recommendations in regard to

greater regulation of big business, some of which were considered socialistic at the time. Many of these were enacted into law and as a result the antitrust laws of the state were strengthened. Also laws requiring better sanitation in factories and enforcement of a law prohibiting the employment of children under thirteen brought better working conditions.

In 1912 the state saw its first popular election for the office of United States Senator. Four of North Carolina's political giants entered the contest — former Governor Charles B. Aycock, Chief Justice Walter Clark, incumbent Senator F. M. Simmons, and Governor W. W. Kitchin. Aycock died during the early stages of the campaign, but the other three candidates fought it out until the end. When the ballots were counted Simmons won with a clear majority over both the other contestants.

After the election, Kitchin completed his term as governor and then began the practice of law in Raleigh with James S. Manning. In 1919, six years after leaving the governor's office, he suffered a stroke and was forced into retirement. He returned to his childhood home in Scotland Neck and there spent his last days. His brother, Claude, was shortly thereafter forced to leave the United States Congress because of ill health and the two spent much time together before Claude's death.

He married Musette Satterfield in 1892. Five children were born of this union: Susan, Annie, Elizabeth, Musette, and Clement Kitchin.

Kitchin died in Scotland Neck on November 9, 1924.

A portrait of Governor Kitchin was given to Person County by R. O. Everett and the State of North Carolina owns a portrait of the former governor which hangs in Raleigh.

For additional information concerning W. W. Kitchin, see: *Reports of the North Carolina Bar Association*, volume 27.

Frederick Koch

Frederick Henry Koch was born in Covington, Kentucky, September 12, 1877. He was one of ten children, born to August and Rebecca Julian Koch.

Shortly after Frederick was born, the Koch family moved from Covington to Peoria, Illinois, where he attended high school and was graduated at the age of seventeen. He received his college education at Caterals Methodist College in Cincinnati, Ohio, Wesleyan University where he received his bachelor's degree in 1900, and Harvard, where he received his master's degree in 1909. He went to the University of North Dakota in 1905 as an instructor in English, and there began his crusade for a people's theater.

When Koch assumed his duties at the University, the only local stage was that of the "Metropolitan Opera House," there being no theater on the campus. The students, however, had a great interest in the stage and Koch soon organized a drama group. The Sock and Buskin Society, as the drama group was named, began writing its own plays and producing them; and in 1917 they changed their name to the Dakota Playmakers. Shortly after this, Professor Koch left to others the continuation of the work he had begun in North Dakota, while he came to North Carolina to plant the seed of another "people's theater."

Dr. Edwin Greenlaw, head of the English Department at the University of North Carolina, was acquainted with the work of Koch in the midwest, and after consulting with University President Edward K. Graham, he wrote and asked him to come to North Carolina. After his arrival in Chapel Hill in 1918, Professor Koch learned that the University offered no course in drama. "Proff," as he came to be known, remedied this with a course called Dramatic Composition. The course was designed to encourage students to write plays with emphasis placed on local traditions, folklore, and contempory life as background material. There was only one male member of this first playwriting class in Chapel Hill, a young man by the name of Thomas Wolfe. Many of "Proff's" students, besides Wolfe, later made a name for themselves in the world of literature: Paul Green, Jonathan Daniels, Betty Smith, Bernice Kelly Harris, Noel Houston, Frances Gray Patton, and many others.

Koch began almost immediately to organize a theater group such as the one he had started in North Dakota. The growth and development of this group, the Carolina Playmakers, was similar to that of the Dakota group. Many of the plays produced by the troup were written by its members. On May 7, 1920, in the third year of their existence, they presented four of their "Carolina Folk Plays" in Greensboro, the first performance outside Chapel Hill. Soon the group began touring neighboring states—South Carolina, Georgia, Virginia, Maryland—as well as North Carolina.

On November 23, 1925, one of Koch's most cherished dreams came true—the dedication of the Playmakers Theater. Smith Hall, erected in 1852, after being used as the University Library, gymnasium, and law center, was now to be the home of the Playmakers.

Koch also organized a Bureau of Community Drama in 1918, the same year he founded the Playmakers. Through this agency schools and other groups could receive assistance in promoting plays, pageants, and festivals. They offered a free play-lending service and the aid of a field representative who would visit the group and help with their productions. Under the supervision of the Bureau, the Carolina Dramatic Association was formed in 1924.

American Folk Plays (1939) and *Carolina Folk Plays* (1941) contain collections of the best plays written in Professor Koch's classes.

Koch, while teaching others to write, did not write a great deal himself. He was too busy inspiring others. In 1902 he wrote *Raleigh, the Shepherd of the Ocean*, a pageant about Sir Walter Raleigh. In addition he wrote many articles.

After leaving Harvard in 1909, Koch went on a tour of Europe. While in Athens, Greece, he met another tourist, Loretta Jean Hanigan, of Denver, Colorado. She and Koch were married on March 24, 1910. Four sons were born to them—Frederick Henry, George Julian, Robert Allen, and William Julian.

Koch was a member of the Drama League of America, American Pageant Association, American National Theatre, National Shakespeare Federation, American Association of University Professors, North Carolina Literary and History Association, North Carolina Folklore Society, American Dialect Society, National Negro Theatre and the Sigma Chi fraternity. He was also a member of the Unitarian Church.

"Proff" died at Miami Beach, Florida, on August 16, 1944. To his memory the Forest Theatre at Chapel Hill was dedicated and became the Koch Memorial Forest Theater. A portrait of him hangs in the Playmakers Theater in Chapel Hill.

For additional information concerning Frederick Henry Koch, see: *Frederick Henry Koch: Pioneer Playmaker*, by Samuel Seldon.

Maude Moore Latham

Maude Moore was born on December 16, 1871, in New
Bern, North Carolina. She was the daughter of James Washington Moore and Sarah Jane Gordon Moore.

She attended Corinne Harrison's private school and the
New Bern public schools, where she was an honor student.
While still quite young, she went to New York City to reside
with her maternal grandparents, attending the public schools
of that city and studying at Hunter College there.

On August 10, 1892, she was married to James Edwin
Latham, of New Bern, a young and promising cotton merchant. Some twelve years later, in 1904, they moved to
Greensboro, where Latham set up headquarters for his cotton
brokerage and commission business as the J. E. Latham Co.

After her marriage, Mrs. Latham became interested in financial and business investments. Her husband occasionally
gave her gold dollars for spending money and instead of buying more clothes, which she loved and for which she became
well-known, she saved her dollars. Surprising her husband
one day, she opened her trunk and pulled out one hundred
and twenty-five gold pieces. She asked him to invest them
for her, so Latham bought Brazilian coffee stock for two dollars a share, thus providing the foundation for her ultimate
personal fortune.

The Latham Memorial Hospital at the Eastern Star and Masonic Home of Greensboro was started by her gift of thirty thousand dollars. She was a member of the First Presbyterian Church of Greensboro and a trustee of the Presbyterian Home for the Aged, to which she was a liberal contributor.

Gardens and garden clubs were among her primary interests. Her own gardens in Greensboro were showplaces and she belonged to the Dogwood Garden Club of Greensboro. In 1939 she helped prepare and finance the book, *Old Homes and Gardens of North Carolina,* for the Garden Club of North Carolina.

She was a member of the United Daughters of the Confederacy, National Society United Daughters of 1812, National Society Daughters of the American Revolution, National Society Daughters of the American Colonists, National Society Daughters of Colonial Wars, National Society Sons and Daughters of the Pilgrims, and Gold Star Mothers of the American Legion Auxiliary.

Well known for her aid in restoration projects, Mrs. Latham was recognized by the North Carolina Society for the Preservation of Antiquities when she was awarded its first Cannon Cup in 1948. She was appointed by Governor Kerr Scott a member of the state commission for the restoration of Governor Charles B. Aycock's birthplace.

A native of New Bern, she had long dreamed of seeing historic Tryon Palace restored to its original importance and beauty as North Carolina's first permanent capitol. On January 26, 1944, she established the Maude Moore Latham Trust Fund of one hundred thousand dollars for the restoration of the building.

Promising to restore the entire structure if the state would purchase the necessary land, she, together with Miss Gertrude Carraway and others, succeeded in persuading the General

Assembly, in 1945, to appropriate one hundred and fifty thousand dollars to the project and to authorize the gubernatorial appointment of a Tryon Palace Commission to supervise the erection and maintenance of the Palace. Mrs. Latham was appointed chairman of the commission by Governor R. Gregg Cherry.

On April 26, 1949, a second trust fund of some one hundred and fifty thousand dollars was set up by Mrs. Latham, and shortly thereafter, the state appropriated an additional seventy-seven thousand dollars for property.

A handsome collection of antique furnishings, valued at one hundred and twenty-five thousand dollars, was given by Mrs. Latham on January 1, 1950, to the state of North Carolina for the restored Palace.

So great was her interest in the project, that following her death in 1951, it was learned that she had bequeathed the residue of her estate, valued at over one million, two hundred and fifty thousand dollars, to the Tryon Palace Commission to assure the complete restoration. Through the able management of her son-in-law, John A. Kellenberger, treasurer and finance officer of the commission, this bequest increased substantially in value through the years. Thanks to Mrs. Latham's generous and unselfish gifts, the Palace was completely restored by 1959.

James Edwin Latham died on April 16, 1946. The couple had two children: Edwin, who died in the service in 1923, and May Gordon, who is Mrs. John A. Kellenberger, present chairman of the Tryon Palace Commission.

Maude Moore Latham died on April 8, 1951, and is buried in Green Hill Cemetery, Greensboro, North Carolina.

16

J. Spencer Love

James Spencer Love was born in Cambridge, Massachusetts, on July 6, 1896, the son of James Lee Love and his wife, Julia Spencer.

He attended the Cambridge Latin School, where he received his preparation for college, entering Harvard upon completion of his work there. At Harvard he completed the normal four-year undergraduate course in three years, but continued his studies for another year at the Harvard Graduate Business School.

Immediately upon leaving Harvard, he enlisted in the Army and after completion of Officers' Training School, was commissioned a second lieutenant in 1917. He soon rose to the rank of major, the youngest major in the American overseas forces during this period of World War I.

After the war he returned to New England to seek a job, but unable to find one to his liking, he came to Gastonia, North Carolina, and took a position as a payroll clerk with the Gastonia Cotton Mills. This was the first cotton mill built in Gastonia and Love's grandfather, R. C. G. Love, had been its first president and had served in this capacity until his death in 1908.

Spencer Love had only $3,000 when he went to Gastonia, but he soon decided to purchase a mill of his own, and was determined not to let the lack of capital stand in his way. He negotiated with the owners of the Gastonia Cotton Mill for its purchase and they put a price of $250,000 on the textile plant. He borrowed $65,000 by pledging the plant's accounts receivable as security, managed to obtain a loan of $15,000 from a local bank, and persuaded the owners to allow him to pay the balance of $170,000 out of the profits of the next several years. So in 1919 Spencer Love owned his first mill.

The cotton textile business remained profitable for but a few years. In 1923 he sold the buildings and land belonging to the mill, keeping only the machinery. The Chamber of Commerce of Burlington, North Carolina, was persuaded to underwrite stock for a new plant and Love moved his machines to this piedmont town. In July, 1924, the first Burlington mill was completed.

The textile business remained depressed and the new plant had to struggle to meet its obligations. Spencer Love then saw the way of the future—synthetic fibers. Rayon was the only such fiber at the time and he began using it in connection with cotton fibers in the manufacture of bedspreads. When this proved successful, he expanded the use of rayon and Burlington made money. Growth came through the building of new mills and the acquisition of existing mills. In the 1950's Burlington Mills engaged in a diversification program so their economic life would not be dependent upon rayon fabrics alone. At Spencer Love's death Burlington had 130 plants in sixteen states and seven foreign countries. It operated sales offices in every part of the United States and in eighty-five foreign countries. The number of employees had risen from 200 to about 65,000.

Spencer Love was a forward looking businessman. He was one of the few textile leaders to recommend a raise in the federal minimum wage. He insisted that his plants be modernized rapidly when possible and that all his employees be given a fair deal. In his words: "You've got to share your success with labor."

In his later years Love began to take an active part in politics, although not seeking any office for himself. On a national scale he served the nation as a member of the Business Advisory Council, a member of the Advisory Committee of Labor-Management Policy, a trustee of the Committee on Economic Development, and a director of the National Safety Council.

Love was a member of the Board of Trustees of the University of North Carolina, the Board of Trustees of Davidson College, and a member of the Visiting Committee of the Harvard Graduate School of Business Administration. Other activities beneficial to education were his efforts in establishing the Burlington Industries Foundation.

Love was a director of the North Carolina Research Triangle, a director of the North Carolina Textile Foundation, a director of the American Cotton Manufacturers Institute, and a member of the Ad Hoc Textile Research Committee of the National Academy of Sciences. His religious affiliation was with the Presbyterian Church.

He was married January 25, 1922, to Sara Elizabeth Love. Four sons were born of this union: James Spencer, Robert Lee, Richard, and Julian. This marriage ended in divorce in 1940. Love was married in 1944 to Martha Eskridge of Shelby, North Carolina. Four children were born of this union also: Charles, Martin, Cornelia, and Lela.

He died January 20, 1962, at his winter home in West Palm Beach, Florida. He is buried in Forest Lawn Cemetery, Greensboro, North Carolina.

For additional information concerning J. Spencer Love, see: *The Spencer Love Story*, a tribute published by Burlington Industries, Inc.

Hugh MacRae

Hugh MacRae was born in Carbonton, North Carolina, March 30, 1865. He was the son of Donald MacRae and his wife, Julia Norton. At the end of the Civil War and the Federal occupation of Wilmington, his family returned to that city. Here and at the Bingham School in Asheville, he received his preparation for college. He entered the Massachusetts Institute of Technology at the age of sixteen and was graduated in 1885.

After receiving his formal education he returned to his native state and took a job as a mining engineer at Burnsville, a position he held until 1889. During this time he became interested in land development. He organized the Linville Company of which he was elected president in 1889 and later chairman of the board of directors. His company developed the mountain resort town of Linville. The company also purchased Grandfather Mountain, one of the major scenic attractions in the western part of North Carolina. In 1895 MacRae became president of the Wilmington Cotton Mills Company. Five years later he also became head of the Wilmington Gas Light Company which was later merged with the Wilmington Street Railway and the Seacoast Railway to become the Consolidated Railways, Light & Power Company. He continued as president of this concern and its successor,

Tide Water Power Company, until 1929 when it was sold.

Real estate development was perhaps MacRae's major interest. Through the Linville Company, he developed not only the mountain resort town, but also the seacoast resort of Wrightsville Beach and the agricultural colonies for which he is best known. He combined his personal real estate holdings and formed the concern of Hugh MacRae & Company.

In addition to his real estate ventures, MacRae established the Hugh MacRae Banking House, which financed the Rockingham Power Company. He served as president of this concern which had headquarters in Wilmington and a branch in New York City.

One of MacRae's favorite sayings and one which was eventually adopted as a slogan for a number of agricultural magazines was: "The South will come into its own when its fields are green in winter." He believed that the South could become the leading beef producing and dairying region in the nation because of its climate. The infrequency of drought and the longer growing season gave the South advantages not found in the beef states of the West or the dairy states of the Great Lakes region. On his farm, Invershiel, near Rocky Point, in Pender County, he experimented with this belief for over thirty years. Here he developed a grazing program which could support a large herd of Black Angus cattle twelve months a year.

The undertakings for which he is best known are his agricultural colonies. MacRae wanted farmers in the eastern part of the state who would practice intensive cultivation. He sent representatives to the midwest with inducements to the farmers there to move to the Wilmington area and undertake such a program. A few were persuaded and came to Wilmington, but became dissatisfied rather quickly and returned to the midwest at MacRae's expense. After this failure he sent representatives to Europe with offers of free transportation to America and a chance to purchase farms as crops were produced on them. People from many countries accepted the offers. The community of Castle Hayne was settled by Hollanders; St. Helena by Italians, Poles and Russians; and Delco by Germans.

Castle Hayne is the best known of these projects and has received the greatest notice. The Hollanders began as truck farmers, practicing the intensive cultivation that was required in Europe because of the crowded conditions there. Then an experiment to see if bulbs would grow in the soil of this area proved successful, and flowers soon took the place of vegetables as the money crop in Castle Hayne.

Ida M. Tarbell in an article in *Collier's* summed up MacRae's work this way: "Most great enterprises start with a vision followed by a definite working plan. Hugh MacRae of Wilmington started with a dream of making life happier, prospects more equal, and rewards more certain for thousands of Americans who want to own their homes and live off the land."

MacRae was a member of the Wilmington Chamber of Commerce, the Cape Fear Club, the Cape Fear Country Club, the Carolina Yacht Club, the National Arts Club in New York, and the Chevy Chase Club in Washington. His religious affiliation was with St. James' Episcopal Church in Wilmington and his political affiliation was with the Democratic party.

He was married to Rena Nelson, daughter of Benjamin Franklin Nelson, on February 4, 1891. Three children were born of this union: Dorothy, Nelson, and Agnes.

Hugh MacRae died October 20, 1951, and is buried in Oakdale Cemetery in Wilmington, North Carolina.

Charles D. McIver

Charles Duncan McIver was born on September 27, 1860, near Sanford, North Carolina, then in Moore County. His father was Matthew Henry McIver, who was born in Scotland. His mother was Sarah Harrington.

McIver began his schooling at eight years of age in a one-room school and when seventeen, he entered the University of North Carolina. He was graduated in 1881 with a degree of Bachelor of Arts. In the fall of that year, he went to work for forty-five dollars a month as assistant headmaster of a small private school, Presbyterian Male Academy, in Durham. Shortly afterwards he was made principal.

McIver's first vote was cast in May 1882, for a local tax to secure the establishment of the Durham public school system. As assistant superintendent, he aided in the organization of the Durham graded schools, and after teaching there for a year and a half, he was called to a similar position in Winston, whose public schools he helped to organize in the spring of 1884. He spent two and one-half years teaching in the Winston public schools, leaving in the fall of 1886 to become principal teacher of the literary department of Peace Institute in Raleigh.

His work at Peace Institute for three years and his residence at the state capital combined to give him knowledge in regard to the education of women and an opportunity to approach legislators. It was with this knowledge and opportunity that he, as chairman of the committee of the North Carolina Teachers' Assembly to memorialize the legislature to establish a normal college, presented before committees and discussed with individual legislators a bill for the establishment of such an institution. The bill passed the Senate by a large majority, but was defeated in the House because there was not enough time to discuss the matter individually with the 120 Representatives as had been the case with the 50 Senators. Instead of establishing a normal college, the General Assembly of 1889 provided for a system of county institutes. Dr. McIver and Edwin Alderman, then superintendent of the Goldsboro graded schools, were elected state institute conductors, and in the fall of 1889 began their work which continued for three years.

For the next few years, they went into every county of the state promoting the idea of higher education for women by making speech after speech on the subject. In 1891, almost without opposition, an act chartering the State Normal and Industrial College at Greensboro, was passed, and in October, 1892, this college began its work with Dr. McIver as president. Under his direction the school grew from a small plant with three or four buildings on ten acres of land into a recognized college for women. The school later became known as the Woman's College of the University of North Carolina, and is now an integral part of the University system.

McIver was widely known as a public speaker and orator, lecturing in teachers' institutes, making campaign speeches for local taxation for better public schools and appearing before legislative committees to secure school legislation. Nearly all his public addresses were on one of two subjects, namely, the education of women and the necessity for increasing taxes for public education. The wide variety of his career as a public servant is indicated by the positions of honor and influence which he held. In addition to fourteen years as president of the College and conductor of state and county normal institutes, superintendent of summer normal schools, and chairman of the committee that secured the establishment of the Normal and Industrial College, he was a participant in the work of the North Carolina Teachers' Assembly and its president in 1892, a worker in the Southern Education Association and its president in 1905, and an active member of the National Educational Association. He was one of the organizers of the Southern Educational Board and a leader in the movement for local taxation for public schools in North Carolina. He organized the Woman's Association for the Betterment of Public Schools. He was trustee and member of the executive committee of the University, which institution conferred on him in 1893 the honorary degrees of Doctor of Letters and Doctor of Laws. He was a member of the State Literary and Historical Association and of the State Library Association.

On July 29, 1885, McIver married Lula V. Martin, of Winston. They had four children.

Dr. McIver died on September 17, 1906, on a train carrying William Jennings Bryan through North Carolina.

For additional information on Charles D. McIver, see: *McIver of North Carolina*, by Rose Howell Holder.

Angus W. McLean

Angus Wilton McLean was born in Robeson County, North Carolina, April 20, 1870. He was the son of Archibald Alexander McLean and Caroline Purcell McLean.

He first attended the local schools and then the McMillan Military School from which he was graduated in 1884. He next attended high school and then went to the University of North Carolina to complete his formal education. At the University he studied law and was graduated in 1892 with the degree of Bachelor of Laws. He returned to Lumberton and began practice with Thomas A. McNeill, a kinsman.

While an able attorney, McLean had a keen interest in business pursuits. At the age of twenty-six he helped organize the Bank of Lumberton and was elected its president after the first president, Thomas A. McNeill, became a state Superior Court judge. In 1895 he helped establish Lumberton's first textile mill, the Lumberton Cotton Mill, and was elected its vice president. He also helped organize two other textile mills—Dresden Cotton Mill in 1906 and the Jennings Cotton Mill in 1909. In 1922 the Lumberton and Dresden mills merged and were reorganized as the Mansfield Mill.

Seeing the need for additional transportation facilities in

the Robeson County area, McLean organized the Virginia and Carolina Southern Railroad.

Other business undertakings in which McLean was involved were the organizaton of the Lumberton Telephone Company in 1898, the Lumberton Improvement Company to build the Waverly Hotel in 1903, and a local building and loan association in 1910. He was also interested in many real estate transactions.

In spite of the time required by these many business activities, McLean still found time to participate in the political affairs of the county, state, and nation. He served as chairman of the Robeson County Democratic Executive Committee in 1892, the same year he began practicing law. In 1912 and 1916 he was the chairman of the presidential campaign committee for Woodrow Wilson in North Carolina, and from 1916 to 1924 he was a member of the National Democratic Executive Committee. He served as a director of the War Finance Corporation from 1918 to 1922 and as its managing director from 1920 to 1921. He was also an Assistant Secretary of the Treasury and chairman of the Railway Advisory Commission while managing the War Finance Corporation.

McLean announced as a candidate for the Democratic nomination for governor in the middle of March 1924, but plans for the race had been made far in advance. In the primary he carried eighty-three of the one-hundred counties to beat Josiah W. Bailey for the nomination. The Republicans nominated Issac Meekins, whom McLean easily beat. Angus McLean was inaugurated governor of North Carolina on January 14, 1925.

McLean's administration was one of applying sound business policies to the functions of government. The introduction of the executive budget system brought the departments and agencies of the state under the direct supervision of the governor, correlating their programs and avoiding duplication. The Department of Revenue was created and given the responsibility of collecting all state funds. Thirty measures aimed at improving methods of government administration were passed in the 1925 General Assembly at Governor McLean's request. The State Department of Conservation and Development was also created.

McLean was a member of the Board of Trustees of the University of North Carolina, Board of Trustees of Flora Macdonald College, American and North Carolina Bar Associations, American Academy of Political and Social Science, North Carolina Historical Commission, Scottish Society of America, Clan McLean Association of Glasgow, Sigma Chi fraternity and the Knights of Pythias. He was also an elder in the Presbyterian Church and trustee of Union Theological Seminary, Richmond, Virginia.

Lumber River Scots and Their Descendants was written by McLean and other people interested in their forebears of this region. It was published after his death with money from his estate.

On April 14, 1904, McLean was married to Margaret French of Lumberton. Three children were born to them. They are Angus Wilton McLean, Jr., Margaret French McLean, who married W. Scott Shepherd, and Hector McLean.

Angus McLean died June 21, 1935, in Washington, D. C. He is buried in Lumberton, North Carolina. A portrait of him hangs in the Executive Mansion in Raleigh.

For additional information concerning Angus Wilton McLean, see: *Papers and Letters of Governor Angus Wilton McLean, 1925-1929*, edited by David Leroy Corbitt; "Angus Wilton McLean, Governor of North Carolina, 1925-1929," by Mary Evelyn Underwood, unpublished doctoral dissertation, University of North Carolina, 1962.

17

John Charles McNeill

John Charles McNeill was born July 26, 1874 in the Spring Hill community, Scotland County, North Carolina. He was born to Duncan McNeill and his wife, Euphemia Livingston.

He first attended school in Spring Hill at the Old Richmond Academy, and then attended the Whiteville Academy, where he completed his preparation for college. McNeill then left North Carolina and went to Georgia where he taught school, but in 1894 he returned to his native state and entered Wake Forest College. He was graduated at the head of his class in 1898. While at Wake Forest he studied law in addition to the regular subjects leading to the A.B. degree and, in 1897, took and passed the oral examination required to obtain a license to practice law. He continued his studies at Wake Forest and was awarded a master's degree in English. Having completed his college work, he went to Mercer University, Macon, Georgia, where he served as professor of English during the absence of one of the regular faculty members.

Teaching did not satisfy McNeill, and the following year he began to practice law in Lumberton, North Carolina. While here he purchased an interest in the *Argus*, a Lumberton weekly newspaper. In 1902 he sold this interest and moved to Laurinburg, where he practiced law in partnership with Angus McLean.

The practice of law was also unable to hold the interest of John Charles McNeill. Many of the hours he was supposed to be devoting to legal work were actually spent writing poetry. In 1902, the same year he moved to Laurinburg, *The Youth's Companion* and *The Century Magazine* began to publish some of his poems. These came to the attention of H. E. C. Bryant, a member of the *Charlotte Observer* staff. He approached McNeill about the possibility of coming to work for the paper, and when McNeill assured him he was interested, he spoke to Joseph Caldwell, the editor, about him. Shortly thereafter McNeill was offered a position on the staff of the paper. Upon assuming this position, he was given no definite assignment but was left to write what he desired. He associated himself with the paper in August of 1904, and this relationship continued until his death three years later.

At the end of his first year with the *Charlotte Observer* he was awarded the Patterson Memorial Cup for having made the most outstanding contribution in the field of literature in North Carolina for the year 1905. The cup was presented to him by President Theodore Roosevelt.

In 1906 McNeill published a volume of his poems under the title *Songs Merry and Sad*. The majority of those verses were ones which had been published in *The Youth's Companion*, *The Century Magazine*, and the *Charlotte Observer*. The edition was quickly sold out, and it has since been reprinted several times.

McNeill intended to publish another volume, but failing health prevented it; however, it was published posthumously in 1907. It is titled *Lyrics From Cotton Land* and has also gone through several printings.

Dr. Archibald Henderson in a tribute to McNeill cited

"To Melvin Gardner: Suicide" as being the one poem "which best expresses the real sweetness, the high seriousness of McNeill's character, and the finer nature of his poetic muse. . . ." The last verse is:

A thousand roses will blossom red,
A thousand hearts be gay,
For the summer lingers just ahead
And June is on her way;
The bee must bestir him to fill his cells,
The moon and the stars will weave new spells
of love and the music of marriage bells—
And, oh, to be dead in May!

Shortly before his death, after his health had begun to fail, McNeill addressed death in these terms:

Patient, O Death, thy reign is hereafter,
Bide thee thy crowning and keep thee apart!
Mine this estate, this lease upon laughter,
Mine all the love in my heart.

John Charles McNeill died October 17, 1907, at Riverton and is buried in the Spring Hill Cemetery. He was only thirty-three years old. Upon his tomb is engraved the stanza of his poem, "Sundown." . . .

We knew, O Lord, so little what is best;
Wingless, we can move so lowly;
But in thy calm all-knowledge let us rest—
Oh, holy, holy, holy!

The poet's birthplace has been restored and is used as a museum and visitors' center for Temperance Hall and the McNeill Memorial Gardens. A portrait of McNeill hangs inside the old homeplace.

For additional information concerning John Charles Mc-Neill, see: *Biographical History of North Carolina*, volume 7, by Samuel A. Ashe, and the December, 1907, issue of the Wake Forest *Student*, issued as a memorial to McNeill.

John M. Morehead

John Motley Morehead was born in Spray, North Carolina, on November 3, 1870. He was the son of James Turner and Mary Elizabeth Connally Morehead.

He attended Bingham Military School in Mebane, North Carolina, before entering the University of North Carolina. He was graduated from the University in 1891 with a Bachelor of Science degree. An exceptional student, Morehead won a Phi Beta Kappa key while in Chapel Hill. Further study was undertaken at Westinghouse Electric and Manufacturing Company, where he was graduated from a special program in 1895. Later he went to Cologne, Germany, and took a special course in oxy-acetylene welding.

He went to work for his father's company in Spray where, in 1892, he accidentally discovered an economic method for producing calcium carbide. He later developed a method for the production of acetylene gas. These developments led to the birth of several chemical companies and ultimately to the founding of Union Carbide and Carbon Corporation. He joined Union Carbide in 1900, the year it was founded by his father and several other industrialists. He worked as an engineer for the company, its branches and subsidiaries, for the greater portion of his life. It was here that he won an international reputation as a designing electro-chemical engineer.

During World War I he received a commission as major and served on the War Industries Board. He was chief of the industrial gases and gas products section.

In 1930 he was appointed by President Herbert Hoover as minister to Sweden, and served from January 22, 1930, until April 15, 1933.

In 1919 he moved to Rye, New York, but he never forgot his home state and especially his alma mater. In 1931 he made the first of many gifts to the University of North Carolina. That year he and Rufus L. Patterson provided the University with the Morehead-Patterson Bell Tower.

In 1945 he set up the John Motley Morehead Foundation as a multi-million-dollar trust. The first project undertaken by the foundation was the erection of the Morehead Building on the Chapel Hill campus. The building was completed in 1949 and houses the Morehead Planetarium and Copernican Orrery, the Genevieve B. Morehead Art Gallery, and the Chapel Hill office of the foundation. The Planetarium was built in Germany and moved to Oslo, Norway, where Morehead purchased it. Because of the excellent reputation of this equipment the American astronauts have been sent here to study as a vital part of their training. The Art Gallery has many rare paintings, two of which are portraits of George and Martha Washington by Rembrandt Peele.

The undertaking of the foundation which has achieved the widest acclaim, is the Morehead Scholarship program. The program was begun in 1951 by Mr. Morehead and the trustees of the foundation. It is patterned after the Rhodes Scholarships and in the words of Mr. Morehead is aimed at providing "tall academic timber" for the University. Each scholarship is designed to meet all of the student's expenses with no strings attached. They are awarded solely on merit;

financial need is not considered. Since the inception of the program, hundreds of the scholarships have been granted representing several millions of dollars.

In addition to his gifts to the University, Morehead has provided funds for the Morehead stadium and chimes at the Tri-City High School in Rockingham County. He also donated $200,000 to the Morehead Hospital in Rockingham County.

In spite of the fact that Mr. Morehead was a Republican, Governor Hodges appointed him president of the North Carolina Railroad. The appointment had special significance since his grandfather, Governor Morehead, inspired and carried through the building of the railroad.

Mr. Morehead was the author of two books: *The Morehead Family of North Carolina and Virginia* and *Analysis of Industrial Gases.* The latter is used chiefly as a textbook.

John M. Morehead was a member of the International Acetylene Association, the American Electro-chemical Association, the American Gas Association, the American Welding Society, the Society of Colonial Wars, the Society of the Cincinnati, the American Legion, and Sigma Alpha Epsilon. He was also a Fellow in the American Institute of Electrical Engineers. His religious affiliation was Baptist.

John Morehead married Genevieve Margaret Birkhoff on July 3, 1915. She died in 1945 and three years later he married Mrs. Leila Duckworth Houghton. No children were born of either marriage.

Mr. Morehead died at his home in Rye, New York, on January 7, 1965, and is buried in that city. At his death his gifts to the University of North Carolina amounted to over $17 millions.

There is a portrait of Mr. Morehead hanging in the Morehead Building in Chapel Hill.

Cameron Morrison

Cameron Morrison was born in Rockingham, North Carolina, October 5, 1869. He was the son of Daniel M. Morrison and Martha Cameron Morrison.

Young Morrison was able to attend school only irregularly because he had to help support his father and the other three children. He worked as a public school teacher and then studied law under Judge Robert P. Dick. Upon receiving his law license in February 1892 he returned to Rockingham to begin his practice.

Morrison entered politics before he began the practice of law. His father was a Republican and he followed him into that political party. In 1891 he was a member of the State Republican Executive Committee, but in the same year he changed his affiliation to the Democratic party.

Young Morrison campaigned vigorously for the Democratic candidates in Richmond and surrounding counties. In 1896 he sought a seat in the State Senate but was defeated as were all the other Democrats in his district. White supremacy was the dominant issue in the campaign two years later, and Morrison, as chairman of the Democratic Executive Committee for his county, played a major part in the election. Like most other white men, Morrison and his father, who by this time had also switched to the Democratic party, joined the Red Shirts. The campaign was perhaps the most violent in the state's history; so violent, that Republican Governor Russell threatened Richmond County with martial law. The violence and threats did not deter Morrison and his followers, and the election was decided in favor of the Democrats. Morrison was not a candidate for any office during this campaign but was elected to the State Senate in the next election. Some years after this he moved from Rockingham to Charlotte where he built a large law practice.

In 1920 Morrison threw his hat into the ring as a candidate for the Democratic party's nomination for governor of North Carolina. He had strong opposition in Robert N. Page, who had been in Congress nearly twenty years, and O. Max Gardner, who was lieutenant governor. In the first primary, held June 3, 1920, Page was eliminated and Morrison received a plurality of eighty-seven votes over Gardner. In the second primary, held one month later, Morrison received the nomination over Gardner. The Republicans offered little opposition in the general election, and the Democratic nominee won easily. Cameron Morrison was inagurated January 12, 1921.

Morrison has become known as the "Good Roads Governor" and not without just reason. During his administration, and on his recommendation, the General Assembly authorized bond issues of $65,000,000 to be used to construct a system of state highways. The bond issues were financed by taxes on automobiles and gasoline. Through his program the principal towns and cities of the state were connected with hard surfaced roads. Other major accomplishments of this administration were: the establishment of a training school for Negro boys in Richmond County, the passage of a bond issue to provide funds for the construction of buildings at the institutions of higher education in the state, the creation of a loan fund to be used by the counties to build new schools, and the strengthening of the state's banking laws.

After his term as governor, Morrison returned to his law practice in Charlotte. In 1930 he was appointed to the United States Senate to fill the seat left vacant by the death of Lee S. Overman, but was defeated in 1932 by Robert R. Reynolds. He was elected to Congress in 1942 and ran for the Senate in 1944, but was defeated by Clyde R. Hoey. He again returned to his law practice as he had done after his defeat for the Senate in 1932.

Morrison was a member of the American and North Carolina Bar Associations, the Sons of the American Revolution, and the Scottish Society of America. He was a member of the Presbyterian Church.

Cameron Morrison and Lottie May Tomlinson were married December 6, 1905. They had one child, Angelia. Mrs. Morrison died November 12, 1919. On April 2, 1924, Morrison married Mrs. Sarah Virginia Ecker Watts.

Morrison died on August 20, 1953. He is buried in Elmwood Cemetery, Charlotte.

For additional information concerning Cameron Morrison, see: *Letters and Papers of Governor Cameron Morrison, 1921-1925*, edited by David Leroy Corbitt.

Howard W. Odum

Howard Washington Odum was born near Bethlehem, Georgia, on May 24, 1884. He was the son of William Pleasant Odum, and his wife, Mary Wiggins. In order that his children could acquire an education, William Odum moved to Oxford, Georgia, then the site of Emory College (now University). Howard attended the public schools of Oxford and then entered Emory from which he was graduated with an A.B. degree in 1904. After graduation he left Georgia and went to Toccopola, Mississippi, where he served as co-principal of a rural school during 1904-05. Howard received a master's degree in the classics from the University of Mississippi in 1906. In 1909 he was awarded a Ph.D. in psychology from Clark University and in 1910 received a second Ph.D., this time from Columbia University in sociology.

After leaving Columbia, he worked for two years with the Philadelphia Bureau of Municipal Research. From 1912 to 1919 he was associated with the School of Education at the University of Georgia. His next move was to his alma mater, Emory, as professor of sociology and dean of liberal arts. He stayed here only one year, leaving in September, 1920, to join the faculty of the University of North Carolina as Kenan Professor of Sociology.

The influence of Odum was felt on the Carolina campus from the first year of his residence there. In 1920 he organized the School of Public Welfare, served as director until 1932, and also established the Department of Sociology. In 1922 he began to edit a journal, *Social Forces,* and served as editor until his death. In connection with this editorship he became an incorporator of the University Press the same year. Two years later he established the Institute for Research in Social Science and served as its director until 1944.

Dr. Odum was a prolific writer. The University of North Carolina Press engaged him to edit a Social Study Series and Henry Holt engaged him to edit a textbook series, the American Social Science Series. In all he wrote over twenty books of a sociological nature, three novels, a book on Negro ballads and a number of articles for magazines and scholarly journals.

A wide range of interests occupied the mind of Dr. Odum, but Negro life and race relations was his main interest. His first real scholarly work, *Social and Mental Traits of the Negro* (1910), dealt with this subject. His three novels, which he called his trilogy, *Rainbow Round My Shoulder* (1928), *Wings on My Feet* (1929), and *Cold Blue Moon* (1930), also concerned themselves with the Negro in daily life. In 1943 he wrote *Race and Rumors of Race,* in which he sought to counteract the rising feeling of hatred between the Negro and the white population. His interest in the Negro continued until his death, at which time he was preparing to write *Agenda for Integration of the Negro.*

In *Annals of the American Academy of Political and Social Science* (1922) and *Systems of Public Welfare* (1925), Dr. Odum addressed himself to the adaptation of the new public welfare systems and their efforts to help those who did not have an equal opportunity. In the latter volume he predicted the involvement of the Federal government in this field.

Dr. Odum, at the request of President Herbert Hoover, was the motivating force behind the production of *Recent Social Trends in the United States* (1933), which consisted of the President's Commission report and thirteen monographs. Odum, with William F. Ogburn, edited these and wrote parts of them.

In 1936 Odum reached the high point of his career when he published *Southern Regions of the United States*. In this he dealt with the South and its development in relation to the nation.

Dr. Odum served as president of the American Sociological Society, chairman of the North Carolina Emergency Relief Administration, chairman of the North Carolina Civil Works Administration, chairman of the North Carolina Committee on Interracial Cooperation, member of the State Planning Board, president of the Southern Regional Council, executive committee member of the American Association for the Advancement of Science, president of the North Carolina Jersey Cattle Club.

He was the recipient of numerous awards for his public service, including the O. Max Gardner Award to the University faculty member making the greatest contribution to the welfare of his fellow man.

In 1910 he married Anna Louise Kranz. Three children were born of this union: Mary Frances, Eugene Pleasants, and Howard Thomas.

Dr. Odum died November 8, 1954, and is buried in Chapel Hill.

A portrait of Dr. Odum is owned by the University of North Carolina.

For additional information concerning Howard Washington Odum, see: *The Kenan Professorships*, by A. C. Howell.

18

Frank Page

Frank Page was born in Cary, Wake County, North Carolina, on February 22, 1875. He was one of eight children born to Francis Allison Page and his wife, Kate Raboteau. Frank's four brothers were all distinguished by their success in the fields they chose as careers: Walter Hines Page was a writer, publisher, and Ambassador to Great Britain during World War I; Robert N. Page was for many years a member of the United States House of Representatives; Henry Page was a banker and railroad president; and J. R. Page was a banker and businessman.

Frank was prepared for college at Davis Military School and then attended the University of North Carolina. Upon leaving the University he went to Aberdeen, where his family had moved, and engaged in the lumber, railroad, and banking business with his father and brothers.

During World War I, Page served in Europe and was discharged a major in the Corps of Engineers. While in Europe he had his first experience with road construction, a field in which he would later become nationally known.

Before the creation of the State Highway Commission, the building and upkeep of roads was left to the counties. This quite naturally resulted in little uniformity of quality and virtually no system of connected road projects. Even within the counties themselves roads were not uniform in quality as part of the county might lie within a "special tax" district whose highways would be better than those a few miles away.

The General Assembly of 1915 created the State Highway Commission. At this time the governor was chairman, but the State Geologist performed the administrative role. In 1919 the law was amended so that the commission was reduced from seven members to three, plus a chairman.

Governor Thomas W. Bickett began looking for a man to fill the position of chairman, and Frank Page was highly recommended to him. The governor called Page to Raleigh and after talking with him offered him the position. Page accepted and thus became chairman.

The salary appropriated for the chairman was $15,000 a year, twice the amount the governor received at that time. He was the highest salaried official in state government.

So it was in 1919 that Page began a program of building an integrated system of highways in North Carolina, starting with only 3,600 miles of roads and the vast majority of this unpaved. Little could be done until the General Assembly saw fit to provide funds with which highways could be constructed. This came in 1921.

It was in this year that the legislature, under the leadership of Governor Cameron Morrison, enacted a highway act providing for a $65,000,000 bond issue and instructions that a system of highways be built to connect each county seat in the state. The act was to be administered by the State Highway Commission. Page and the Commission were given wide latitude in the methods they might employ to carry this act into effect. The types of roads to be constructed and their location was left entirely to their discretion. Page was reappointed as the chairman by Governor Morrison and served until 1929. During this ten-year period he supervised the spending of $115,000,000 in road bonds and saw the mileage of roads in the state more than doubled.

A plaque was placed in the new State Highway Building in 1953 in memory of Page. Its inscription reads:

"Frank Page — 1875-1934; Chairman, State Highway Commission, 1919-1929.

"His response to an unprecedented challenge made North Carolina one of the first American states to build an integrated system of highways drawing more closely together the people of one hundred counties.

"By his leadership, his wisdom, his integrity and fidelity, he set an example for distinguished service faithfully emulated but never surpassed.

"His organization of highway craftsmen endures as his living memorial."

Page was president of the American Road Builders' Association and the American Association of State Highway Officials. He was appointed by President Hoover as chairman of his Highway Safety Council and had earlier been appointed by President Coolidge as one of five appointees to the Pan-American Road Congress, which was held in South America. After leaving the Highway Commission he served as a member of the State Public Works Advisory Board. He was also a member of the Rotary Club and by religious affiliation was a Methodist.

He was married to Ella B. Martin on June 17, 1896. Three children were born of this union: Allison M. Page, Frank M. Page, and Clara F. Page.

Frank Page died December 20, 1934 in Raleigh. He is buried in Bethesda Cemetery, near Aberdeen.

For additional information concerning Frank Page, see: *North Carolina Roads and Their Builders,* by Capus Waynick—printed by Edwards & Broughton Co.

Walter Hines Page

Walter Hines Page was born in Raleigh, North Carolina, on August 15, 1855. He was the son of Allison Francis Page, and his mother was Kate Raboteau.

Though he first attended an old field school kept by Adolphus Jones, he was prepared for college at Bingham School in Mebane. For a few months, he was a student at Trinity College, and then for four years at Randolph-Macon College, in Ashland, Virginia, where he was graduated in 1876. From Randolph-Macon, he went to Johns Hopkins University, where he did graduate work, holding a fellowship in Greek.

After study in Germany in 1877, some lecturing at the 1878 summer school session of the University of North Carolina, and a year of teaching in Louisville, he decided to go into journalism. He could find no place in North Carolina, so by advertising, he got a position as a reporter with the St. Joseph, Missouri, *Gazette*. Within a year, he became the editor of the paper. He began, in addition to his newspaper work, to write for magazines, first for the *Atlantic Monthly*, articles dealing especially with the South. In 1881, he went to the Atlanta Exposition as special correspondent for the *New York World*, and for that paper he wrote reviews, literary notes and editorials in New York and Washington.

Returning to North Carolina, Page started the Raleigh *State Chronicle* and never was there such a stirring of dry bones in the state. The young editor wrote what he thought about everything that took place, and he advocated policies that were revolutionary in his day. He stood for industrial education and development of public schools. But the paper did not pay and he left North Carolina in February, 1885, "without a dollar or a job."

He soon got employment with the *Brooklyn Union* and then spent two years on the New York *Evening Post*. He was offered first the management, then the editorship, of the *Forum*, a position he held until 1895, piloting the tottering magazine to solvency.

In 1895 he was called to Boston as literary adviser to Houghton, Mifflin & Company, and in the following year was given the position of editor of the *Atlantic Monthly*. The *Atlantic*, which had been identified in a special way with the group of New England authors, was much broadened under Page's editorship, as he put it into more vital connection with the life of the country.

Although now living an almost ideal life in Cambridge and connected with one of the two great publishing houses of America, he found a salaried editorship too narrow. Wanting a magazine of his own, he and F. N. Doubleday, in 1899, organized the firm of Doubleday, Page & Company, which quickly made its way to a leading position among American publishers. Here, Page made *The World's Work* magazine his own special sounding board of national life.

As his *State Chronicle* was a failure, so was his novel, *Nicholas Worth, Southerner*, also a failure, for much the same reason. He loved the South deeply and would have preferred to live in North Carolina, but he was eaten up by the zeal of the reformer at a time when such zeal was defeated by local mores, traditions, and superstitions.

Nevertheless, he was a leading spirit of the Watauga Club in Raleigh that brought about the establishment of the State College of Agriculture and Engineering, now part of the consolidated system of the University of North Carolina. His speeches on "The Forgotten Man" and "The Rebuilding of Old Commonwealths" are generally believed to have exercised profound influence in assisting in bringing about North Carolina's educational crusade and popular awakening. In later years, his work on the Southern Education Board and the General Education Board was constructive, helpful, and generally beneficial to the state. As founder and editor of the magazine of industry, education, and economics, *The World's Work*, he did much to foster and encourage the South's economic development.

In the spring of 1913, President Woodrow Wilson appointed Page to be the United States Ambassador to Great Britain, where he remained through the difficult years of the first World War.

Page married Willia Alice Wilson on November 15, 1880. They had four children.

He died on December 21, 1918, and is buried in Old Bethesda Churchyard near Pinehurst.

For additional information on Walter Hines Page, see: *The Life and Letters of Walter H. Page*, by Burton Jesse Hendrick.

John Parris

John Parris was born in Sylva, North Carolina, on November 23, 1914. He attended school in Sylva.

Parris began writing at an early age, taking a job with a local weekly, the *Jackson County Journal,* when he was only thirteen years of age. In this capacity he covered sports and general assignments. Also while a teen-ager he worked as a local correspondent for the *Asheville Citizen-Times.* In 1934 he went to Raleigh and joined the United Press news bureau, being the youngest capitol correspondent in Raleigh. United Press transferred him to the New York bureau where he did a daily by-lined feature. He resigned his position with UP in 1937 and became a roving reporter for the *Winston-Salem Journal-Sentinel,* an assignment he held for two years before he rejoined UP as night bureau manager in Memphis, Tennessee. About six months later he was again transferred to New York, this time as assistant night cable editor. In March, 1941, he was sent to London to cover the diplomatic beat for UP, an assignment he filled until he left UP and joined the Associated Press news bureau in 1944. Before leaving UP he covered the invasion of North Africa, actually landing with the troops at Arzew. In this position with AP he continued to cover the news in the diplomatic circles in London until May 1946.

His work as a foreign correspondent formed the basis for two books which he co-authored, *Springboard to Berlin* (1943) and *Deadline Delayed* (1946). He wrote another book, *The White Eagle,* a biography of the Yugoslav guerrilla leader, Draja Mihailovitch, which was accepted for publication in 1942. However, the UP refused permission to publish the book while Parris was employed by them on the grounds that it would cause the Russians to attack his objectivity as a diplomatic correspondent. In his position he was to have no published controversial opinions. About five years later when it would have been possible to publish the book because of a change in attitudes, the only complete manuscript had been destroyed in a London air raid.

Also during the war he did some work with the Belgian underground, for which he was decorated with the Order of Chevalier of the Order of Leopold II.

In 1946 he was transferred to New York to cover the United Nations. In this capacity he reported the San Francisco World Conference, the United Nations Preparatory Commission, and the first Assembly in London.

Parris returned to western North Carolina in 1947, leaving the Associated Press to devote his time to creative writing. He recorded the history of the Indians of western North Carolina in *The Cherokee Story* (1950). In the fall of 1950 he was appointed public relations director of the Cherokee Historical Association and the drama *Unto These Hills,* which is sponsored by the Association.

In February, 1955, Parris began writing a regular column for the *Asheville Citizen-Times,* "Roaming the Mountains." Later that same year many of these were collected into a book by the same name as the column. Two years later his columns were again collected into a book, *My Mountains, My People.*

"He always presents our people in a favorable light, a

people of great dignity and simplicity of character: he describes vividly the manifold beauties of our wonderful mountain region; he ferrets out and records for posterity the old stories, traditions and legends which without his labor of love, would have been lost for all time."

In 1967 many of his columns were again collected into a book, *Mountain Bred*.

In 1958 Parris accepted the position as regional editorial representative for the *Asheville Citizen-Times*. In this capacity he continued his regular column in the paper, but also worked with correspondents in various communities to develop better news coverage.

Governor D. K. Moore appointed Parris chairman of the North Carolina State Parks and State Forest Study Commission in 1967. The duty of this commission was to study these state facilities and report their findings and recommendations to the 1969 General Assembly.

Since returning to North Carolina, Parris has been active in the promotion of the mountain area of the state. In addition to his position with the Cherokee Historical Association, he has served as president of the Western North Carolina Highlanders and as secretary of the Southern Highlands Attractions Organization. He is a member of the National Association of Travel Organizations, the North Carolina Travel Council, and the American Travel Writers Association.

He is married to Dorothy Luxton Klenk, an artist-designer from Topeka, Kansas, and New York. She has provided illustrations for his books.

For additional information concerning John Parris, see: *North Carolina Authors: A Selective Handbook*, prepared by a joint committee of the North Carolina English Teachers Association and the North Carolina Library Association.

Richmond Pearson

Richmond Pearson was born in Yadkin County, North Carolina, on January 26, 1852. He was the son of Richmond Mumford Pearson, jurist and law teacher, and Chief Justice of the Supreme Court of North Carolina from 1858 until his death in 1878. His mother was Margaret McClung Williams.

Pearson's early education was received at Horner's School at Oxford, North Carolina. He entered Princeton University in 1868, at the age of sixteen, and received his Bachelor of Arts degree in 1872, delivering the valedictory address for his class.

Upon leaving college he returned to North Carolina for two years. He studied law under his father, and in 1874 was licensed to practice. On June 19 of that year, President Grant appointed him a consul to Verviers and Leige, Belgium, when he was but twenty-three years of age. In 1875 he paid a brief visit to the United States and delivered the master's oration at Princeton in that year. He was awarded the Master of Arts degree.

On April 22, 1877, Pearson resigned from the consular service and returned to the United States. Later he formed a law partnership with John D. Davis, with offices in St. Louis, Missouri. Shortly afterwards, the death of his father made it necessary for him to return to North Carolina and finding it impossible to return to St. Louis, he gave up the practice of law.

Entering politics, he was elected to the North Carolina General Assembly in 1884 and again in 1886 as a Democrat. Eight years later he was elected to Congress and served three terms, carrying the Ninth District, which had been Democratic for years, by the largest majority ever given a Republican.

At the time he made his campaign for Congress, it was the custom for the candidates to appear at the different county seats in the district and discuss the issues before the people in joint debate. Pearson was truly a great debater, and through this medium he defeated his first opponent in a close and hard fought race. The next time he ran, he gave his Democratic opponent a terrific political beating, carrying the district by a large margin.

During the time he was a member of Congress, he was one of the leaders of the Republican Party in the state. Moreover, both Presidents McKinley and Roosevelt regarded Pearson as one of the ablest men in the party, and he was a close friend of both these men. His political constituents in the district admired him for his fairness and for his strict attention to duty as a congressman. As a member of Congress he served on the important Committee of Foreign Affairs, and on the sub-committee of three which drafted the resolutions authorizing war on Spain. He espoused the cause of sound money, the gold standard, in 1894 and 1896, and did it in such a way as to give him considerable prominence. It was this that first attracted the attention of the Republican national leaders, and it gave him a place in the public eye for a number of years.

He occupied a conspicuous place in the social life of the capital. He was a member of the Metropolitan Club, taking an interest in all its activities, especially in those embracing a number of international chess games.

Recognizing Pearson's ability as a statesman, and his scholarly learning, President Roosevelt appointed him, on December 10, 1901, United States Consul at Genoa, Italy. He was so successful that a year later the President promoted him and made him Minister to Persia, stationed at Teheran. An excellent speaker, being possessed of a brilliant mind and a forceful and fascinating manner, and speaking French, German and Italian fluently, he is credited with having been the first American minister to Persia to present his credentials to the Shah, addressing him in French, the court language of the country. For five years he discharged the duties of his post with such success that President Roosevelt appointed him Envoy Extraordinary and Minister Plenipotentiary to Greece and Montenegro, with headquarters at Athens, which post he held for two years.

In 1909, Pearson resigned from the diplomatic service and returned to the United States, retiring from public life. His last years were spent at his home on Richmond Hill near Asheville.

On March 30, 1882, he married Gabrielle Thomas, daughter of James Thomas, Jr., of Richmond, Virginia, one of the wealthiest tobacco planters of his day. They had two children, Marjorie and Thomas.

Pearson died on September 12, 1923, and is buried in Riverside Cemetery in Asheville.

Clarence Poe

Clarence Hamilton Poe was born in Chatham County, North Carolina, on January 10, 1881. He was the son of William B. Poe and his wife, Susan Dismukes. His formal education was received in a one-room clapboard school which was operated only eleven weeks out of each year.

When Poe was fourteen years of age, an uncle offered him a year's subscription to the *Progressive Farmer* if he would pick a field of late cotton. A couple of years later he sent an article to the farm journal urging the adoption by the state of a six-month school term. The editor, J. L. Ramsey, liked the article and being in need of an office boy, wrote to Poe and asked him to come to Raleigh. So at the age of sixteen, Clarence Poe became a writer and office boy for the *Progressive Farmer*. Two years later he took over the editor's chair.

When Poe became editor of the journal, its future was in some doubt. It was a weekly with about 5,000 readers and total physical assets of under $1,000. However, after serving as editor for four years, he formed the Progressive Farmer Company in 1903 and purchased the magazine for $7,500.

Serving as head of the *Progressive Farmer* is the only occupation Clarence Poe ever pursued. From the small beginning when he became editor, he built the magazine into the leading farm journal in the South and one of the leading ones in the nation. During the first twenty years of Poe's ownership of the magazine, fourteen Southern farm journals merged with the *Progressive Farmer.*

Through the years Clarence Poe used the *Progressive Farmer* to carry on many crusades for the betterment of social and economic conditions of citizens living in the rural South. Once when asked what he considered his most important contribution to Southern agriculture, he answered: "The campaign for 'two-arm' farming. . . . " In this campaign, carried on through writings and speeches, he urged the Southern farmer to raise both crops and livestock. Before this time the farmers were relying almost entirely on the crops of cotton and tobacco for their incomes. This practice he branded as "one-arm" farming and urged that the other arm be used to raise livestock.

Other campaigns included a fight for a better and more practical system of education in rural areas; a campaign for the abolition of the crop lien as the system of advancing credit to farmers; the insistence that the Negro be given a fair deal; a crusade for cooperative marketing among the farmers of their products; and many other fights aimed at helping the rural citizen improve his standard of living.

Poe never sought political office, but was mentioned for various offices at different times. The two highest offices for which his name was offered were for United States Secretary of Agriculture after the election of Woodrow Wilson and for governor in 1940 at the insistence of the farmers of the state. In both instances Poe made clear his desire that his name be withdrawn from consideration.

In 1907 Poe went to Europe and upon his return wrote a book which was to win him his first Patterson Cup—*Southerner in Europe.* A few years later he toured the Orient and from this experience came his book, *Where Half the World is Waking Up*, and a second Patterson Cup. Some of his other books are *True Tales of the South at War*, *How Farmers Co-operate and Double Profits*, and the *Life and Speeches of Charles Brantley Aycock*, written and edited in cooperation with R. D. W. Connor.

Many awards were bestowed upon Poe besides the Patterson Cups. Two of these were the American Freedom Association's World Peace Award in 1962 and one of the first North Carolina Awards in 1964.

He was a trustee of State College, the University of North Carolina, and Wake Forest College. He served from 1913 to 1931 as a member of the State Board of Agriculture. At different times he has served as president of the following organizations: State Farmers Convention, State Press Association, State Dairymen's Association, State Forestry Foundation, and the State Literary and Historical Association. He was a member of the Watauga Club and the Rotary Club, among others. His religious affiliation was with the Baptist Church.

In 1912, Poe married Alice Aycock, daughter of Charles Brantley Aycock, governor of North Carolina 1901-1905. Three children were born of this union: Charles Aycock, Jean, and William Dismukes.

Clarence Poe died October 8, 1964. He is buried in Oakwood Cemetery in Raleigh.

For additional information concerning Clarence Hamilton Poe, see: *My First 80 Years*, an autobiography.

Leonidas LaFayette Polk

Leonidas LaFayette Polk was born in Anson County, North Carolina, on April 25, 1837. He was the son of Andrew Polk and his wife, Serena Autry.

Polk's early formal education was in the neighborhood one-room schoolhouse. His parents died when he was a young teen-ager, and for four years he lived on farms of his relatives and attended the community schools. In the fall of 1855 he entered Davidson College as an "irregular" student, one who could plan his own schedule and take those courses he desired. After ten months at Davidson, where he studied all available subjects related to science and agriculture, he returned to Anson County and began farming the tract of land left him by his father's estate.

In 1860, at twenty-three years of age, Polk was elected by the Whigs to the state legislature. Immediately faced with the issue of secession, he fought against it with all earnestness, until Lincoln called on North Carolina to furnish troops for war against her sister Southern states. From that time on, he was heart and soul in the fight for the Southern cause. Commissioned a colonel, he saw action in several campaigns. In 1864 he was elected by his comrades as the "army candidate" for the North Carolina legislature. Here, his services on the Committee of Education gave him more accurate knowledge of the educational situation in North Carolina.

When the war was over, Polk returned to his Anson County farm. He was destined for a larger service, however, and was overwhelmingly elected to the Constitutional Convention of 1868. His hand in the Constitution may be seen in the provision requiring that there be established in connection with the University of North Carolina "departments of agriculture, mechanics, and mining."

In April, 1874, Polk published the first issue of *The Ansonian,* a farm and local news weekly sponsoring the Grange and farmers' clubs and specifically demanding the establishment of a State Department of Agriculture. In 1877, after three years of zealous activity in this regard, he met in Goldsboro with the State Grange and representatives of the University, the State Agricultural Society, and members of the legislature. Polk was elected chairman of this meeting, the outcome of which was the creation by the legislature in 1877 of a State Department of Agriculture. Polk was named the state's first Commissioner of Agriculture, and served for three years.

Although it was not until after he founded *The Progressive Farmer* magazine in 1886 and organized the farmers' clubs in the state that his dream of a Land Grant Agricultural College would be realized, his fight began as early as 1872, when, at the Agricultural Fair, he addressed the crowd gathered there and advocated the establishing of an agricultural college.

In 1887 his dream became a reality. A legislature composed largely of farmers had been elected and Polk called a mass meeting of all the organized farmers' clubs of the state in Raleigh. The huge gathering remained in Raleigh for two days and named Polk on a committee to present its plan to the legislature. The farmers called for an agricultural and mechanical college which would annually receive funds appropriated by the state. On March 3, 1887, the General Assembly embodied this idea and two years later the "North Carolina College of Agriculture and Mechanic Arts," now the North Carolina State University at Raleigh, began its fruitful career.

In addition to securing the establishment of an agricultural college for men, Polk set out to secure a college for girls in the denomination of which he belonged. Hence, at the 1888 Baptist State Convention at Greensboro, he proposed the appointment of a committee, named by him in the resolution, to investigate the feasibility of creating a Baptist woman's college. The resolution was amended by adding Polk as chairman of the committee. In 1889, he was elected president of the Baptist State Convention and named chairman of the Board of Trustees to establish the proposed school for Baptist girls. He arranged for the purchase of a site in Raleigh. While he did not live to see it, one of his most cherished dreams became a reality when the "Baptist Female University," now Meredith College, opened its doors in October, 1899.

Polk was chosen three times by acclamation president of the Interstate Farmers' Association of eleven cotton states. In 1889, when the several farmers' organizations consolidated at St. Louis and formed the Farmers' Alliance and Industrial Union, he was elected President and twice re-elected by acclamation. Under his direction the National Farmers' Alliance reached a membership of two and one-half million.

Polk was married on September 23, 1857, to Sarah Pamela Gaddy, daughter of Joel Gaddy, a prosperous Anson County planter. They had six daughters.

Polk died on June 11, 1892, and is buried in Raleigh.

For additional information on L. L. Polk, see: *Leonidas LaFayette Polk, Agrarian Crusader,* by Stuart Noblin.

William Louis Poteat

William Louis Poteat was born in Caswell County, North Carolina, on October 20, 1856. His father was James Poteat and his mother was Julia Annise McNeil.

During his first school years, he was under the instruction of a governess. Later he attended the village academy at Yanceyville. In 1872 he entered Wake Forest College, graduating in 1877 with the Bachelor of Arts degree. In 1889 he received the Master of Arts degree.

Poteat had begun to read law, when, a year after his graduation, the trustees of Wake Forest elected him a tutor. His acceptance of this position determined his life's work. In 1881 he became assistant professor of natural science; and in 1883 was placed in full charge of the Chair of Natural History, now known as the Chair of Biology, becoming professor of biology at that time.

Poteat was the first man who introduced the biological method, that is, the laboratory method, as opposed to the recitation method, in the teaching of biology in the South. In 1888 he went to Germany to study at the University of Berlin, mainly to get some information about the methods of teaching. In 1893 he attended a course at the Marine Biological Laboratory at Woods Hole, Massachusetts.

In 1905 Poteat was elevated to the presidency of Wake Forest College, a position which he held for twenty-two years.

Poteat was called to teach the most revolutionary of the sciences in a period when the biological revolution and the teaching of evolution were taking shape. He, as well as others, was learning that what he knew in biology was in direct conflict with what he had been taught in the field of religion. But here, he made one of his most important discoveries, that is, that religion was one thing and intellectual effort to account for it was another thing.

He had long been an open and courageous pioneer in the teachings of Darwin and of Darwinian evolution. As early as 1882, when he introduced the first course in laboratory biology in the South, he had published an article entitled "Darwin." In 1884 he made an address at Kinston College on "The Groundless Quarrel," in which he explained the futility of the argument between the evolutionists and the non-evolutionists.

In the early twenties, the evolution controversy broke out like a brush fire throughout the South, and Poteat became a focal point, among both Baptists and North Carolinians.

Believing in academic freedom and the pursuit of truth wherever it might be found, he did not back down. He published several open letters in the *Biblical Recorder* in response to inquiries as to whether there were teachings adverse to the Christian doctrine being taught in Southern Baptist schools. He defended the teaching of evolution as the "divine method of creation," believing it to be fully in harmony with the fundamental tenets of the Baptists.

In 1925 he pleaded successfully against a move to put North Carolina on record as opposed to teaching Darwinian evolution in the state schools before the legislative committee considering this bill. While other states proceeded to make it unlawful to teach the theories of Darwin, suffering subsequent academic embarrassment, Poteat helped to keep North Carolina sane.

Although involved in the controversy over evolution with fundamentalists who once caused him to remark, "It was thought that my head would be cut off by the State Baptist Convention," his election as president of that Convention in 1936 showed how completely he had been vindicated.

In addition, Poteat was an active prohibitionist for more than twenty years, and as president of the United Dry Forces in North Carolina and the Anti-Saloon League of North Carolina, he led an unsuccessful fight to prevent passage by the General Assembly of the county liquor bill and the repeal of prohibition.

Poteat was a member of the North Carolina Utilities Commission, president of the North Carolina Teachers' Assembly, North Carolina Academy of Sciences, and the North Carolina Literary and Historical Association. He was a lecturer for the Gay Foundation at the Southeast Baptist Theological Seminary and for the Brooks Foundation at Hamilton Theological Seminary, Colgate University.

He received honorary degrees of the Doctor of Law from Baylor University in 1905, the University of North Carolina in 1906, Brown University in 1927, and from Mercer University in 1933.

Poteat was a nationally known lecturer and author. Some of his books are *Laboratory and Pulpit*, *The New Peace*, *Can a Man Be a Christian Today*, *The Way of Victory*, and *Stop Light*.

Poteat married Emma Purefoy on June 24, 1881. They had three children: Hubert, Louis and Helen.

He died on March 12, 1938, and is buried in Wake Forest.

For additional information on William L. Poteat, see: *William Louis Poteat, Prophet of Progress*, by Suzanne Cameron Linder.

Julian Price

Julian Price was born on November 25, 1867, near Richmond, Virginia. He was one of six children born to Joseph J. and Margaret Hill Price. He received his formal education in a one-room country school.

Meherrin was a railroad stop and it was with the railroad that Julian found his first jobs. He performed such odd tasks until he was sixteen at which time he had learned the Morse Code and, thus qualified, he was soon employed as telegraph operator and dispatcher for the Southern Railroad. In 1895 he moved to North Carolina with the railroad, first to Durham and shortly thereafter to Greensboro. He remained with the railroad until 1903, when he became a traveling representative of the American Tobacco Company out of Durham.

The insurance business lured Julian away from the American Tobacco Company and he went to work for the Greensboro Life Insurance Company in 1905. In a very short time he became general agent for the company and in only four years, in 1909, was taken into the office as secretary and agency manager.

The Greensboro Life Insurance Company, The Security Life Annuity of Greensboro, and the Jefferson Standard Life of Raleigh merged in 1912 and became the Jefferson Standard. Upon their consolidation Price assumed the position of agency manager and two years later was also given the position of vice president. In 1919 he stepped up to the presidency, a position he held until January, 1946, when he became chairman of the board of directors and his son became president.

Under the guidance of Julian Price, Jefferson Standard grew into one of the outstanding insurance companies in the nation. When he became president, the company had assets of under $10 million and total insurance in force of under $82 million; when he left the presidency, the assets had reached over $174 million and the insurance in force had climbed to over $655 million. At this time, Jefferson Standard ranked thirteenth among the insurance companies in the country.

In 1930 Jefferson Standard acquired controlling interest in Pilot Life Insurance Company and its affiliated companies. Price served as chairman of the board of directors of Pilot.

Perhaps one of the most talked about business ventures that Price engaged in was his purchase of the controlling interest in the *Greensboro Record* shortly after World War I. The reported price was $40,000 and he is reported to have sold this interest nine years later for a profit of $360,000. In 1930 he contributed financially to the merger of the *Record* and the Greensboro *Daily News*.

It was also in 1930 that Price became president of the Atlantic and Yadkin Railway, a position he held until his death.

From 1924 to 1928, he served in the administration of Governor A. W. McLean as head of the state Salary and Wage Commission. In this capacity he worked to ensure a fair pay schedule and employment system for state workers.

There were many other activities, both of a civic and

business nature, in which he was interested. During World War II he served as Chairman of the Victory Bond Committee; he was an executive committeeman of the Greensboro Council of Catholics, Jews, and Protestants; an executive committeeman of the Elon College Foundation; he served as a trustee of A. and T. College in Greensboro, and he served as a Director of Institute of Life Insurance.

After the death of his wife in 1943, Price made a donation of $400,000 for the erection of a Catholic church and rectory in Greensboro to be built in her memory. The church is called "Our Lady of Grace."

In addition to the civic organizations, in which Price was active, he was also active in a number of social organizations. He was a Mason, a Rotarian, a member of the Greensboro Country Club, a member of the Sedgefield Country Club, a member of the Southern Society of New York, and a member of the Elks.

On August 22, 1897, he married Ethel Clay. Two children were born to this union: Mrs. Joseph McKinley Bryan and Ralph Clay Price.

Julian Price died October 25, 1946, as the result of injuries sustained in an automobile accident. He is buried in Green Hill Cemetery in Greensboro. In his memory his children have established a professorship in life insurance at the University of North Carolina at Chapel Hill which is funded with an endowment of $80,000. They have also deeded their father's estate in the mountains of North Carolina to the United States government as a part of the Blue Ridge Parkway and it is called the Julian Price Memorial Park.

A portrait of Price is owned by the Jefferson-Pilot Corporation.

For additional information concerning Julian Price, see: *The Jeffersonian*, November, 1946.

20

D. Hiden Ramsey

Darley Hiden Ramsey was born in Gretna, Virginia, on September 24, 1891. He was the son of Simeon Clay Ramsey and his wife, Lucy Pinckard. In 1903 the Ramsey family moved from Virginia to Asheville, North Carolina. It was here that Hiden attended high school, graduating in 1908 as valedictorian of his class. He attended the University of Virginia and was awarded his A.B. degree in 1912. He continued his studies at the Virginia institution and received his master's degree the next year.

Two years after leaving college, Hiden became interested in the idea of changing the method of city government of Asheville. At that time the city was run by a board of aldermen and he preferred the commission form of city government. He associated himself with a young men's club interested in the change and they promoted a successful campaign. He was elected commissioner of public safety in the new governmental organization, taking office in 1915. In 1919 he was defeated for re-election and went to Winston-Salem where he served as commissioner of safety for a short time.

The position of associate editor of the Asheville *Citizen* enticed him to return to that city in 1920. The next year he and two associates purchased the Asheville *Times*. He served as editor of the *Times* until 1925 when the paper was purchased by Don S. Elias. One year later he returned to the staff of the paper as general manager.

In 1930 the *Times* and the *Citizen* were consolidated and Ramsey was made general manager of the combined enterprise. He served in this capacity and that of vice president until his retirement in 1954.

Ramsey was the recipient of the North Carolina Press Association Award for the best editorial of the year 1940. The editorial concerned itself with the conditions in the Negro hospital in Asheville.

Some measure of national acclaim came to him as a noted "paragraph" writer, a form of expression which was popular in the 1930's in which the writer expressed a single idea in a short article. The *Literary Digest* often reprinted his contributions.

Outside of his work as an editor, education was perhaps Ramsey's prime area of interest. He served on the State Board of Education for eight years and when the State Board of Higher Education was established in 1955, he was named its first chairman. He served the state in that capacity until 1959. During this period he was a prime force in getting the General Assembly to adopt the prospective teachers scholarship loan fund. Through this fund needy students can acquire the money to attend college. If they teach in North Carolina, then a part of the amount advanced will not have to be repaid. If they leave North Carolina or do not teach, then the advancement is treated as a loan. Also during this time, he started the fire insurance fund for state school buildings, a project which has saved the state a large amount of money.

For ten years he served on the Board of Trustees of Western Carolina College, nine of these as chairman of the board. He also rendered services to Asheville-Biltmore College and in appreciation for this and his services to education in the state, they named their new library in his honor in 1964.

The idea of a program to interest people in health careers originated with Ramsey, and such a program was started in the western part of the state. Later the program, Health Careers for North Carolina, became state-wide and received national attention.

On May 17, 1940, he delivered the keynote address at the State Democratic Convention in Raleigh. The same year he served as temporary chairman of the convention and Democratic elector-at-large.

Ramsey was a member of the Asheville Chamber of Commerce, the Civitan Club, Executive's Club, North Carolina Press Association, North Carolina Conference for Social Service, North Carolina Society for Crippled Children and Adults, and the North Carolina Rhodes Scholarship Committee. He received special awards in 1958 from the Western North Carolina Historical Association and the Society for the Preservation of Antiquities for his efforts to have the state restore the birthplace of Zebulon B. Vance. He served as treasurer of the School of Journalism Foundation of North Carolina and was vice president of the Medical Foundation of North Carolina.

He was married January 30, 1926 to Mary Summer. One child, D. Hiden Ramsey, Jr., was born of this union.

Hiden Ramsey died February 18, 1966. He is buried in Riverside Cemetery, Asheville.

Watson Smith Rankin

Watson Smith Rankin was born in Mooresville, North Carolina, on January 18, 1879. He was the son of John Alexander Rankin and Minnie Isabella McCorkle.

He spent his early life in the area of his home, attending the public schools of Mooresville and Statesville. He studied medicine at the North Carolina Medical College at Davidson College for two years and received his Doctor of Medicine degree from the University of Maryland, at College Park, in 1901. Rankin did post-graduate work at the Johns Hopkins University Medical School for one year before becoming a resident physician in obstetrics at the hospital of the University of Maryland. After six months he became resident pathologist at the Johns Hopkins University Hospital in Baltimore, where he remained for some thirteen months.

In 1903, Rankin returned to North Carolina to become a professor of pathology in the medical department of Wake Forest College in Wake Forest. In 1905 he became dean of the Wake Forest College School of Medicine.

Leaving Wake Forest in 1909, Dr. Rankin took over the position of health officer for the state of North Carolina. On July 1, 1909 he became the state's first full-time public health officer.

His first work was one of public relations, that is, of public enlightenment. In 1909 the state of North Carolina was spending a mere twenty-five thousand dollars per year on public health work through the state board, but when Dr. Rankin resigned his position in 1925, the state was spending four hundred and fifty thousand dollars annually for this work.

As part of his enlightenment program, Dr. Rankin enlarged the *Bulletin* of the North Carolina State Board of Health. In addition, many popular educational pamphlets on the more important public health problems were printed and distributed.

Numerous programs and legislation were introduced during Dr. Rankin's tenure as the state's public health officer. The State Board of Health used public health exhibits at state and county fairs and operated a public health truck for mobile demonstrations of public health methods. He stressed sanitation strongly and a department of sanitary engineering with ten full-time inspectors for inspection of state and county institutions and food handling establishments.

The laws controlling the spread of communicable diseases were expanded and more rigidly enforced. A state-wide vital statistics law requiring the registration of births and deaths was passed by the General Assembly in 1913. This was perhaps the single act of the legislature that pleased Dr. Rankin most. With an appropriation of ten thousand dollars to enforce it, he regarded this law as an essential tool to measure the progress of the public health service in North Carolina. In 1916 North Carolina was admitted to the federal Registration Area, a great step forward.

Perhaps the most important accomplishment of Dr. Rankin's sixteen years of administration was the development of full-time county health work. In 1912 Guilford County became the first county in North Carolina to employ a full-time county health officer. When Dr. Rankin retired in 1925, there were thirty-six counties in the state with full-time health departments.

Under Dr. Rankin a campaign was begun which eradicated the hookworn from North Carolina. Working in co-operation with the Rockefeller Foundation, which contributed a million dollars for this work in the South, and the United States Public Health Service, Dr. Rankin and the North Carolina State Board of Health waged a war on the hookworm with eminent success.

In 1925, Dr. Rankin resigned his position to become the director of the Hospital and Orphans Section of the Duke Endowment. The foundation has provided a great deal of money in North Carolina in assisting in the construction and maintenance of hospitals. Dr. Rankin spent the next twenty-five years helping hospitals with the funds at his disposal and encouraging others to provide more such funds.

Retiring from this post in 1950, he remained with the Duke Endowment as a consultant. He was a trustee of the Endowment from 1925 until his death. He was the recipient of the honorary Doctor of Science degree from Duke University, Davidson College, and Wake Forest College.

Dr. Rankin was a trustee of Wake Forest College from 1909 to 1925. He was a member of the American, North Carolina, and Mecklenburg County medical societies, and a member and president of the American Public Health Association. He was president of the Conference of Secretaries of State and Provincial Boards of Health and a member of the North Carolina Conference for Social Service. He was a vice-president for the national associations for the study and prevention of tuberculosis and of infant mortality. He was a trustee of the American Hospital Association from 1935 to 1939.

On August 14, 1906, he married Elva Margaret Dickson. They had one son, Jesse Dickson. Dr. Rankin died on Sept. 8, 1970 and is buried in Charlotte, North Carolina.

Richard J. Reynolds

Richard Joshua Reynolds was born at No Business Mountain, in Patrick County, Virginia, on July 10, 1853. He was the sixth of fifteen children born to Hardin William Reynolds and Nancy Jane (Cox) Reynolds.

Reynolds went to school at home, until leaving to attend Emory and Henry College in Emory, Virginia, which he left before graduation in 1871.

At the time, Reynolds' father, brother and brother-in-law were engaged in the manufacture of tobacco at the home place, and after returning from Emory and Henry, Reynolds went on the road to sell the finished product.

Feeling the need of additional education and preparation for business, he entered Bryant and Stratton's Business College of Baltimore in 1874. Upon his return home, Reynolds took charge of his father's factory, superintended the manufacture of the tobacco, introduced new and improved methods, and ran it with marked success.

As conditions improved from the poverty of the Reconstruction years the business of manufacturing plug tobacco began to assume large proportions and to take definite shape. Studying the situation carefully, Reynolds decided to move to Winston, North Carolina, and go into business for himself. On October 19, 1874, he purchased property on which to construct a factory. By 1875, with a mere seventy-four hundred dollars in capital, he had completed his first small factory.

In the beginning, Reynolds employed just two regular workers and about a dozen seasonal workers to make chewing tobacco plugs. Lacking equipment for redrying tobacco for storage, he manufactured his products during the tobacco harvesting season. During the remainder of the year, he concentrated on marketing. Not one to stick to tradition, the young businessman abandoned the consignment system of selling and made personal visits on horseback to his customers.

The business prospered and by 1888, Reynolds was worth more than two hundred and fifty thousand dollars. On January 7, 1888, a partnership agreement was signed by Reynolds, his brother, William Neal, and by Henry Roan. On February 11, 1890, the R. J. Reynolds Tobacco Company was incorporated under the laws of North Carolina, with the founder holding seventeen hundred of the nineteen hundred shares of stock issued. Roan, believing that the company was overexpanding, withdrew from the business in 1893. In the meantime, another Reynolds brother, Walter, had joined the firm.

In the late 1890's the company began to feel the effects of James B. Duke's efforts to bankrupt or absorb competing tobacco firms. By 1899 it was necessary for the R. J. Reynolds Tobacco Company to reorganize and to seek more capital. Selling two-thirds of the company's stock to Duke, Reynolds found himself nominally controlled by Duke's American Tobacco Company. In 1911, however, the Supreme Court of the United States split up the giant enterprise; and its holdings of R. J. Reynolds stock were ordered distributed.

By 1906, R. J. Reynolds Tobacco Company was producing one-seventh of the nation's plug tobacco, and by 1912 it was turning out one-fourth of the total. Recognizing the potential market for smoking tobacco, Reynolds had entered this field in 1895, and in 1907 he developed "Prince Albert" smoking tobacco. This Burley mixture immediately became a favorite of pipe smokers and roll-your-own cigarette smokers, and today is the largest-selling smoking tobacco in the United States.

In 1913, motivated by a long-standing economic battle with "Buck" Duke, Reynolds launched head-long into the cigarette field. Combining flue-cured, Burley and Turkish tobaccos, he began manufacturing his "Camels," the brand that became the most popular cigarette ever produced. Because this emphatically Burley flavored blend contained less of the imported Turkish leaf, "Camel" was able to undersell the typical Turkish brand. By World War I, "Camels" were capturing over thirty per cent of the nation's cigarette business, and wartime shortages of Turkish leaf further hobbled oriental blends just as "Camel" was hitting its stride.

By the time of Reynolds' death in 1918, his company had achieved forty per cent of the nation's cigarette business and twenty per cent of its chewing and smoking tobacco volume.

Today, the company produces the nation's best-selling filter cigarette, "Winston," and its largest-selling menthol-flavored cigarette, "Salem." From Reynolds' original investment of seventy-four hundred dollars, total assets of the R. J. Reynolds Tobacco Company and its subsidiaries have grown to more than one billion dollars.

Reynolds was married on February 27, 1905, to Mary Katherine Smith of Mount Airy, North Carolina. They had four children: Dick, Mary, Nancy and Zachary Smith.

Richard Joshua Reynolds died in Winston-Salem, North Carolina, on July 29, 1918.

Charles Phillips Russell

Charles Phillips Russell was born in Rockingham, North Carolina, on August 5, 1884. He is the son of Moses H. Russell and Lucy Phillips Russell.

Russell attended the public schools of Rockingham, and it was there that he wrote his first published composition. It concerned a visit to an orphan asylum which was published in the local newspaper. In 1900, he entered the University where he was editor of the *Carolina Magazine*, and of the student newspaper, the *Tar Heel*. He was graduated in 1904 with the degree of Bachelor of Arts.

After leaving Chapel Hill, he found a job as a reporter for the Charlotte, North Carolina, *Observer*, where he worked for two years. While serving his apprenticeship there, he recalled his youthful dreams of working in New York, and in 1906 Russell secured a job on the staff of the New York *Press*, which later became the *Evening Sun*. Newspapers were not so departmentalized at that time, and he found himself serving as a reporter, copyreader, rewriter, assistant literary editor and make-up artist.

In 1914 Russell and a friend worked their way to Europe to search for adventure. With only fifty dollars between them, they lived by picking up jobs here and there. Late in July, they left Paris on foot for Belgium, arriving just hours before the German army. Making their way to the North Sea, Russell and his companion gained ship passage to London. Landing in England shortly after war was declared, he was twice thrown into prison as a German spy. In October of 1914, he returned to New York, gaunt and hungry; so he went to work for the newspapers once again.

Russell lived in New York almost fifteen years, and while not working on a newspaper, was employed by the McClure Syndicate or did free lance writing. His first notable short story was "The Troubadour," published in *The Smart Set*, a magazine of humor and cleverness.

In 1920 he returned to Europe, visiting England, Scotland, Wales, Belgium, France and Italy. He made his home in London until 1925, where he worked chiefly for the London *Daily Express*.

Russell returned to the United States in 1925, and in 1926 his book, *Benjamin Franklin, The First Civilized American,* was published, winning for the author immediate recognition. This was his first book and his best selling one. Several years later Russell's fine biography, *John Paul Jones, Man of Action,* was published. His novel, *The Fumbler,* was written prior to the two biographies, but did not appear in print until 1928.

The urge to travel not yet sated, Russell made a trip with the English artist, Lynn Underwood, to Yucatan where they explored the lost cities of the Mayan culture. Out of this trip came the travel book, *Red Tiger,* written by Russell and illustrated by Underwood.

Ralph Waldo Emerson, The Wisest American, which Russell thought was his best book to that time, appeared in 1930. The book added stature to his literary reputation and received much acclaim from national critics.

In 1931, Russell returned to North Carolina to join the

faculty of the University as an instructor of creative writing, a new course in the School of Journalism.

Although he achieved distinction by his own literary productions, his course in creative writing has resulted at least indirectly in the authorship of numerous books by his pupils and outstanding success by many of them in the writing field. One of singular prominence is Robert Ruark.

Not content only to teach, Russell continued to write. After coming to Chapel Hill, he wrote a biography of William the Conqueror; a book of essays entitled *The Harvesters; The Glittering Century*, dealing with American life in the eighteenth century; and *North Carolina in the Revolution*. His biography of his great-aunt, Cornelia Phillips Spencer, *The Woman Who Rang the Bell*, won for him the Mayflower Cup Award for the best book by a North Carolinian in 1949.

In the spring of 1955, Russell retired after twenty-four years as a professor in the School of Journalism of the University. He then devoted most of his time to the Chapel Hill *News-Leader*, a semi-weekly newspaper which he established in May of 1954. He was editor of the paper until it stopped publishing in January, 1959.

In 1968 Russell was selected a winner of the North Carolina Award in literature "for his creative work in writing and teaching others to write."

He was married shortly after returning to Chapel Hill in 1931 to Caro Mae Green, sister of playwright Paul Green. They had two children, Claire and Avery. In addition, he had a son, Leon, by a previous marriage to an English girl, while he lived in London.

Though he owns a farm outside the town where he spends much of his time relaxing, Russell resides at 300 Chase Avenue in Chapel Hill, North Carolina.

Terry Sanford

Terry Sanford was born in Laurinburg, North Carolina, on August 20, 1917, the son of Cecil LeRoy Sanford, a merchant and realtor, and Elizabeth Martin.

He attended the public schools in Laurinburg before going to Presbyterian Junior College. A semester later he entered the University of North Carolina and graduated from there in 1939 with the Bachelor of Arts degree. Returning to the University's Law School, he received the Bachelor of Laws degree in 1946.

Sanford served as a special agent of the Federal Bureau of Investigation from 1941 to 1942 when he enlisted in the United States Army. He served in the 501st Parachute Infantry Regiment and the 517th Parachute Combat Team from 1942 to 1945. When released from active duty in December, 1945, he held the rank of first lieutenant.

Sanford was the organizer and first commanding officer of the Fayetteville unit of the North Carolina National Guard. He is a former Judge Advocate of the North Carolina Department of the American Legion and a member of the Veterans of Foreign Wars.

After receiving his law degree, he worked as assistant director of the Institute of Government at Chapel Hill from 1946 to 1948, at which time he established his law office in Fayetteville. In 1960 he withdrew from the private practice of law after his election as governor.

Sanford was elected president of the North Carolina Young Democratic Clubs in 1949. He served as a member of the State Ports Authority from 1950 to 1953. Sanford was elected to the North Carolina State Senate in 1953.

On June 25, 1960, he won the Democratic nomination for governor of the State of North Carolina and on November 8 of that year, was elected to that office. Sanford set about immediately to inaugurate a Quality Education Program in North Carolina. When he threw the weight of his administration behind its adoption, the General Assembly cranked out the Higher Education Act, establishing a network of community colleges across the state, creating three new senior colleges in Wilmington, Charlotte, and Asheville.

Under Sanford's leadership were established the Governor's School at Winston-Salem, the North Carolina School of the Arts, the Advancement School, the Learning Institute of North Carolina, Operation Second Chance, and others.

With an interest in the mentally retarded, he pushed through the General Assembly funds for the establishment of a Center for Mental Retardation at Chapel Hill, and for an allotment to the State Board of Health for identification and evaluation of retarded children.

The Governor met the race question head-on and began early in his administration to lay the ground-work for major and positive action in this regard. His establishment of the Good Neighbor Council was one of a number of important acts in his encouragement of peaceful and progressive race relations during a time of upheaval in America.

In addition, Sanford's administration saw the first court reform in North Carolina in the twentieth century, the establishment of the State Board of Science and Technology, the first reapportionment of the State House of Representatives in twenty years, prison policies that led to a decreasing prison population, a sound budget policy in which some of the largest surpluses in the state's history were compiled, and the construction of thousands of miles of new secondary, primary, and interstate roads.

He returned to Fayetteville in 1964. In Fayetteville, Sanford was active in the affairs of his community. He served as chairman of the Fayetteville Chapter of the American Red Cross, as president of the United Services Fund, and as a director of the Children's Home Society of North Carolina.

As a Methodist, Sanford was for several years District Lay Leader, and was the first chairman of the Board of Trustees of Methodist College.

In addition to several pamphlets on education, Sanford's book, *But What About the People,* was published in 1966.

In December, 1969, Sanford was elected president of Duke University.

On July 4, 1942, he married Margaret Rose Knight. Governor and Mrs. Sanford are the parents of two children: Betsy and Terry, Jr. The Sanfords reside in the president's house on the Duke University Campus.

For additional information on Terry Sanford, see: *Messages, Addresses, and Public Papers of Terry Sanford,* edited by Memory F. Mitchell.

William L. Saunders

William Laurence Saunders was born in Raleigh, North Carolina, on July 30, 1835. He was the son of James H. Saunders, an Episcopal minister.

Saunders was prepared for college at the old Raleigh Academy and in 1850 entered the University of North Carolina from which he was graduated four years later. He continued his education in Chapel Hill the next year by studying under Judge William H. Battle. He was licensed to practice law in 1856, but continued to study and received his LL.B. degree in 1858.

Saunders chose Salisbury as the place to begin the practice of his profession. While here he also worked as one of the editors of a Democratic newspaper, the *Salisbury Banner*. The outbreak of the Civil War brought his legal career to a close.

Immediately after the beginning of the war, in April, 1861, he volunteered as a private in the Rowan Rifle Guards and went with the unit to Fort Johnston near Smithville, now Southport. Two months later he was made a lieutenant and was transferred to Reilly's Battery with which he went to Virginia. In January of 1864 he was elected colonel of the Forty-sixth North Carolina Regiment. Saunders saw action during all of the war and was wounded twice.

After the war he moved to Florida where he lived for a short time seeking to regain his health which had been impaired by the hardships of war. Upon his return to the state he made his home in Chapel Hill.

In the election of 1870, the Conservatives gained control of both houses of the General Assembly and the Senate for that session elected Saunders as chief clerk. By process of re-election he served in this position four years. During this same period he was an associate editor of the Wilmington *Journal*.

Colonel Saunders had taken an active part in public affairs during the Reconstruction Period and was believed by many, including a Congressional Committee of 1877, to be the Emperor of the Invisible Empire, better known as the Ku Klux Klan. Upon being informed that Federal authorities were planning to send him to Washington to testify before the committee, the Colonel left town for a few days to make his plans and arrange his private affairs. Before his return he was approached by a friend and told that a large sum of money had been raised to enable him to slip out of the country and live abroad for the rest of his life. This offer he refused and submitted to arrest by the officials.

He was taken to Washington and appeared before the committee which asked him over a hundred questions, all of which he refused to answer.

Colonel Saunders had moved to Raleigh in 1876, where he and Peter M. Hale founded the *Observer*. It quickly became one of the leading newspapers in the state, but Saunder's association with it ended in 1879 when he was forced to retire on the advice of his doctor.

That same year he was appointed Secretary of State to fill the vacancy left by the death of Major Engelhard, his brother-in-law. He was continuously re-elected to the post and served in it until his death.

Shortly after he took office as Secretary of State, Colonel Saunders began the task for which he will always be remembered by those interested in the history of the state, the compilation of the *Colonial Records of North Carolina*. The ten-volume work was eleven years in preparation. The only reward Saunders received for his task was a vote of thanks from the General Assembly.

Saunders served as a trustee of the University of North Carolina from its reopening in 1875 until his death. Part of this time he was secretary and treasurer of the board. The University named a lecture hall in his honor.

He was married on February 3, 1864, to Flordia Cotton, the daughter of John W. Cotton of Edgecombe County. His wife died in July, 1865.

Saunders died April 2, 1891, and is buried in Calvary Churchyard in Tarboro. Among the lines carved on his tomb are these: "For Twenty Years He Exerted More Power in North Carolina Than Any Other Man." And the last line, "I Decline To Answer."

A portrait of Colonel Saunders is owned by the University of North Carolina at Chapel Hill.

For additional information concerning William Laurence Saunders, see: *Southern Exposure*, by Peter Mitchel Wilson, and *Biographical History of North Carolina*, volume 4, by Samuel A. Ashe.

W. Kerr Scott

William Kerr Scott was born near the community of Haw River, Alamance County, North Carolina, April 17, 1896. He was the son of Robert W. "Farmer Bob" Scott and Elizabeth Hughes Scott. Robert and Elizabeth Scott were the parents of eleven children.

He attended the public schools of Alamance County and in 1913 was graduated from Hawfields High School. In 1917 he received the degree of Bachelor of Science from North Carolina State College, now North Carolina State University at Raleigh.

A short time before he completed his course at State College, the United States became an active participant in World War I and upon his graduation Scott received an appointment as a special Emergency Food Production Agent. This position carried with it military service draft exemption. Kerr resigned this position after only a few months and enlisted in the Army where he served in the Field Artillery.

Coming home from the war, Scott discovered that jobs were not easy to find. After the war Scott borrowed $4,000 from his father and purchased a tract of farm land. Much of the land was wooded and young Scott set himself to the task of clearing it and putting it to productive use. In 1920

Scott became Alamance County farm agent. He continued
in this position for ten years and used his pay to meet his
current expenses as well as to purchase additional farm
land. The Scott farm grew to some 1,300 acres.

Kerr Scott expanded his range of service from the county
level to the state level in 1930 when he became Master of
the North Carolina State Grange. President Franklin D.
Roosevelt appointed him regional director of the Farm Debt
Adjustment Administration. In this position he helped the
farmers of seven southern states overcome the hardships of
the depression.

With the 1936 Democratic party primary well under
way, Kerr Scott filed as a candidate for his party's nomination for the North Carolina Commissioner of Agriculture.
When the votes were counted, Kerr Scott was the victor. He
was re-elected in 1940 and 1944. During his terms as Commissioner of Agriculture, North Carolina became the first
state in the nation to rid itself of Bangs Disease among cattle.
Also as a result of Scott's efforts feed manufacturers would
no longer add sawdust as a filler in livestock feed, and
fertilizer manufacturers were forced to stop the practice of
putting sand in fertilizer.

In 1948 Scott filed as a candidate for the Democratic
nomination for governor of North Carolina, and won the
general election in November. "The Squire of Haw River,"
as Kerr Scott came to be known across the state, was inaugurated governor on January 8, 1949.

Scott's "Go-Forward Program" ran into substantial opposition from the state legislature. In order to overcome this
opposition, he appealed directly to the people through the
medium of radio and sought their help in getting the legislature to act on his proposals. This direct appeal to the
people worked, and most of the "Go-Forward Program"
was adopted by the General Assembly. Some of the more

important accomplishments of the Scott administration were: the paving of more miles of roads than had been paved in all of North Carolina's history; the building of 8,000 new classrooms, 175 gymnasiums, and 350 lunchrooms for the public schools; an annual appropriation of over one-half million dollars for a public school health program; and the construction of deep water ports at Wilmington and Morehead City at a cost of seven and one-half million dollars.

After his term as governor was completed in 1952, Scott returned to his farm at Hawfields for a short period. He ran and was elected to the United States Senate in 1954 where he served until his death.

Kerr Scott was a member of the American Jersey Cattle Club, North Carolina Jersey Cattle Club, North Carolina Cotton Growers' Association, American Legion, Junior Order American Mechanics, and a member of agricultural boards and commissions. In 1947 he received the "Man of the Year" award from the *Progressive Farmer*, and in 1950 he received the "Man of the Year" award from the North Carolina State Grange. His religious affiliation was with the Hawfields Presbyterian Church.

On July 2, 1919, William Kerr Scott married Mary Elizabeth White. Three children were born of this union: Osborne W. Scott, Robert W. Scott, and Mary Kerr Scott.

Senator Scott died April 16, 1958, at Burlington, North Carolina. He is buried in the Hawfields Presbyterian Church Cemetery.

A portrait of Governor Scott is owned by the state and hangs in Raleigh.

For additional information concerning William Kerr Scott, see: *Addresses and Papers of Governor William Kerr Scott, 1949-1953*, edited by David Leroy Corbitt.

Susie Marshall Sharp

Susie Marshall Sharp was born on July 7, 1907, in Rocky Mount, North Carolina, although she was reared in Reidsville. Her father was James Merritt Sharp, a lawyer, and her mother was Annie Britt Blackwell.

She attended the public schools of Reidsville and it was here that she decided she wanted to share her father's legal profession. When Miss Sharp was in high school, she was a debater and so many people said "you ought to be a lawyer" that she took them seriously. She went to Woman's College, now the University of North Carolina at Greensboro, and studied chemistry for two years, then entered the University of North Carolina Law School as the only girl in a class of sixty boys, where she excelled. She received her Bachelor of Laws degree as an honor graduate of the class of 1929. She was one of the student editors of the *North Carolina Law Review* and a member of the legal honor society, the Order of the Coif. She was admitted to the North Carolina Bar in August, 1928.

Miss Sharp was awarded an honorary Doctor of Laws degree from Woman's College in 1950 and from Elon College in 1963, and the honorary degree of Doctor of Humane Letters from Pfeiffer College in 1960 and from Wake Forest College in 1965.

Her father never pressured her into following in his footsteps, yet when she did so, he went all out to help her. He took her into his firm as a partner, and they called the firm Sharp and Sharp. While practicing with her father, she served as Reidsville's city attorney from 1939 to 1949, the first and only woman to hold that post in Reidsville.

She was vice chairman of the Democratic Executive Committee of Rockingham County for ten years and has been a member of the State Democratic Executive Committee. She was Secretary of the 11th Judicial Bar Association from the time it was organized in 1931 until it was split and Rockingham County became a part of the 21st District. She was secretary of the 21st District Bar until she resigned in 1943.

Miss Sharp is an experienced campaign manager. She headed Governor R. Gregg Cherry's campaign in Rockingham County in 1944 and Congressman John Folger's campaign in 1946. She was Governor W. Kerr Scott's manager in her county in the second primary. As vice chairman of the county executive committee, she of course helped with a number of county political campaigns.

Since the beginning of her career she has been regarded as unusual because she chose law as her profession. When she had been practicing for three days, an old colored man entered the office and asked whether she was "that woman lawyer" he had been hearing about. She acknowledged that she was and asked what she could do for him. "Nothing, ma'am, thank you," he replied, "I just wanted to see what you looked like."

Her biggest job as a lawyer came while she was city attorney for Reidsville. It involved the condemnation of properties for the city airport, and the legal battles raged for a period of years in which she "fought injctions, shotguns, astronomical valuations of real estate, private graveyards, dwelling houses and irate farmers." She and the city won, and Reidsville got its airport after two Supreme Court decisions in March, 1944.

On July 1, 1949, Governor W. Kerr Scott appointed Miss Sharp as North Carolina's first woman Superior Court judge. She immediately plunged into a case that brought a beginning to prison reform in North Carolina. She sentenced a prison camp superintendent who had assaulted a prisoner by ordering him handcuffed to the bars for some 52 hours.

Climaxing a thirty-three year legal career, Miss Sharp was sworn in as North Carolina's first woman justice of the State Supreme Court on March 14, 1962. She has since been backed by the North Carolina General Assembly for a seat on the United States Supreme Court.

She served as a member of the North Carolina Constitutional Commission of 1959. She holds honorary memberships in Phi Beta Kappa, Delta Kappa Gamma and the Altrusa Club. She has been cited for achievement and distinguished service by the state Federation of Business and Professional Women's Clubs, Chi Omega social sorority and the Order of the Valkyries, University of North Carolina Leadership Society.

Miss Sharp resides at 629 Lindsey Street, Reidsville.

James E. Shepard

James Edward Shepard was born in Raleigh, North Carolina, on November 3, 1875. He was the son of Augustus Shepard, a minister, and his wife, Hattie Whitted.

He received his preparatory education in the public schools of the state and then attended Shaw University in Raleigh from which he was graduated in 1894 with a degree in pharmacy. Immediately after graduation he opened a pharmacy in Durham. Being unsatisfied in this work, he went to Washington, D. C., in 1898 where he was employed as a comparer of deeds in the recorder's office. The following year he returned to his native state and assumed the position of Deputy Collector of Internal Revenue for the United States government. He continued in this position until 1905.

In 1910 Shepard was instrumental in establishing a school known as the National Religious Training School and Chautauqua. It was begun on a twenty-five-acre tract of land given by the citizens of Durham. Shepard was made president of the institution. He devoted all of his energies to the development of this school and served as its president until his death.

The first years of the school, like those of many others, was characterized by a high degree of interest, but a shortage of funds. In spite of this, by 1912 ten buildings had been erected on the campus. During this early period the support for the school came from the fees paid by students and donations from private sources. Fees were low by necessity; room rent being only $7 per month and tuition $1 per month. Faculty members were paid between $500 and $1,000 per year, depending upon the degree they held and their experience. The school began with a total staff of twenty-one and an enrollment of 109.

The initial plans for the school were to establish it as a four-year college; however, it was found impractical during the beginning years to carry out this plan. Shepard found it desirable to include a high school course, as well as a four-year college, a commercial school, a home economics school, and a training school for ministers.

Financial difficulties continued to plague the institution and in 1915 the school had to be sold. Mrs. Russell Sage of New York enabled the continuance of the college by a donation which permitted the repurchase of the property. At this time the school underwent a reorganization and became known as the National Training School.

Even before this financial crisis was over, World War I brought another financial depression to the struggling educational center. Two plans were considered to enable the school to continue—either allow some religious denomination to assume control or deed the property to the State and allow it to be administered as a public institution. The latter plan was adopted and the school's name was again changed, this time to the Durham State Normal School.

The year 1925 marked one of the high moments in the history of this school. Shepard, along with his supporters, concluded a successful legislative campaign to make the school the first state-supported Negro liberal arts college. This time the name of the school was changed to North Carolina College for Negroes. New funds, $42,000 from B. N. Duke, $8,000 from citizens of Durham, and $100,000 from the state, enabled the school to expand its physical facilities substantially.

The depression of 1929 brought a period of lower enrollment, but also a period of expansion for the college.

Before the death of its first president, the college underwent one more name change — to North Carolina College at Durham. Shepard lived to see his creation grow into an outstanding educational institution. At his death it was one of only four Negro colleges in the nation to be fully accredited by the Association of American Universities. Its faculty had grown to over seventy and its student body to 1,500.

After the death of President Shepard, the James E. Shepard Memorial Foundation, Inc. was established as a tribute to him. Funds for this came from donations from citizens and organizations across the state. The major portion of these funds is used as a loan and scholarship fund for students attending the college.

Shepard served as Grand Master of the Masons of North Carolina, Grand Patron of the Eastern Star, a member of the Knights of Pythias, and president of the North Carolina Teachers' Association. At the World Sunday School Convention in Rome, Italy, in 1910, Shepard was the only Negro speaker.

On November 7, 1895, he married Annie Day Robinson and two daughters were born to the couple: Marjorie and Annie Day.

Shepard died on October 6, 1947. He is buried in Beechwood Cemetery in Durham.

For additional information concerning James E. Shepard, see: "James E. Shepard Memorial Foundation, Inc." (a pamphlet).

Furnifold M. Simmons

Furnifold McLendel Simmons was born on January 20, 1854, near Pollocksville in Jones County, North Carolina. He was the son of Furnifold Green Simmons, and Mary McLendel Jerman.

He was frail in his youth so he was coached by a family tutor at home and attended a private school near there. He entered Wake Forest College in 1868 but a year later matriculated at Trinity College, now Duke University. He was graduated in 1873 with the Bachelor of Arts degree.

He was admitted to the bar on January 3, 1875, shortly before turning twenty-one years of age.

For nearly two years he practiced law in Jones County, then opened an office in New Bern. At different times he had law partnerships with W. T. Faircloth of Goldsboro, H. L. Gibbs of Hyde County, Clement Manly of New Bern, James H. Pou of Raleigh, E. W. Pou of Smithfield, M. A. Allen of Kinston, and P. M. Pearsall and A. D. Ward of New Bern.

Simmons was twice an unsuccessful candidate for a seat in the state legislature before being elected to a seat in the United States House of Representatives in 1886. The Republican vote in his district was split when each of two Negroes claimed to represent that party. Although admirably serving in the House from 1887 to 1889, being named to the Committee on Claims and obtaining record appropriations for his home section, he was defeated for re-election by a Negro, Henry P. Cheatham. In 1890 he withdrew from the Congressional race rather than accede to the demands of the North Carolina Farmers' Alliance which he considered dangerous and unconstitutional.

In 1892 Simmons became chairman of the State Democratic Executive Committee. Working untiringly, he helped carry North Carolina for the Democratic Party. President Grover Cleveland rewarded him for his splendid management and leadership by naming him Collector of Internal Revenue for the Eastern District, which post he held for four years.

In 1898 he again became state chairman of the Democratic Executive Committee, serving in this capacity for four more terms. As chairman, Simmons led the "Red Shirt" revolt against Republican and Negro "misrule" in 1898 and returned the state to white supremacy under the Democratic party. He supervised the drafting of the constitutional amendment limiting suffrage in North Carolina, and as state chairman led the campaign for its adoption. He wrote and sponsored the Watts Bill and the Ward Bill for prohibition.

In 1901 Simmons took his seat in the United States Senate. He was re-elected in 1906, 1912, 1918, and 1924. His thirty years in the Senate make him the longest serving North Carolinian ever in the upper house of the national Congress.

As a member of the commission to investigate waterways in other countries, he was instrumental in obtaining for North Carolina such coastal improvements as the deepening of the Cape Fear, the Neuse and the Trent rivers, the construction of a breakwater at Cape Lookout, and the construction of ship canals.

Simmons began his labors for improved highways in 1904. In 1912 he obtained one-half million dollars for experimental improvement of roads on rural mail delivery routes. In 1917 an appropriation of eighty-five million dollars was passed for this purpose.

In 1909 he became a member of the Democratic Steering Committee and was placed on the committees of Finance and Commerce, becoming thereby one of the most influential men in the country. He was an early advocate of construction of the Panama Canal and was the recognized spokesman for President Wilson on this matter. During President Wilson's administration, Simmons was chairman of the Senate Finance Committee.

Known as a tax expert, he guided through the Senate the Simmons-Underwood Tariff Bill and his own plan for reduction of income taxes, both plans adopted over the opposition of the majority Republican party.

In 1928, however, Simmons refused to support Alfred E. Smith for the Democratic nomination for the presidency and after the latter's nomination he declined to support Smith's campaign. For this reason he resigned from the Democratic National Committee, a post he had held for some time. It led to his defeat for renomination to the Senate in 1930.

Simmons was married to Eliza Hill Humphrey in 1875, and they had three children. She died in 1883, and on July 29, 1886, he married Belle Gibbs; to them were born two children.

He died on April 30, 1940, and is buried in Cedar Grove Cemetery, New Bern.

For additional information on Furnifold McLendel Simmons, see: *F. M. Simmons, Statesman of the New South*, by J. Fred Rippy.

Asa T. Spaulding

Asa Timothy Spaulding was born on July 22, 1902 in rural Columbus County, North Carolina, the son of Armstead Spaulding and Annie Bell Lowery.

During his first sixteen years he was able to attend a school for only a few months of each year. When Dr. A. M. Moore, a native of Columbus County who had moved to Durham, suggested that he come to Durham for secondary schooling, he followed the advice. In 1918 he entered the National Training School (now North Carolina Central University). Dr. Moore, who was responsible for his coming to Durham, was a founder and official of North Carolina Mutual Life Insurance Company and he saw to it that Asa got a job with the company during the summer.

By the fall of 1923 Spaulding had acquired the equivalent of a high school education and in the fall of that year he returned to Columbus County. Here he served for one year as a teacher and principal of the school at Farmers' Union, where he had first started school. The next year he went to Washington, D. C., where he entered Howard University and pursued an accounting course. At the end of his first term at Howard his funds were exhausted and he had to return to North Carolina Mutual for work.

After about two years of working and saving he was again

able to pursue his education. He entered New York University from which he was later graduated magna cum laude. At N.Y.U. he studied in the School of Commerce, Accounts and Finance, where he came under the influence of Professor S. B. Ackerman, who was one of the leading insurance actuaries in the nation and interested Spaulding in this field.

In 1930 he entered the University of Michigan, on borrowed money, and two years later was awarded an M.A. degree in actuarial science. He then returned to Durham where he served his apprenticeship under F. B. Dilts, the actuary for Home Security Life of Durham.

In January of 1933 the board of directors of North Carolina Mutual named Spaulding full-time actuary for the company. He rose in the organization holding the positions of assistant secretary, controller, vice president and in 1959 he was elected president. He retired as head of the company on December 31, 1967. North Carolina Mutual is the largest Negro owned and Negro operated insurance company in the world. Its main offices are in Durham with branches in ten states and the District of Columbia.

Other business organizations in which Spaulding is interested include: director of Mutual Savings and Loan Association, director of Mechanics and Farmers Bank, director of Realty Services, Inc., director of W. T. Grant Company, and chairman of the board of Bankers Fire and Casualty Company.

Education has always been one of Spaulding's chief interests. In 1965 he was selected as the chairman of the board of trustees of Shaw University, a leading Negro educational institution. He is also a trustee of Howard University and a member of its finance committee, and has served as president of the North Carolina College (now North Carolina Central University) Alumni Association.

Spaulding has been called on by several North Carolina

governors to help in race related matters. He has served as vice chairman of the Durham Bi-Racial Human Relations Committee and vice chairman of the North Carolina Advisory Committee to the Commission on Civil Rights.

Presidents Eisenhower, Truman, and Johnson have sent Spaulding on various diplomatic missions. He represented the United States at the inauguration of President William Tubman of Liberia, he made a trade tour of Central America for Secretary of Commerce Luther Hodges, and he went on a trade mission to four African countries for Secretary of Commerce John T. Conner. He was also a member of the United States Delegation to the UNESCO General Conference in New Delhi, India, in 1956.

He is the author of numerous papers and articles, the best known being *Negro Insurance in the United States*. Several of his addresses have been printed and distributed, some of which are: *Discrimination and the Negro in the United States* and *Moral and Spiritual Values: America's Greatest Need.*

Some of the organizations to which he belongs are: the National Negro Insurance Organization, James E. Shepard Memorial Foundation, National Urban League, the North Carolina Council of Churches. He is a director of the John Avery Boys' Club and the United Fund of Durham. His religious affiliation is with the White Rock Baptist Church.

He was married on June 22, 1933, to Elna Bridgeforth of Athens, Alabama. Four children have been born of this union: Asa T., Jr., Patricia Ann, Aaron Lowery and Kenneth Bridgeforth Spaulding.

For additional information concerning Asa T. Spaulding, see: *North Carolina Lives*, by William S. Powell, and the Raleigh *News and Observer*, June 6, 1965.

Francis Speight

Francis Speight was born on the family farm between Windsor and Lewiston in Bertie County, North Carolina, September 11, 1896. He was the son of the Reverend Thomas Trotman Speight and Margaret Otelia Sharrock.

Speight first attended school in a schoolhouse in his yard. His father employed a teacher and had a private school for his children and the children of a few other families. He later went to a public school and then to high school in Lewiston. Although he did not finish high school, Speight was enrolled at Wake Forest College in 1915, where he studied for two years. During those two years, in addition to his regular studies, he took art lessons on Saturdays with Miss Ida Poteat at Meredith College in Raleigh. His chief interest at the time was to be a writer, and the art lessons were his sister Tulie's idea. She thought he might like to illustrate his own writings.

In 1919, Speight went to Washington, D. C., where he studied several months in a commercial art studio, Chanderly Art School. Then in January, 1920, he went to the Corcoran School of Art and studied for a semester. At the Corcoran he saw an exhibition of the drawings of Daniel Garber, who was a teacher at the Pennsylvania Academy of Fine Arts. It was this exhibition, along with the interest of his sister, Tulie, that led him to go to the Pennsylvania Academy of Fine Arts in the fall of 1920. He remained at the Academy for some forty years before returning to North Carolina in 1961.

Speight studied at the Academy for five years, from 1920 to 1925. He spent two years as a student-teacher, and thirty-three years as a teacher. While a student there, he won two Cresson Traveling Scholarships, each of which provided a summer of travel and study in Europe.

He is best known for his landscapes though he has done some drawing and even a few abstractions in school in 1923 and 1924. Most of his painting was done in the suburbs of Philadelphia, chiefly in the manufacturing district of Manayunk, a hilly industrial area along the Schuylkill River. He lived and painted one year at New Hope, Pennsylvania, and one summer in Applebacksville, Pennsylvania. On various occasions he painted at Wierton and Coaldale, towns much like Manayunk, but expressed in different color terms.

Speight has also painted some in North Carolina, and was the first person to be employed by the University of North Carolina to teach art there, which he did as a visiting instructor in the summer school sessions of 1934 and 1935.

At the Pennsylvania Academy of Fine Arts, he taught figure and landscape painting, doing his own painting in his spare time.

In September, 1961, Speight returned to North Carolina, becoming artist-in-residence and professor of art at East Carolina College at Greenville, North Carolina.

He has received many awards and prizes: first prize at the 38th annual exhibition of the Washington Society of Artists in 1929, the Bronze Medal and Third Clark Prize from Corcoran Gallery in 1937, the Altman Prize for Landscape in 1951 and 1953, the Obrig Prize from the National Academy in 1955, a grant of one thousand dollars by the National Institute of Arts and Letters in 1953, first prize in the Pennsylvania Academy of Fine Arts Regional Exhibition, and the Gold Medal Award of the Pennsylvania Academy of Fine Arts.

In 1960 Speight was elected to membership in the National Institute of Arts and Letters. He has been a member of the National Academy of Design since 1940. In 1962 he was awarded an honorary Doctor of Humane Letters from Wake Forest College. In 1964 he received a North Carolina Award for his work as a painter and for the honor he has brought to the state.

His canvases hang in the permanent collections of the Metropolitan Museum, Pennsylvania Academy, The Art Gallery of Toronto, Butler Institute of American Art, Norton Gallery in Palm Beach, Memorial Art Gallery in Rochester, Museum of Fine Arts, Boston, Pennsylvania State University, Gibbs Gallery in Charleston, the Corcoran Art Museum in Washington, and the North Carolina Museum of Art, as well as in some thirty other museums, galleries and private collections.

The "Francis Speight Retrospective Exhibition" was held in the North Carolina Museum of Art in 1961. In 1956 his work was exhibited in a New York show entitled "Thirty North Carolina Artists." In 1953 the Ranger Fund of the National Academy of Art purchased one of his works to present to the Rochester Museum of Art. The American Academy of Arts and Lectures has purchased his work. In 1936 he won his first commission, which was to paint a mural for the Gastonia, North Carolina, post office.

On November 7, 1936, Speight married Sarah Jane Blakeslee, a former student of his. The Speights have two children, Thomas Blakeslee and Elisabeth Sharrock. They reside at 501 Eighth Street, Greenville, North Carolina.

23

Cornelia Phillips Spencer

Cornelia Ann Phillips was born in Harlem, New York, on March 20, 1825. She was the daughter of James Phillips and Julia Vermeule.

In May, 1826, when Cornelia was barely a year old, Dr. Phillips moved to Chapel Hill, North Carolina, to fill the professorship of mathematics and natural philosophy. Her education was acquired through the instruction of her parents and self study.

On June 20, 1855, she married James Munroe Spencer, of Greene County, Alabama.

Her husband died on June 24, 1861, and she and her daughter returned to Chapel Hill, where she lived with her parents.

Her marked influence upon public events began upon her return to North Carolina in 1861, and yet she never appeared in public, either to speak or to read, or even to occupy a seat on a public platform. Her public work was accomplished through others or through the pen, for she was an intimate, personal and trusted friend of the state's most prominent men: William A. Graham, David L. Swain, and Zebulon B. Vance.

The Civil War created a severe hardship for the University of North Carolina, but it continued throughout the struggle. When the reconstructionists took control in 1869, they dismissed all the old faculty of the institution and appointed others. The University was carried on for two years in this manner but was shortly compelled to close for lack of students. In 1868 Governor W. W. Holden had closed its doors, and when it was reopened in 1869 with a new president, Soloman Pool, who had replaced the kindly David Swain, Mrs. Spencer launched her campaign.

It was in 1869 that she contributed to the Raleigh *Sentinel* her *Pen and Ink Sketches of the University,* which stirred up public feeling and interest in the school and brought her a certain measure of fame. She wrote tirelessly to the press concerning the incompetence of the University administration and faculty during the Pool regime. During those years she wrote largely for the *North Carolina Presbyterian,* in a weekly feature entitled "The Young Lady's Column." The University closed in 1870.

To Cornelia Phillips Spencer can be given more credit than to anyone, with the possible exception of Kemp P. Battle, for the reopening of the University in September, 1875.

When Dr. Battle telegraphed her from Raleigh on March 20, 1875, that the bill had passed the legislature giving the University seventy-five hundred dollars annually from the landscrip fund, Mrs. Spencer climbed the stairs to the attic of South Building and rang the bell for an hour.

After the opening of the University, the purpose to which she had devoted her energies for so long, she continued her writing. She contributed reports of the University to the state press from 1877 to 1884. In 1888 she published her last work from Chapel Hill, a child's history of North Carolina entitled *First Steps in North Carolina History.*

In 1867 her papers written for Dr. Deems' New York weekly, *The Watchman,* were collected in one volume and titled *The Last Ninety Days of the War.* Her *Old Times in Chapel Hill* was published by the *University of North Caro-*

lina Magazine in seventeen numbers from 1884 to 1890. In 1889 she compiled and edited the first edition of the *Catalogue of Officers and Students of the University,* a laboriously constructed alumni directory containing five thousand names.

Mrs. Spencer was greatly concerned about the development of the young women of the Presbyterian Church and for six years she regularly pointed out to them through "The Young Lady's Column" the path in which they should walk.

She heartily supported efforts to establish a state normal and industrial college for women and it has been said that she "held up the hands" of Charles McIver and Edwin Alderman in their labors to establish the State Normal and Industrial College. A dormitory at the University of North Carolina at Greensboro bears her name in recognition of her efforts. The University at Chapel Hill named its first woman's building after her.

Mrs. Spencer did not think of herself as a poet but rather as an occasional "versifier." She did, however, highly prize the poet's art, and showed her interest in it with several papers as well as through a number of songs, odes, hymns, and poems. The University Hymn, first sung at the celebration of University Day in 1879, has continued to be used for that day and on other occasions. In 1895 at the University Centennial Celebration, the Centennial Ode written by Mrs. Spencer was sung. The University also conferred upon her the honorary degree of Doctor of Laws, the first such distinction to be conferred by it to a woman.

In 1894, because of failing health, Mrs. Spencer moved to Cambridge, Massachusetts, where she resided with her daughter Julia, and her son-in-law, James Lee Love. She died on March 11, 1908, and was buried in Chapel Hill on the 14th.

For additional information on Cornelia Phillips Spencer, see: *The Woman Who Rang the Bell,* by Phillips Russell and *Old Days in Chapel Hill,* by Hope Summerell Chamberlain.

James Sprunt

James Sprunt was born in Glasgow, Scotland, June 9, 1847. He was the eldest son of Alexander and Jeanie Dalziel Sprunt. When James was five years old his family moved to the United States and settled in Wilmington, North Carolina. He had attended school one year in Glosgow and attended private schools in North Carolina for an additional seven years.

Because of circumstances brought about by the Civil War, Sprunt was forced to quit school and begin work at the age of fourteen. Three years later he became purser on the blockade runner *North Heath*. During the course of the war he served as purser on several blockade runners and on many occasions narrowly escaped with his life.

On one of these voyages he brought ten barrels of sugar into Wilmington, sold them, and invested the proceeds in twenty-five bales of cotton. His intention was to take the cotton out on the next voyage, but circumstances prevented this. Instead it was taken to Fayetteville for safety, but when Sherman marched through this city he burned eleven of them. After the war the remaining bales were sold and the money was used as capital for the export firm of Alexander Sprunt & Sons. Initially the firm dealt mainly in naval stores, but gradually switched to cotton. After the death of his father in 1884, James became the sole proprietor of the business. Later a younger brother, William H. Sprunt, became a partner. The firm grew and prospered and at its peak had branch offices or agencies in Liverpool, Le Havre, Barcelona, Rotterdam, Milan, Manchester, London, Charlotte, Houston, and Savannah. During the active years of the firm over one billion dollars in drafts were negotiated and not a single one of these was ever refused.

In 1880 Sprunt's father-in-law, Colonel K. M. Murchison, purchased "Orton" plantation. At Murchison's death in 1906, Sprunt purchased the plantation as a gift for his wife. It is due to his restoration and expansion that "Orton," established in 1725 by "King Roger" Moore, is the show place of present times. He added the wings to the house and further restored the grounds. He also built the little chapel which overlooks the Cape Fear River.

Sprunt was always interested in the Cape Fear River and ways to improve it. It was largely through his efforts that the city acquired an anchorage basin and a channel deep enough for ships to come to the port without fear of being grounded. Mr. Sprunt consulted with the Secretary of Commerce and acquired his recommendation for another lightship off Frying Pan Shoals. Through an amendment introduced by Senator Overman to the Sundry Civil Bill, $115,-000 was provided for this purpose. In 1910 Mr. Sprunt went to Washington and testified before the House Committee on Interstate and Foreign Commerce concerning the inadequate condition of the lights by the Big Island and Old Brunswick. Due to his testimony, in part at least, a modern and efficient lighting system was installed and maintained.

Sprunt was a noted North Carolina historian, with a special interest in the lower Cape Fear area. He contributed many articles to local newspapers and periodicals on this subject. In addition, he also published several books. Among these are: *Information and Statistics of Wilmington, N. C.* (1883),

Tales and Traditions of the Lower Cape Fear (1896), *Tales of The Blockade of the Cape Fear* (1910), *The Chronicles of the Cape Fear, 1660-1916* (1917), and *Derelicts* (1920). Much of the information in these books and papers on blockade running would have been lost if Mr. Sprunt had not chosen to preserve it. Having served on several blockade runners, he had access to facts which were never recorded in any official records.

James Sprunt was a member of the North Carolina State Literary and Historical Association, the North Carolina Folklore Society, Board of Commissioners of Navigation and Pilotage, the Board of Trustees of the University of North Carolina, and the Board of Trustees of Davidson College. He succeeded his father as British vice-consul at Wilmington, serving for thirty-one years, and also served as German consul of North Carolina for five years. He was very active in the Presbyterian Church and gave liberally to its support. He built a number of Presbyterian churches; maintained a mission and hospital in China; erected a home for missionaries in Kiangyin, China, where he also built the James Sprunt Boys' Academy and the Luola Murchison Sprunt Girls' Academy; and he established a lectureship at Union Theological Seminary, Richmond, Virginia.

Sprunt was married to Luola Murchison on November 27, 1883. They were the parents of three children: Kate, James Laurence, and Marion. Both girls died in childhood, and in memory of Marion, Mr. Sprunt built the Marion Sprunt Hospital for the care of women and children.

James Sprunt died on July 9, 1924. He is buried in Oakdale Cemetery, Wilmington, North Carolina.

For additional information concerning James Sprunt, see: *James Sprunt: A Tribute From the City of Wilmington.*

Henry Jerome Stockard

Henry Jerome Stockard was born in Chatham County, North Carolina, December 15, 1858. He was the son of James Gibbs Stockard and his wife, Mary Johnson.

He was prepared for college at Graham High School, after which he went to the University of North Carolina to take some special courses. He next attended Elon College from which he took the degree of Master of Arts.

Upon completing his college training he began teaching school in Alamance and after several years became principal of Graham High School, and later superintendent of the Alamance County schools. Shortly thereafter he returned to the University as assistant professor of English. His next move was to Fredericksburg College in Virginia as professor of English and political science. Four years later in 1896, he returned to North Carolina where he assumed the position of professor of Latin at Peace Institute, Raleigh, in 1900. His connection with Peace continued until his death. In 1907 he was made president of Peace and served in this capacity until 1912 when he resumed his position as professor of Latin.

In 1886 Eugene G. Harrell, editor of the *North Carolina Teacher,* offered a prize of five dollars in gold for the best poem submitted to the journal. Stockard entered the contest

and his poem "The Review of Our Dead" won the five dollars. From this beginning he went on to write a number of
poems and to acquire fame throughout the nation for them.

His work was published in leading magazines in the nation
such as *Harper's, Scribners, Century,* and *Atlantic Monthly.*
He published two volumes of verse: *Fugitive Lines,* a collection of some of his poetry, and *A Study in Southern Poetry,*
a textbook which also contained some of his verse. Some
of his poems can also be found in Stedman's Anthology,
Representative Sonnets by American Poets, and *Songs of the
South.*

James Y. Joyner, in an address before a meeting of the
State Literary and Historical Association at Raleigh in 1914,
grouped Stockard's poetry into five classes based upon subject matter and content.

Under the poems of patriotism, Joyner lists "The Last
Charge at Appomattox" as being the most notable. It begins:

> Scarred on a hundred fields before,
> Naked and starved and travel-sore,
>   Each man a tiger, hunted,
> They stood at bay as brave as Huns,
> Last of the Old South's splendid sons,
> Flanked by ten thousand shotted guns,
>   And by ten thousand fronted.

As characteristic of his poems of meditation and sentiment, Joyner recited "A Christmas Memory." The poem concludes with these lines:

> Thank God for Christmas! Man ne'er grows
>   So old but that he loves the snows,
>   And bells of Christmas ringing!

As illustrative of Stockard's poetry dealing with faith and
spiritual yearning, Joyner thought "The Hand That Binds the
Star" to be typical:

The Hand that binds the star
In its far centre, and around it rolls
Through space its worlds, with never halt nor jar,
No less my steps controls.

Among his poems on nature, Joyner chose "An Evening Song." Its last verse concludes:

Earth calls her weary ones to rest,—
Good-night!
The sickle moon sinks down the west,
The shadows veil the mountain's crest,
The fires burn low where sunk the sun,
To sleep! The long, long day is done,—
Good-night, good night!

In his selections of miscellaneous sonnets, Joyner chose "Homer" as one. Its final lines are:

I hear the Odyssey and Iliad rise
With deeper rhythm than that of Chios' surge,
And there upon the blue Aegean's verge,
Unchanging while the centuries increase,
After three thousand years, before me lies
The unveiled shore of old sea-cinctured Greece!

His political affiliation was with the Democratic party and his religious affiliation with the Presbyterian Church.

Stockard was married twice. His first wife was Sallie J. Holleman of Morrisville. After her death he married Margaret Lula Tate of Graham. He was the father of ten children.

He died at his home in Raleigh in 1914.

A portrait of Henry Jerome Stockard is owned by Peace College in Raleigh, a gift of the Stockard family.

For additional information concerning Henry Jerome Stockard, see: *Biographical History of North Carolina*, volume 5, by Samuel A. Ashe.

Lamar E. Stringfield

Lamar Edwin Stringfield was born near Raleigh, North Carolina, on October 10, 1897. His father was O. L. Stringfield, a Baptist minister. His mother was Ellie Beckwith.

He attended both Mars Hill College and Wake Forest College, and played in the band at each school.

In 1916 Stringfield joined the army, serving with the First North Carolina Infantry on the Mexican border and with the 105th Engineers of the Thirtieth Division in France during World War I. It was there that he first took up the study of the flute, tinkering with the instrument during his off-duty hours.

Returning to North Carolina he began a serious study of the flute. After a year of study under Emdil Medicus, he entered the Institute of Musical Art in New York City, where his teacher was the famous flutist, George Barrere. While there, he studied composition under the guidance of Percy Goetschins, Franklin Robinson, and George Wedge. After four years he received the artist's diploma in flute-playing and a prize in composition, these coming in 1924. He also received diplomas from the American Orchestral Society for orchestral playing and for conducting. Stringfield studied conducting with Chalmers Clifton and Henry Hadley. In

1928 he studied more composition under Nadia Boulanger
in Paris.

Stringfield played with the Chamber Music Art Society
for two seasons and the New York Chamber Music Society
for three seasons. He conducted symphonies in Aeolian and
Carnegie halls, was guest conductor of the Newark Phil-
harmonic and the Nashville Symphony in 1926 and 1927,
conductor at the Washington National Opera Association in
1927 and 1928 and at the English Folk-dance Festival in
New York in 1928 and 1929. In 1930 he conducted the
Baltimore Symphony and the Barrere Symphony at the
Spartanburg Festival.

During the summer of 1927, Stringfield organized and
conducted the Asheville Symphony Orchestra, achieving
amazing results with a handful of players. When the suggestion was made that Asheville have a symphony orchestra,
he carried his fight to the businessmen of the city.

In 1930 while he was recuperating from an automobile
accident, Stringfield decided that he would remain in his
native state to work. He conceived the idea of organizing
a department on the campus of the University of North
Carolina which would form a connecting link between the
Music Department, the Carolina Playmakers, and the Institute for Research in Social Science. This department became
the Institute of Folk Music.

Stringfield, in wishing to enlarge upon the civic symphony
orchestra plan, turned to the idea of a state-wide symphony
group, and in 1932 his idea culminated in the formation of
the first state-supported symphony in America. The North
Carolina Symphony Society was organized in 1932 and head-
quartered in Chapel Hill at the University of North Carolina.
Stringfield directed the North Carolina Symphony Orchestra
from 1932 to 1938.

Stringfield became known as an authority on ballads and

folk music of the South. He left approximately one hundred and fifty published works, including the orchestral suite *From the Southern Mountains,* for which he was awarded the Pulitzer Prize in music, this honor coming in 1928. He was the musical collaborator with Paul Green in "The Lost Colony," with LeGette Blythe in "Shout Freedom," and with Hubert Hayes in "Thunderland," all North Carolina historical dramas produced in outdoor theatres. His compositions include:

For the theatre: *Tread the Green Grass,* music for Paul Green's "Fantasy" (1930); *The Mountain Song,* opera in three scenes (1931); music for "Aeolik Fragment" (1937).

For orchestra: *Indian Legend,* symphonic poem (1925); *From the Southern Mountains,* suite (1927); *The Seventh Queue,* symphonic ballet (1928); *At the Factory,* symphonic fantasy (1929); *A Negro Parade,* symphonic patrol (1931); *The Legend of John Henry,* symphonic ballad (1932); *Moods of a Moonshiner,* suite (1934); *From the Blue Ridge,* symphonic sketches (1936); *Mountain Dew,* serenade for string orchestra (1937).

Chamber music: *Mountain Sketches* (1923), *Indian Sketches* (1924), *The Ole Swimmin' Hole* (1924), *At Evening* (1927), *From a Negro Melody* (1928), and *A Mountain Episode* (1933).

He was a member of the American Society of Composers, Authors and Publishers, the National Association of Composers and Conductors, the Composers-Authors Guild and the Bohemians.

He was married about 1927 to Caroline Crawford, but they were divorced some ten years later. They had one daughter, Meredith.

Lamar Stringfield died in Asheville, North Carolina, on January 21, 1959.

24

Louis V. Sutton

Louis Valvelle Sutton was born in Richmond, Virginia, on August 6, 1889. His father, Lee Edwards Sutton, was a tobacco manufacturer. His mother was Ella Wagner.

Sutton had the opportunity of going into his father's business but he chose to follow an early interest in electrical engineering. Lee Sutton, sparing no effort in helping his son develop this talent in the field of electricity, built his son an electrical workshop in the back yard of the home.

In 1902, when Sutton was fourteen, he moved with his family to Petersburg, Virginia, where he attended Petersburg Academy (the old McCabe Academy). On graduating from the Academy, he enrolled at Virginia Polytechnic Institute. While there, he was a cadet captain, an adjutant and a member of the football team. In 1910 he was graduated with a Bachelor of Science in electrical engineering.

Shortly thereafter, he was selected as an apprentice engineer in General Electric's training program at Lynn, Massachusetts.

Sutton, however, had his eyes on a job in North Carolina as soon as an opening occurred in some power company there. When he missed out on the first such opportunity, he immediately wrote to Paul Tillery, the chief engineer of Carolina Power and Light Company, and asked for a job

— any job. When an indefinite answer came back, he took a train to Raleigh to make a personal appeal. He finally persuaded Tillery to give him a job as statistician at a sacrifice in salary.

Sutton's salary and titles gradually rose. As commercial manager, he supervised local office managers and sales managers, never missing a chance to stress the opportunities of company growth in serving domestic customers. He had installed in the Meredith College home economics department one of the first electric ranges ever built. When it was tested and proven, he put a similar range in his home. While his wife tested recipes, he took notes, subsequently publishing the first "electric cook book."

He became assistant to Tillery while the latter was still chief engineer and continued as assistant when Tillery took over executive responsibility for the operation of the company.

In August, 1924, Sutton accepted the position of assistant general manager of the Arkansas Central Power Company. After three years at Little Rock, Arkansas, he became vice president and general manager of the newly-formed Mississippi Power and Light Company at Jackson, Mississippi.

In 1932 Sutton returned to Raleigh, North Carolina, as vice president of Carolina Power and Light Company. Mr. Tillery was deathly ill and died in January of 1933. Sutton was elected president and general manager on March 23, 1933.

Taking over the company during the depression years was no easy task but Sutton was no ordinary man. Depression-pinched customers were using less and less electricity, but Sutton, rather than increase rates for residential users to make up the deficit, reduced these rates! Facing this new "inducement rate," domestic customers doubled their usage of electricity in two years. This residential use of electricity rose at a rate never since equaled in the company's history.

Sutton's problems were by no means confined to rates. In addition, the early thirties found electric utilities facing the prospect of being nationalized. As he had done in Mississippi, Sutton steadfastly resisted government competition. His staunch support of investor-owned utilities won recognition throughout the industry, which in 1950 made him president of the Edison Electric Institute. In 1944 he had been awarded an honorary degree of Doctor of Engineering by North Carolina State College, and in 1953 he received the award of the year from the North Carolina Society of Engineers for "outstanding engineering achievement."

Sutton was a director and president of the Carolinas, Virginia Nuclear Power Association, director and president of Capitan Corporation, a member of the board of directors of the North Carolina State College Engineering Foundation, president and director of the Business Foundation of the University of North Carolina, president and director of Southeastern Electric Exchange and director of the Research Triangle Foundation.

In 1953 *The State* magazine selected him as North Carolinian of the year. In 1961 he was awarded the Distinguished Alumnus citation by Virginia Polytechnic Institute. In 1967 he was named by *Dixie Business Magazine* as "Man of the South" for 1966.

In thirty-six years as head of Carolina Power and Light Company, Sutton watched it grow from 75 million dollars to 600 million dollars in assets. He retired as chief executive officer of the company on December 31, 1968, but continued as chairman of the board until his death.

Sutton married Cantey McDowell Venable, daughter of a past president of the University of North Carolina, on April 30, 1912. They had two children: Louis, Jr. and Sarah.

Sutton died on January 5, 1970, and is buried in Montlawn Cemetery, Raleigh, North Carolina.

Benjamin F. Swalin

Benjamin Franklin Swalin was born on March 30, 1901, in Minneapolis, Minnesota. His father was Benjamin N. Swalin and his mother was Augusta Johnson.

Swalin took up the violin when he was seven years old, and by the time he was sixteen, he was teaching violin in the St. Paul Conservatory of Music.

Right out of high school, he joined the violin section of the Minneapolis Symphony Orchestra, where he was the youngest member of the whole troupe. He left the Symphony in 1921 to study violin under Franz Kneisel. Swalin studied with Kneisel from 1921 until 1926.

He earned the money to pay for these lessons by playing in the orchestra at the Capitol Theatre and in musical shows on Broadway. After Kneisel's death in 1926, he studied with Leopold Auer, also at the Institute of Musical Art. In the meantime, his musical credits and extra courses won for him a Bachelor of Science degree from Columbia University in 1928.

In 1929 he became concert master of the WOR Concert Orchestra. In 1930 Swalin received his Master of Arts degree in English from Columbia. While there, he won an exchange fellowship in music which he chose to take at the University of Vienna and the Hochschule fur Musik in Vienna. He left

Austria in 1933 with a Doctor of Philosophy degree and two diplomas in music.

Armed with these years of study, Swalin began his college teaching career in 1933 at De Pauw University in Indiana, where he taught violin and theory for two years. In 1935 an opening occurred on the music faculty of the University of North Carolina and Swalin moved to North Carolina to teach at the University, where he served as associate professor of music until 1949.

Almost as soon as he was settled in his new post he began to study the orchestral situation. He noted that the North Carolina Symphony was gradually being liquidated as a federal music project and its musicians were scattering. Swalin thought it deplorable that the orchestra might be lost completely and in 1937 he started doing something about it, appealing to various committees for support. In 1938 he began coaching instrumentalists with a view to working up the needed membership for an orchestra.

At the time he became the Symphony's director in 1939, musicians performed with the orchestra on a purely volunteer basis and attendance at rehearsals generally depended on the weather. The General Assembly, in 1943, set a musical precedent by appropriating four thousand dollars for the two-year period of the legislative biennium. This was not enough, however, to put the musicians on regular salaries, and the orchestra's troubles continued.

Finally Swalin had assembled a sufficient number of players to make up a good orchestra, but by 1944 he had decided either to quit or to go professional by binding the musicians under contract at stipulated pay. A campaign to raise one hundred and fifty thousand dollars actually produced sixty-five thousand dollars for the 1945-1946 season, covering one hundred and four concerts.

The balance of income is made up primarily by the sale

of individual and group season subscriptions to the North Carolina Symphony Society.

Under Swalin's directorship, the North Carolina Symphony has grown into a sixty-five musician traveling orchestra. It performs some eight months out of the year and travels over ten thousand miles annually. One of the principal features of the North Carolina Symphony Orchestra is to arrange and present free concerts to the children of the public schools of the state.

Swalin has also composed music and written about it. In 1941 The University of North Carolina Press published his book *The Violin Concerto: A Study in German Romanticism.* He is the author of various articles in music journals. He has composed a symphonic overture called *Maxaben,* and numerous smaller pieces for violin and chamber ensembles.

In 1949 he was invited to Mexico as guest conductor of the Symphony Orchestra of Guadalajara. While there he also conducted with the University of Mexico Symphony Orchestra at Mexico City.

In 1967 Swalin received a North Carolina Award in the area of fine arts for his twenty-five years as conductor of the North Carolina Symphony and for his untiring efforts to carry good music into every part of the state. In 1968 he received the Morrison Award for his achievements and contributions to the performing arts in North Carolina.

Benjamin Swalin was married on January 1, 1935, to Martha Maxine McMahon of Waukee, Iowa. The Swalins reside on Jones Ferry Road, Chapel Hill, North Carolina.

Charles E. Taylor

Charles Elisha Taylor was born in Richmond, Virginia, on October 28, 1842, the son of James Barnett Taylor and Mary Williams Taylor.

Taylor attended one of the academies in Virginia's capital city to prepare for college. In the fall of 1858 he entered Richmond College and studied there until April, 1861, when Virginia seceded from the Union. With the outbreak of the war, he joined Company F of the First Virginia Regiment and spent the first months of his military service helping train new recruits. He was next assigned to the Twenty-first Virginia Regiment and participated in the West Virginia campaign under General Robert E. Lee. In December of 1861 his brigade was transferred to the command of Stonewall Jackson. On March 23 of the following year he was wounded in the Battle of Kernstown, an injury from which he suffered the rest of his life. After a short period spent at home recovering, he was assigned to the Signal and Secret Service Corps and served in the cavalry under the leadership of J. E. B. Stuart. He was promoted to acting adjutant of the Signal and Secret Service Bureau in Richmond in 1863 and remained in this capacity until the war's end.

When the University of Virginia reopened in 1865 he entered the institution and was graduated in 1870. On

August 12, 1870, the Board of Trustees of Wake Forest College elected Taylor an assistant professor of language and in the fall of that year he assumed the duties of this position.

In 1883 he was made Professor of Latin and in 1885 Professor of Moral Philosophy. The latter title he held until 1915.

After assuming his duties at Wake Forest, he decided to preach and was ordained on April 23, 1871. He served as minister to the Baptist churches of Franklinton and Louisburg, and at Perry's Chapel. When the Wake Forest Church needed someone to fill its pulpit temporarily, he was often called upon.

The Board of Trustees of Wake Forest met in Raleigh on November 11, 1884, and elected Taylor president to fill the vacancy created by Dr. T. H. Pritchard's resignation.

Increasing the endowment of the college was a goal which Taylor had recognized even before his elevation to the presidency. As early as 1875 he had been requested by the Board of Trustees and the Executive Committee to seek additional patronage for the college. There is evidence of further requests and also evidence that he was successful in his efforts. Taylor had sought an interview with John D. Rockefeller in his efforts to raise funds. Although not donating any money himself, Rockefeller advised Taylor to approach Jabez A. Bostwick concerning the matter. This he did. However, a few days after this meeting, the college received a rather large donation in the form of stock in the Standard Oil Company. Additional donations were made in later years by Mr. Bostwick: $12,000 in 1885, $50,000 in 1886, and $13,000 in 1891. These formed the basis upon which the college grew during the latter part of the nineteenth century and the early part of the twentieth.

The curriculum of the school was broadened substantially

while Taylor was president. In 1887 he introduced the elective system at Wake Forest. Under this system a student had a choice of six different programs by which he might acquire a Bachelor of Arts degree. The School of Law was organized in 1894 and the School of Medicine established in 1902. In addition to these two schools, a number of departments were added: modern language in 1888, religion in 1896, history and political science in 1898, physics in 1899, and both education and physical culture in 1900.

Seven professors constituted the faculty when Taylor became head of the college; when he left there were seventeen. The number of students increased to 328, over twice the enrollment of 1884. He resigned as president in 1905 but continued to teach until his death.

His most notable published work is *Story of Yates, the Missionary* (1898), which is the biography of a North Carolina missionary to China. He also wrote "Gilbert Stone," a poem (1891); *How Far a State May Educate* (1894); and several scholarly papers.

He married Mary Hinton Prichard on September 11, 1873. She was the daughter of Dr. John L. Prichard. Six daughters and one son were born to the couple: Charles Elisha, Jr.; Fanny, Mary, Ethel, Jane, Agnes, and Edith, wife of Elliott Earnshaw.

Taylor died at Wake Forest on November 5, 1915.

A portrait of Dr. Taylor is owned by Wake Forest University, Winston-Salem, North Carolina.

For additional information concerning Charles Elisha Taylor, see: *Biographical History of North Carolina*, Volume 1, by Samuel A. Ashe.

Frances Tiernan
(Christian Reid)

Frances Christine Fisher was born in Salisbury, North Carolina, on July 5, 1846, the daughter of Colonel Charles Frederick Fisher and his wife, Elizabeth Caldwell.

Frances' education was acquired mainly at the direction of her aunt, Christine Fisher, although she did spend one semester at St. Mary's College in Raleigh. She had access to a fine family library, and her aunt was more than a capable teacher.

Early in life she developed a desire to write and her aunt encouraged this desire. At the age of nine she dictated to her aunt an "Autobiography of an Old Oak Tree." Finally one morning she announced to a somewhat skeptical family that she intended to write a novel. Shortly thereafter, in 1870, *Valerie Aylmer* was published. This marked the true beginning of her literary career. This novel, like her later ones, was published under the pen name Christian Reid, and it was by this name that she became known to thousands of readers.

Dr. Archibald Henderson divides her literary career into four periods based upon the influence of events in her life. The first of these was from 1869 to 1879. During this period her more noteworthy works were the novels, *Morton House* (1871), *A Daughter of Bohemia* (1874), and *A Question of*

Honor (1875). It was during this period also that she wrote a short travel-sketch called *The Land of the Sky* (1876). This book described in narrative form a journey through the mountains of western North Carolina and because of this work, that area is known today by that name.

The second period of her career began in 1880, after the completion of a European tour, and ended in 1887. Much of her time in Europe was spent in Paris and Italy where she collected source material for *Heart of Steel* which was published shortly after she returned home. Other works produced during this time include *Armine* (1884), *Reslyn's Fortune* (1885), *A Child of Mary* (1887), and *Miss Churchill* (1887).

The events which marked the beginning of the third period of her career were her marriage and moving to Mexico, where her husband had extensive mining interests. The books which she wrote during this period all have settings in that country. One of these, *The Picture of Las Crucas* (1896), had the distinction of being translated into French. One of her better known works of this period is her travel-sketch, *The Land of the Sun* (1894). In this she described the Mexican cities, the architecture, and the people as they went about the daily tasks of their lives. The death of her husband in 1898 marked the end of this period of her career. Some of her other books during this time were *Carmela* (1891), *A Cast of Fortune* (1893), *A Little Maid of Arcady* (1893), and *The Man of the Family* (1896).

The final period of Christian Reid's writings was devoted primarily to religious themes. She became a devout Roman Catholic and in these novels her lack of respect for the Protestant faith is illustrated in such passages as the following from *The Light of the Vision* (1911): "He knew so well the Protestant point of view — which considers one religion as good as another, and holds no claim higher than that of human love." Some other novels of this period are: *The War-grave Trust* (1912), *The Daughter of a Star* (1913), *A Far Away Princess* (1914), and *The Secret Bequest* (1915).

The works which have been mentioned are all novels; how-ever, two dramas and many poems were also the products of her pen. The best known of the dramas is *Under the Southern Cross* (1900), a play dealing with the Civil War. The play was first produced in Salisbury and later in cities throughout the South. The copyright was given to the United Daughters of the Confederacy. The other drama by Christian Reid was *Princess Nadine* (1908), written as a play, but published in the form of a novel.

In 1909 Christian Reid was honored as the recipient of the Laetare Medal given by the University of Notre Dame. This gold medal is awarded each year to a Catholic lay mem-ber who had made some outstanding contribution to the fields of science, literature, art, statesmanship, or philanthropy.

Before her death Mrs. Tiernan produced over forty novels in addition to many shorter works. She remains one of the most prolific writers produced by North Carolina.

She was a member of the French Society; The Order of the Golden Rose; the United Daughters of the Confederacy, in which she held high offices; the Salisbury Book Club; and the St. Monica's Reading Circle, which she helped establish.

On December 29, 1887, she became the wife of James Marquis Tiernan of Maryland. Most of their life together was spent in Mexico.

Mrs. Tiernan died March 24, 1920, and is buried in Chestnut Hill Cemetery in Salisbury.

For additional information concerning Frances Christine Fisher Tiernan, see: *Biography of Christian Reid*, by Kate Harbes Becker.

Daniel A. Tompkins

Daniel Augustus Tompkins was born in Edgefield County, South Carolina, October 12, 1851. He was the eldest of three children born to Dr. DeWitt Clinton and Hannah Virginia Smyly Tompkins.

Tompkins' first formal education was received in the county schools near his home. Later he attended an academy in Edgefield. In 1867 he entered South Carolina College (now the University of South Carolina) and studied there for two years. On the advice of one of his professors, General E. P. Alexander, he entered Rensselaer Polytechnic Institute, at Troy, New York, in the fall of 1869. He was graduated in 1873 with a degree in civil engineering.

After graduation he became the assistant of Alexander L. Holley, who built the first Bessemer steel plant in America. While working with Holley, Tompkins made the detailed drawings for the Bethlehem Iron Works, at Bethlehem, Pennsylvania. In 1874 he took a job with the Bethlehem plant. Early in 1883 he received a contract with the Westinghouse Machine Company to sell and install their steam engines and other machinery in North and South Carolina. By this time he had gone into business for himself in Charlotte, North Carolina, under the sign of "D. A. Tompkins, Engineer, Machinist, and Contractor."

At the same time his business of selling and installing Westinghouse steam engines was expanding, Tompkins became interested in the cottonseed oil industry. In 1886 he and Fred Oliver began promoting the Southern Cotton Oil Company. The company was finally organized in 1887 with a capital stock of $2,500,000. By the time the 1887 cotton crop was ready, the company had constructed eight mills in seven Southern states. Both Tompkins and Oliver, however, severed their relationships with the company, when in 1889 the board of directors entered into a "working agreement" with the American Cotton Oil Company, their major competitor, which neither man felt acceptable.

Tompkins continued his interest in cottonseed oil mills, but now his efforts were expended through the D. A. Tompkins Company. The company either built, or helped build, mills in nearly all the Southern states. Their facilities in Charlotte were expanded and they also began building cotton gins and electric light plants.

In 1893 the Chester Manufacturing Company and the Catawba Manufacturing Company, both cotton mills, were forced into receivership. When they were put up for sale, Tompkins purchased them. Thus began his interest in constructing cotton mills, and like his building of cottonseed oil mills, he was soon erecting them in many of the Southern states.

Tompkins was firmly convinced that manufacturing alone could not raise the South from its economic depression—it would also take education. He began promoting textile schools. He helped with the organization of and built such schools in North Carolina, South Carolina, and Mississippi.

In 1891 Tompkins purchased the *Charlotte Observer* which was having financial difficulty. He immediately overhauled the machinery and expanded the physical plant. He then persuaded the editor of the *Statesville Landmark*, Joseph P.

Caldwell, to move to Charlotte to head the paper and become part owner. Later he began publishing an evening edition, *The Evening Chronicle*, and acquired controlling interest in the Greenville, South Carolina, newspaper, *The News*.

In spite of his busy schedule managing his many interests, Tompkins found time to write several books. Most of these were designed to be used as textbooks for textile schools and handbooks for managers of mills. Among these are: *American Commerce: Its Expansion, Cotton Mill: Processes and Calculations, Cotton Mill Commercial Features, Cotton and Cotton Oil,* and *Cotton Values in Textile Fabrics.* In addition to these books in the industrial area, he also wrote *A History of Mecklenburg County and the City of Charlotte* in two volumes.

D. A. Tompkins was president of the Manufacturers' Club at Charlotte, an organization promoted by him; member of the Engineers' Club of New York. He was also president of the D. A. Tompkins Company, the Atherton Cotton Mills, the High Shoals Cotton Mills, and the Edgefield Manufacturing Company.

While in the employment of Holley, in New York, Tompkins met and became engaged to Harriet Brigham. In 1884, before they were wed, she died. He never married.

Illness forced Tompkins into early retirement and he spent his last years at his summer home at Montreat. Tompkins died on October 18, 1914 at Montreat. He is buried in Elmwood Cemetery, Charlotte.

For additional information concerning Daniel Augustus Tompkins, see: *A Builder of the New South, Daniel Augustus Tompkins,* by George T. Winston; "Daniel Augustus Tompkins: An American Bourbon," by Howard B. Clay (unpublished doctoral dissertation, University of North Carolina 1951).

Richard Tufts

Richard Sise Tufts was born in Medford, Massachusetts, March 16, 1896. He was the son of Leonard and Gertrude Ware Sise Tufts. He received his formal education at Middlesex School in Concord, Massachusetts, and at Harvard University, being graduated from the latter institution in 1918. He served during World War I as an ensign in the United States Navy.

Richard Tufts was the grandson of James W. Tufts, a Boston millionaire who in June of 1895 began construction of a model New England village to be built in the sandhills section of North Carolina and to be called "Pinehurst." He had purchased 5,000 acres of land for this purpose and by 1896 the development was far enough along that the first guests were taking advantage of James Tufts's dream.

James Tufts continued his supervision over his project until his death in 1902, at which time his son Leonard took over active management. During this time golf was increasing in popularity in the United States and Pinehurst was increasing in reputation as a golf center. Leonard directed the operations at the village until 1930, when he turned them over to his son, Richard Tufts.

Richard assumed management at a bad time. Even though Pinehurst enjoyed an enviable reputation among resorts at the time, this did not prevent the depression from dealing it a hard blow. The financial condition of the resort reached the point of being in debt over one million dollars.

A successful effort was made to attract convention business and this helped increase revenues. With the beginning of World War II Fort Bragg and Camp Mackall expanded and business began to boom. With the increased activity, profits began to replace losses and the huge debt began to decline. After the war, business continued to increase until the resort reached a popularity exceeding the days before the depression. In 1967 Tufts received the North Carolina Distinguished Citizen Award for his outstanding career in the field of resort management.

In addition to maintaining a resort with a worldwide reputation as a golf center, Richard Tufts has made substantial contributions to the game of golf itself. He is the author of two books concerning the game, *Principles Behind the Rules of Golf* and *The Scottish Invasion.*

Tufts has long been associated with the United States Golf Association of which he served as president 1956-1957, having held many committee chairmanships previously in the association. Through these committees he has exerted great influence on the manner in which the game is played. While on the rules committee, he helped write and negotiate the present code. He was a driving force in the beginning of USGA's Junior and Senior Championships. He has also through these committees had a profound influence on course architecture. He served as non-playing captain of the Walker Cup Team in 1963.

The development of the Carolina Golf Association is largely due to his guidance. During this period the association became one of the largest district associations with over 240 clubs and over 9,000 individual members.

Tufts has received a number of awards from the sports

world. Among the more outstanding are: the Golf Writers Association of America's William B. Richardson Award for Service to Golf, 1950; the American Seniors Golf Award for Distinguished Senior, 1963; the United States Golf Association's Bob Jones Award for Sportsmanship, 1967; the Atlantic Coast Sports Writers Award for Service to Sports, 1968; and election to the North Carolina Sports Hall of Fame, 1968.

He is a member of a number of golf associations, among which are: Carolina Golf Association, Southern Golf Association, United States Senior Golf Association, American Seniors Golf Association, and the American Society of Golf Course Architects.

He holds membership in several golf clubs, one of these being the oldest such club in the world, the Honourable Company of Edinburgh Golfers, at Gullane, Scotland.

In addition to his service to sports, Tufts has served North Carolina in other respects. He served on the National Advisory Committee for the state of North Carolina at the New York World's Fair, 1939; he has served on the Governor's hospitality committee; he has served as a member of the North Carolina Board of Conservation and Development; he was a founder and director of the North Carolina Travel Council; and has been a director of the Moore Memorial Hospital.

His religious affiliation is with the Episcopal Church and his political affiliation with the Democratic party.

He was married on August 10, 1925, to Alice Vail of Glen Cove, New York. Two children were born of this marriage: Peter Vail and Sara Crane Harrington.

For additional information concerning Richard S. Tufts, see: *North Carolina Lives*, 1962, by William S. Powell and *The State*, April 15, 1950, Raleigh, North Carolina.

Zebulon B. Vance

Zebulon Baird Vance was born in Buncombe County, North Carolina, on May 13, 1830, the son of David and Mira Margaret Baird Vance.

As a boy, Vance attended the neighborhood schools. In 1843 he went to Washington College in East Tennessee. He studied there about one year, returning home at the news of the illness of his father who died shortly thereafter. He did not return to Washington College, but in 1851 entered the University of North Carolina where he studied law. He obtained his license to practice in 1852.

Asheville was his choice of places to practice, and almost immediately after his arrival there, he was chosen solicitor of Buncombe County. He soon won a reputation at the bar as an able advocate.

Politics quickly drew his interest and he was elected to the North Carolina General Assembly in 1854. He moved rapidly up the political ladder and was elected to the United States Congress, where he served from December 7, 1858, to March 3, 1861, being forced to leave because of the secession of North Carolina from the Union. During this period of growing secession sentiment in the South, Vance supported Union measures and sought to prevent the disruption of the nation. However, after Lincoln's call for troops he supported the Southern cause.

Before North Carolina had officially left the Union, Vance organized a company of "Rough and Ready Guards" in Asheville. This company, of which he had been elected captain, first saw active duty in the summer of 1861 along the coast of North Carolina. Near the end of the summer he was elected colonel of the 26th North Carolina Regiment and in this capacity saw action in the New Bern campaign and the Seven Days Battle near Richmond.

In 1862 the Conservative Party nominated Vance as their candidate for governor. Vance won by a large majority and was inaugurated on September 8, 1862. Two years later he was elected to a second two-year term by defeating his former supporter, W. W. Holden, editor of the *North Carolina Standard*.

His administrations were characterized by constant controversies with the Jefferson Davis administration. Davis and his advisors considered Vance's election to be a sign of Union sentiment in North Carolina and thus never fully trusted him. This distrust of Vance was unfounded as can be seen from the part North Carolina played in the war under his leadership.

On May 13, 1865, at the end of the war, Vance was arrested on orders of President Andrew Johnson and imprisoned in Old Capitol Prison in Washington, D. C. He was released on July 6 of the same year. While in prison, he applied for a pardon which was finally granted in March, 1867.

Following his release, Vance returned to his native state and the practice of law in Charlotte. In 1870 he was elected to the United States Senate, but unable to have his disabilities under the Fourteenth Amendment removed, he surrendered his certificate of election two years later. Shortly thereafter these disabilities were removed by Congress.

Vance again became a candidate for governor in 1876. The Democrats were seeking to gain control of the state from the Republicans and repudiate much of the work of the Reconstruction. Judge Thomas Settle was the standard bearer for the Republicans. Vance won the election and was inaugurated on January 1, 1877.

During this administration, he could devote himself to the betterment of the state and its people. During this time railroad construction was resumed; education for both races was advanced; both industry and agriculture were promoted; and the financial structure of the state was put on a sound basis.

With only two of his four-year term filled, Vance was elected to the United States Senate. He won re-election twice, serving the state in this capacity until his death. As a Senator Vance served as a mediator between the North and the South. He defended the South and sought to explain the motivations and feelings of her people to the North; at the same time, he encouraged the South to bind up its wounds and look to the future.

Vance was married to Marriette Newell Espy, of North Carolina, on August 3, 1853. Four sons were born of this union. Marriette died November 3, 1878. In 1880 he married Mrs. Florence Steele Martin of Kentucky, but they had no children.

After experiencing failing health for several years, Vance died in Washington, D. C., on April 14, 1894. He is buried in Asheville.

For additional information concerning Zebulon Baird Vance, see: *Life of Zebulon B. Vance* by Clement Dowd, and *Zeb Vance: Champion of Personal Freedom* by Glenn Tucker.

Stephen B. Weeks

Stephen Beauregard Weeks was born in Pasquotank County, North Carolina, February 2, 1865. He was the son of James Elliott Weeks and his wife, Mary Louisa Mullen Weeks.

Weeks's first education was gained in the country schools which were generally poor. At the age of fifteen he was sent to the Horner School at Henderson. He next studied at the University of North Carolina where he received the degree of A.B. in 1886. He continued his studies at the University and took a masters degree the following year and in 1888 earned his Ph.D. in English.

In 1888 Stephen entered Johns Hopkins University as an honorary Hopkins scholar. It was here that he was influenced by Professor Herbert B. Adams to change his major field of interest from English to history. After studying here for three years, he received another Ph.D. degree, this one in history.

In the fall of 1891 Dr. Weeks took a position on the faculty of Trinity College in Randolph County. When the college moved to Durham, he moved with it and continued in his position with the school. While here he established the Trinity College Historical Society and organized the department of history. As professor of history at Trinity, Weeks was the first full-time professor of history in any Southern institution of higher learning. Before this, history had always been taught in connection with some other subject such as government or geography. Weeks left Trinity in June of 1893 because of a dispute with the president.

The academic year of 1893-94 was spent in study as a "fellow by courtesy" at Johns Hopkins University. Weeks went to Washington, D. C., in July of 1894, where he held a position with the United States Bureau of Education. This job gave him more time for historical research and he wrote a number of monographs based upon these studies. He had previously written several other scholarly monographs dealing with North Carolina history.

While in Washington, Dr. Weeks was one of the founders of the Southern History Association. He often contributed to the publications of the association as well as to other outstanding historical journals.

Ill health forced him to leave his job in Washington in 1899 and move to the West. He obtained a position with the United States Indian service as principal teacher in the Santa Fe, New Mexico, school. While in the West, Weeks wrote numerous biographical sketches of outstanding North Carolinians which were published in S. A. Ashe's *Biographical History of North Carolina.*

By 1909 his health was restored to the point that he could again return to his native state. He took the position as principal of the Trinity School in Randolph County and served there for two years. Leaving in 1911, he once again went to Washington and a position with the United States Bureau of Education.

Dr. Weeks was a prolific writer; a list of books, articles, and pamphlets written by him contains almost 200 entries. The most notable of all his works is his four-volume index to the *Colonial and State Records of North Carolina.* This index to the 26 volumes of records makes them useful to historians and not merely a depository for thousands of documents. For a listing of the writing of Weeks, see: *Stephen Beauregard Weeks, 1865-1918, A Preliminary Bibliography*, by William S. Powell.

Weeks not only wrote and studied about North Carolina, but he collected books, magazines, pamphlets, church minutes, autographs and any other type of North Caroliniana which he could find. This collection, which contained around 10,000 items, was purchased by the University of North Carolina and formed the bases for the North Carolina Collection. This Collection is today one of the most outstanding of its kind in the United States.

Stephen B. Weeks was a member of the American Historical Association; an honorary life member of the Southern History Association, which he helped form; a corresponding member of the Wisconsin Historical Society; and a member of the Maryland Historical Society.

He was married to Mary Lee Martin, daughter of the Reverend Joseph Bonaparte Martin, on June 12, 1888. Two children were born of this union: one dying in infancy and Robertson Jackson Weeks. Mary Weeks died in 1891. On June 28, 1893, he married Sallie Mangum Leach, the daughter of Colonel Martin W. Leach. Four children were born of this union: Willie Person Mangum Weeks, Thomas Weeks, Stephen B. Weeks, Jr., and Sallie Preston Weeks.

Dr. Weeks died in Washington, May 3, 1918. He is buried in the Mangum family cemetery near Durham.

A portrait of Weeks hangs in the North Carolina Collection at the University of North Carolina, Chapel Hill.

For additional information concerning Stephen Beauregard Weeks, see: *Biographical History of North Carolina*, volume 5, edited by S. A. Ashe.

Henry Horace Williams

Henry Horace Williams was born on August 16, 1858, at Sunbury in Gates County, North Carolina, the eldest of eight children. He was the son of Elisha Williams and Mary Taylor Williams.

When he was nineteen years of age, his mother, along with some relatives, gathered together enough money to enroll him in the Boys' School in Murfreesboro, North Carolina. Though the farm boy clashed violently with the knowledgeable schoolmaster at first, Williams went on to spend two years at the school, becoming a favorite of the master. He later declared that "Mr. Conrad showed me the intellectual process."

Conrad urged him to go to college, but the family was quite poor. Not to be denied, he took a job in a country store in Belvidere on a month's trial without pay. At the end of the month he was hired at a salary of one hundred and twenty-five dollars for the year. He saved one hundred dollars the first year. When his salary was raised to one hundred and seventy-five dollars for the second year, he saved another hundred.

Taking his two hundred dollars he left home during the Christmas season of 1879 and enrolled at the University of North Carolina. Williams was graduated in 1883 with highest honors. He received the degrees of Bachelor of Arts and Master of Arts.

Almost immediately he went to La Grange, North Carolina, and began teaching in a preparatory school, La Grange Collegiate Institute; but experiences there led him to believe that he was not as yet adequately "educated." Consequently, he resigned his position and enrolled at the Yale Divinity School in New Haven, Connecticut. At the end of a year came an urgent appeal from Trinity College, now Duke University, for Williams to return to North Carolina and teach Greek and German there. Though absorbed in his work at Yale, he went to Trinity and taught for a year. In June, he took the four hundred dollars he had saved and went to Germany for the summer. He wanted to hear the Germans talk, and it amused him that several times he passed for a German.

During the middle of the next term he was "forced" to leave Trinity, for the school could no longer afford him; he had asked for a salary higher than that of the president of the college. Returning to Yale at Christmas, he began his work again.

In due course he was graduated from Yale with a Bachelor of Divinity degree. A paper written at Yale had won for him a Williams Fellowship to Harvard University at Cambridge, Massachusetts, and in the fall of 1888 he entered the Harvard Divinity School. There his outlook changed. He realized that he did not want to go into the ministry, but rather into teaching. He delved deeply into the subjects of religion and logic, and emerged ready to teach his favorite subjects.

In the fall of 1891 Williams was called to his Alma Mater, the University of North Carolina, to fill the chair of philosophy and psychology, a brand-new field of instruction at the University. For fifty years thereafter he headed the department of philosophy, becoming a Kenan professor in 1920.

Williams' aim was to school the state's leaders in the techniques for discovering truth; but his philosophy inspired so much individualism that he practically turned the state upside down. He puzzled fellow academicians and enraged the trustees. The fundamentalists sought his scalp. He was accused of heresy and atheism and republicanism.

He was the author of three volumes: *The Evolution of Logic, Modern Logic,* and *The Education of Horace Williams.* While he had no real style and no flair for writing, his books being poorly written, in the classroom he was another person. He did not fill his lecture with objective facts. He was not a scholar in the usual sense. He created his own system, inviting the students to participate in his experimentation with it. He asked questions the students had never thought about. He did not distribute facts; he distributed doubts. He made the students think for themselves.

Not many of his students remembered the substance of his philosophy. They remembered mostly the impact of his personality. He left his imprint on individuals, not in books.

Williams married Bertha Colton on June 10, 1891, but she died in 1922. The couple had no children.

He died on December 26, 1940, and is buried in the Chapel Hill Cemetery, Chapel Hill, North Carolina.

For additional information on Henry Horace Williams see: *The Education of Horace Williams,* his autobiography, and *Horace Williams, Gadfly of Chapel Hill,* by Robert Watson Winston.

Louis Round Wilson

Louis Round Wilson was born in Lenoir, North Carolina, on December 27, 1876. His parents were Jethro Reuben and Louisa Jane (Round) Wilson.

After spending a year in preparation at Davenport College in Lenoir, Wilson attended Haverford College in Haverford, Pennsylvania, from 1895 to 1898. At that time he transferred to the University of North Carolina where he was graduated in 1899 with the degree of Bachelor of Arts.

After two years of teaching in private schools, he returned to Chapel Hill to become librarian of the University in 1901. Besides this work, he continued his studies and received the Master of Arts degree in 1902 and the Doctor of Philosophy degree in 1905, both from the University.

Wilson was the University's librarian from 1901 until 1932. When he took over the position there were about 3,800 volumes in the library. By 1932, the book collection totaled over 235,000 volumes. The present library structure was erected in the years 1926 to 1929. He developed a staff of twenty-three trained librarians by 1932, though he had worked from 1907 until 1915 with one assistant. By 1932 there were assembled some 47,000 related items of the North Carolina Collection. A Southern Historical Collection, specializing in the acquisition of manuscript materials, was on his agenda as early as 1904; and he cooperated in its development. In May of 1932 he organized the Friends of the Library of the University of North Carolina.

In his annual report for the year 1906-1907, he formulated a program for increased extension work, with the library as the pivotal agency in the plan. In 1912 he became director of the Bureau of Extension of the University, greatly expanding it. He held this post until 1921, editing its *Bulletin* from 1913 to 1921 and its *Leaflets* from 1917 to 1921.

In 1904 Wilson helped organize the North Carolina Library Association, serving as its secretary from 1904 to 1909 and its president during the years 1909-1910, 1921-1923, and 1929-1931. In 1909 he helped organize the North Carolina Library Commission and served as its chairman until 1916. He was president of the Department of Libraries of the Southern Educational Association in 1911.

From 1907 to 1912 he was an associate professor of library administration at the University, professor of library administration from 1912 to 1920 and Kenan professor of library science from 1920 to 1932. In 1931 he established the school of Library Science and served as its first director.

He served at various times as a member of the President's Advisory Committee, the Administrative Group, the Board of Governors of the Institute for Research in Social Science, Board of Governors of the University Press, administrative boards for the schools of medicine, public health, and education, committees on honorary degrees and relations with alumni, and the Weil Lecture Committee.

He was a member of the editorial board of the University *News Letter* from 1914 to 1932; editor of the University *Record* for several years; one of the original incorporators and first director of the University of North Carolina Press; and a member of the Commission on University Consolidation from 1931 to 1932.

In September of 1932 Wilson resigned as University librarian to become dean of the Graduate Library School of the University of Chicago, a position which he retained until 1942. He was president of the American Library Association from 1935 to 1936, and of the Association of American Library Schools from 1938 to 1939.

Returning to Chapel Hill in 1942, Wilson became a professor of library administration in the University's School of Library Science. He taught there until 1959. From 1945 to 1955 he was chairman of the Friends of the Library. He was director of the University of North Carolina Sesquicentennial Celebration from 1944 to 1946.

In 1932 he received the honorary degree of Doctor of Laws from Haverford College and of Doctor of Literature from the University of Denver. In 1934 the University of North Carolina conferred upon him the honorary degree of Doctor of Laws. In 1944 Catawba College conferred upon him the honorary Doctor of Humane Letters.

In 1954 he was the recipient of the Herbert Putnam Award of the American Library Association and in 1956 the main library building of the University of North Carolina was named the Louis Round Wilson Library.

Wilson was a prolific editor and writer. His books include: *The History of the University of North Carolina, 1900-1930* and *The Library of the First State University*, as well as his edited work, *The Selected Papers of Cornelia Phillips Spencer*.

Wilson was married on June 10, 1909, to Penelope Bryan Wright. They had four children: Elizabeth Wright; Penelope; Mary Louise; and Louis Round, Jr.

Dr. Wilson resides at 607 East Rosemary Street, Chapel Hill, North Carolina.

For additional information, see: *Louis Round Wilson, Librarian and Administrator*, by Maurice Falcolm Tauber.

Richard H. Wright

Richard Harvey Wright was born near Louisburg, in Franklin County, North Carolina, on July 13, 1851. He was the son of Thomas D. Wright and Elizabeth Glover Harris Wright.

His formal education was gained at the Davis High School in Louisburg and at the school of T. J. Horner, in Granville County, where he prepared for college. Financial hardship forced him to forget his plans of a college education.

He became the apprentice of J. H. Hunt in his general merchandise store in Oxford in 1869, and received his board and $50 per year for three years. At the end of this period Hunt and Wright formed a partnership and opened a store at Tally Ho in Granville County. The business was doing well when one night in 1874, while Wright was away from home, a fire destroyed the store. Due to this, and the fact that the insurance policy had expired, he found himself $6,000 in debt. He contemplated giving up, but instead returned to Tally Ho, reopened the store, and soon paid off the debt.

The opportunities in the manufacturing of tobacco became apparent to Wright, and in 1877 he entered R. H. Wright and Company in Durham. He traveled extensively in the West seeking customers for his "Wright's Orange Durham" smoking tobacco. While on one of these selling tours he met

Washington Duke and greatly impressed him with the volume of his sales. The Dukes decided it would be advantageous to have him as a partner and spent several weeks trying to persuade him to join their firm. In 1880 Wright purchased an interest in Washington Duke's firm and became the chief traveling salesman for the company. He made his headquarters in Chicago for two years and then in 1883 he made a world tour through which he introduced the products of Washington Duke & Sons abroad. In 1884 a branch house was established in New York City, due largely to his efforts. The next year Washington Duke repurchased from Wright his interest in the company.

Wright moved to Lynchburg, Virginia, and purchased an interest in the Lone Jack cigarette factory. While in Lynchburg he was able to secure the exclusive right to sell an automatic cigarette machine in China, Japan, India, Africa, and the Philippine Islands. He held these rights to this machine invented by James Bonsack until 1907. In order to promote the machine effectively in China, he found it necessary to establish a cigarette manufacturing company there. This was the first such company in China. Wright had difficulty marketing the machine in South Africa because of that country's low tariff on manufacturers. Wright was able to persuade the government to reverse the tariffs, thus placing a high tariff on imported cigarettes and a low one on imported leaf. This gave a stimulus to the manufacture of cigarettes in South Africa and created a market for Wright's machine.

After the expiration of his rights to sell the Bonsack machine, Wright began concentrating his efforts on selling an automatic cigarette machine of his own. He worked in Durham as president of Wright's Automatic Tobacco Packing Machine Company. This company was not limited to tobacco products for it also held the rights for a power press for the manufacture of soap, a stamping device, and other machines.

Wright had many interests other than those related to tobacco. In 1901 he organized the Durham Traction Company of which he was president until 1912 when he sold his interest to the Henry L. Doherty Company of New York. Under his guidance this company built a street railway system, an amusement park, an electric light plant, and an ice plant in Durham. He also owned and was president of the Interstate Telephone and Telegraph Company of Durham. This company grew from one furnishing 700 telephones to one furnishing over 5,000. Wright also served as president of the Southern Fire Insurance Company and the Public Hardware Company and in addition was a member of the board of directors of the Tomlinson Chair Company of High Point, the Locke Cotton mills of Concord, and the Yarborough mills of Durham.

Having been an orphan himself, children without parents were a special concern of Mr. Wright's. He was the founder of the Wright Refuge, an orphanage located near Durham to which he gave $100,000. He also gave $100,000 to Louisburg College at Louisburg, part of which was used to construct the Pattie Julia Wright dormitory.

He was a Mason, a Democrat, and a member of Trinity Methodist Church of Durham.

In June, 1884, he married Mamie Exum of Wayne County, North Carolina. She died the following year. A daughter, who died at the age of four, was born of this union.

Mr. Wright died March 4, 1929. He is buried in Maplewood Cemetery in Durham.

For additional information concerning Richard Harvey Wright, see: *Biographical History of North Carolina,* volume 5, by Samuel A. Ashe.

Appendix

THE EDWARDS & BROUGHTON COMPANY

It was the spring of 1871. The printing industry in Raleigh was at a low state. The chief printers were Nichols & Gorman. Owing to Mr. Gorman's skill as a printer, this firm was doing excellent work. In addition, job printing was done in the offices of nearly all the periodicals of the city—the *Sentinel;* the *Christian Advocate;* the *Friend of Temperance;* the *News;* and the *Biblical Recorder.*

Although the work done in some of these shops was good, much of the printing for people of the state was going to Northern houses, which, it was believed, could do better printing, in shorter time, and do it for less.

Such was the state of the art when two young printers of Raleigh, Cornelius Bryant Edwards and Needham Bryant Broughton, aspired to set up a printing office, which they avowed from the first to make of such excellence that it would no longer be necessary for the people of North Carolina to go out of the state for the best of their printing.

Both of these young men were masters of their art, honest, industrious, of good character, social, and interested in their church, their city and their state, and ready to help build a new South on the wreckage of war and reconstruction. As a further inspirational influence each had recently married and had a happy home.

The one thing lacking to these young men was the means to buy and equip an office. At this time the outfit of the old *Standard*, south of the Yarborough Hotel on Fayetteville Street, was for sale. A mortgage on it was held by Major W. A. Smith of Johnston County, popularly and affectionately known as "Blow Your Horn Billy." He was doing some printing under the name "W. A. Smith & Co." Learning of the young printers, he decided to give them a start. He sold them the old *Standard* almost entirely on credit, and lent them a hundred dollars to help pay for necessary supplies.

Major Smith appreciated their industry and aspiration and had confidence in them. He told them he would look in from time to time and that he would never foreclose the mortgage so long as he found them with their coats off and hard at work. The mortgage was not foreclosed—it was paid. "Work" might well have been their motto. They were soon advertising that they did their own work and guaranteed it.

Soon the young printers began to advertise in the papers. They were practical book and job printers with ten years experience and would respectfully inform the citizens of Raleigh and the state generally that they had a complete outfit for a first class job and book printing office; they had on hand a large assortment of type, espe-

27

cially adapted to book-work, and were prepared to print, in the best of style, minutes of associations and conventions or any kind of book or pamphlet. They could furnish on short notice tobacco labels, bands and notices and on as reasonable terms as could be found anywhere.

Before the end of their first year, they had made considerable improvement. They now had one of the most complete printing establishments in the South; they were prepared to print all manner of "catalogues, pamphlets, circulars, cards, letterheads, billheads, and fancy work." Clerks of associations, principals of schools, would do well to put their printing with them, and tobacco manufacturers were told that they could not get their work done cheaper or better anywhere, in the state or out of it, and they were ready to furnish bronzed labels and bands, etc., all done in the latest style of the art.

Without a word of explanation, today's reader may not understand the type of printing the young company was soliciting. For instance, it is chiefly in connection with their engraving department that the Company of today would think of business cards, but it was an entirely different kind of card they were offering to furnish in 1871. They were cards by which the merchants of Raleigh and other market centers sought to gain customers for their goods and wares from the trade generally but in particular from the farmers who came to market with their produce in covered wagons. They backed their wagons up to the old Market House, and soon had cash for their loads and money to spend, and the Raleigh merchants wanted to let them know where they could spend it to the best advantage. They did this by means of printed cards, about the size of a post card, but somewhat narrower. These were not ordinary cards, but were neatly printed in the best style of the printer's art in order to call attention to the house and its goods. Some had pictures on them —a hat, an overcoat, a cook stove, a plow, hoes and shovels, a mortar and pestle, a fish, a double-barrel shot gun, an assortment of groceries. Most of the farmers carefully preserved them and carried them home with them. Thus the names of many firms became household words. Great numbers of these cards were printed, and added not a little to the printer's income.

It might also be noted that the only manufacturers whose printing was solicited were manufacturers of tobacco. These were probably more numerous than any other in North Carolina in 1871. The laws required that every package of tobacco, chewing or smoking, carry a printed notice identifying the maker and declaring that the manufacturer had complied with all requirements of the law, and warning all persons not to use that package for tobacco again.

Manufacturers of smoking tobacco found it profitable to have attractive labels on the little white bags in which such tobacco was then sold, telling the brand of tobacco therein. Since some of the better known brands of smoking tobacco had bronze labels, some of the smaller manufacturers copied after them. Therefore all of them were patrons of printers. Edwards & Broughton, of course, was ready to print for big and little factories and told in big letter type that they could print labels in bronze, which all the companies wanted.

In their first years, the company began to print the annual minutes of Baptist associations, and before the turn of the century were doing this printing for most of the fifty or sixty associations of the state. These minutes from the first show the characteristics of the company's work through all the years. Every copy seems to indicate that the printers were masters and had ideals which they sought to realize in every piece of work that left their shop.

In July, 1873, two years after beginning operations, Edwards & Broughton had already established a statewide reputation. Their trade had expanded, and they were in need of a larger plant, new presses, a greater variety of type, and machinery for their own bookbinding and blank-book manufacturing department. They were also in need of more capital to enable them to keep on hand larger stocks of paper and inks to meet the growing demand.

It was at this time that the aspiring young printers joined in a partnership, known as Edwards, Broughton & Company, with the *Biblical Recorder,* "The Organ of the North Carolina Baptists." John H. Mills, who had been editor of the paper since 1867, was retiring. A. F. Redd, a native of Virginia, who had come to North Carolina four years earlier as a teacher in the Horner School in Oxford, and for the past two years a teacher in the Raleigh Female Seminary, acquired the property and subscription list and good will from Mr. Mills. (The subscription list at this time was approximately 3,000.)

Mr. Redd contributed all these to the partnership of Edwards, Broughton & Company, becoming a partner with one-third interest on equal terms with Mr. Edwards and Mr. Broughton. The *Biblical Recorder* had been doing much job printing on its own presses both for individuals and for churches and associations and other religious and fraternal bodies. This equipment and the established trade over the state no doubt was an asset to the young firm. The first paper published under the new partnership was dated July 23, 1873. An immediate improvement in the appearance of the paper was noted. Old and worn type had been replaced by that which was new and sharp and better assorted. The pages were neater and more attractive. Thus began a partnership which continued for fourteen years, until July 1, 1887.

The addition of a "complete bindery" proved, as was expected, immediately profitable. They were now able to bind or rebind books for individuals and libraries, any volumes they themselves might print, and those printed by other printers who did not have binding facilities. They also added a department for blank-book manufacture, for which there was a large demand.

The firm soon outgrew its limited quarters. In October 1873 it moved to the third floor of a building recently erected at 216 Fayetteville Street, and extending to Salisbury Street. This building still stands and for many years was occupied by Boylan-Pearce & Company. Here the company operated for the next eight years. By this time the quarters were again becoming inadequate, and it was also feared the jar of the presses was affecting the walls of the building. Early in October 1881, it moved to a new building erected by the grocery firm of Williamson and Upchurch, at the southeast corner of Hargett and Salisbury streets. The company had entrances at 17 and 19 West Hargett Street and at 203 South Salisbury Street, occupying nearly all the lower floor and all of the second floor.

Perhaps one of the most important single jobs produced by the young company in its early years was the printing and binding of *Battle's Revisal*. North Carolina had had no new code of laws since the *Revised Code* of 1855. Accordingly, the legislature of 1872-73 authorized the publication of a new revisal which had already been prepared by William H. Battle, who had been a justice of the Supreme Court of the state and earlier professor of law at the University of North Carolina. Passing up all the older established firms, he asked the young printers to publish the work which was to be his chief legal monument, *Battle's Revisal*. This was a monumental volume of 987 pages, bound in tooled calf. It was no small accomplishment to have produced a book which does not suffer in comparison with the work of those famed Boston printers, Little, Brown and Company, who had published the *Revised Code*. It is interesting to note that Edwards, Broughton & Company received, for printing and binding 5,000 volumes of the work, the sum of $9,967.80. Compensation, however, was not all immediately financial. The good work done on this great volume gave the new firm an open door to others who had printing entrusted to them, especially state printers, most of whom, having no presses of their own, owed their appointments to political influences. Thereafter for many years, the Edwards and Broughton firm did much of the State printing, sometimes on appointment of the government, but until the close of the century much more often when employed by those who were the state printers.

Let us now return briefly to the company's association with the *Biblical Recorder*. A. F. Redd had been serving as editor for two years, but in the summer of 1875, he accepted appointment as professor of the Natural Sciences at the University of North Carolina. Several prominent Baptist ministers urged Edwards and Broughton to purchase Mr. Redd's interest, but not succeeding in this, they had another plan. Through their arrangement Rev. C. T. Bailey, the Baptist pastor at Warrenton, came to Raleigh. There he found Edwards and Broughton already well disposed towards accepting him as a partner. Mr. Bailey had been educated in law at William and Mary College. However, feeling called to the ministry, he went to Richmond College to prepare himself for that work. On the outbreak of the War Between the States, he volunteered as a private and served for two or three years, being discharged on account of rheumatism. Until the close of the war, he served as pastor of rural churches in Virginia. When the war was over, he returned to North Carolina as principal of Reynoldson Academy in Gates County. After two years, he gave this up to become pastor of the churches in Edenton and Hertford. In 1871, he came to Warrenton as the pastor of the Baptist church in that town.

Mr. Broughton himself, through his connection with the Baptist State Convention, well knew Mr. Bailey's qualifications to be editor of the paper. An interesting sidelight here is that Mr. Redd wanted $5,000 for his part of the partnership, which Mr. Bailey had to borrow. Hereafter in advertising, where the names of the partners were given, it read: "C. B. Edwards. N. B. Broughton. C. T. Bailey." Thus it came about that the firm of Edwards, Broughton & Company came to be associated in the minds of the Baptists of the state with the *Biblical Recorder*, and the company took pains that this association should work in their favor. Early in the partnership the firm was sometimes referred to as "The Recorder Printing House and Book Bindery." This partnership continued until 1887, when Mr. Bailey withdrew, taking as his part the *Biblical Recorder*.

Under the terms of the dissolution of the contract, if the *Biblical Recorder* was ever to be disposed of, Edwards & Broughton should have the refusal of it at the price offered. Upon Mr. Bailey's death in 1895, Mrs. Bailey continued to operate it until the end of the year, when she decided to sell it. Her son, Josiah William Bailey, who had edited the paper during his father's illness and since his death, offered to pay $16,000 for it. Edwards & Broughton, however, exercising their right under the contract with Mr. Bailey, matched this price and again came into full possession of it. They retained Mr. J. W. Bailey as editor, he also being the choice of the Baptist State Convention.

This arrangement continued until February 1901. During that period the paper was prosperous, and gained and kept 8,000 paying subscribers. But for some time before the meeting of the Baptist State Convention in Raleigh in December 1900, "the owners and the editor were agreed that one or the other should retire."

The question of the control and ownership of the paper had been brought before the Convention at its meeting in Asheville in December 1899, and a committee had been appointed to represent the Convention, supposedly for the purchase of the paper. At any rate this was their recommendation to the Convention at the meeting in Raleigh in 1900. This was turned down by the Convention, but it authorized the creation of a stock company to purchase and own the paper. This company was soon organized. The purchase price, by previous agreement, was $16,000, the amount Edwards & Broughton had paid for it in 1895. They delivered their interest in this property to other hands in February 1901. They had printed the paper since July 1873, and were to continue to print it for a score of years longer.

During all this time, the company continued to prosper and make normal progress, maintaining the lead it had already established among the printing establishments of the state, even though they now had the competition of other well-equipped printing plants. It was a well ordered business, with a division of labor between the two partners, each doing that for which he was most capable. On the first floor were what would now be called the executive offices and the accounting department. Here sat Needham B. Broughton. Through his office ran much of the life not only of Raleigh but of the state as well. He was the public relations man of the firm since its formation. He was active in the civic affairs of his city, serving continuously on numerous committees, more often than not as chairman. Broughton was at home with the public, always ready to make a worthwhile speech when called upon. He served in the state Senate, as director of the Deaf Institute, on the board of agriculture, as trustee of State College, and of the Oxford Orphanage. He had other affiliations too numerous to mention.

Upstairs was the mechanical end of the business, and here amid the thump of the presses and the whir of the pulleys could be found C. B. Edwards. It was entirely a steam plant, and when the whistle blew at 7:00 a.m., he was right there. Edwards ruled the mechanical part, for he was a past master of his craft. If any of the machinery broke down, he could and did fix it himself, for he was a skilled mechanic; there was nothing above the first floor he could not control with his own hand. He was an artist in his line. He delighted in fine work, and it was not unusual for him to stop the old hand presses to get a slightly different impression on even one letter; or experiment with his inks to get the exact consistency or color. This was, of course, before the days of the linotype, and all type setting was done by hand, and all press work on old flat-bed presses. When necessity demanded, Edwards himself could set a stick of type with the best of his hired help. Too, he was a patient man, for a print shop in those days was as full of afflictions as was Job.

Being the man that he was, it was, of course, easy for Mr. Broughton to solicit and secure work for the firm, as it was also easy for Mr. Edwards to see that the work was so well done that the customer was pleased with it. With this combination the business continued to grow and prosper.

We come now to the year 1906. Both men were advancing in years, Mr. Edwards now 62, Mr. Broughton 58 years of age, each feeling the wear of 35 years of the ownership and conduct of their ever-expanding business. With justifiable pride in the good name and rank their business had among other printing plants in the state, they were desirous of seeing it continued when the time came for them to give it up.

So it was that the partners came into communication with Dr. Charles Lee Smith. They well knew his character and ability, for he had served as associate editor of the *Biblical Recorder* in the years 1885-86, then owned and published by Edwards & Broughton. In the 20 years intervening, their former employee had won considerable reputation as a scholar, author, teacher, lecturer, administrator and executive with three eminent educational institutions—Johns Hopkins University, William Jewell College, and Mercer University.

Upon Dr. Smith becoming a member of the firm, the company was re-organized as a corporation, the charter being granted on September 15, 1906. The corporate name became the Edwards & Broughton Printing Company, the chief stockholders being, in approximately equal amounts, Mr. Edwards, Mr. Broughton, and Dr. Smith. Mr. Broughton became president, Dr. Smith, vice president and secretary-treasurer, and Mr. Edwards, general manager.

In the spring of 1910, Mr. Edwards withdrew from the company, disposing of his holdings equally to Mr. Broughton and Dr. Smith, they now being the sole owners except for a few shares owned outside. Upon Mr. Broughton's death on May 26, 1914, Dr. Smith, by previous agreement, purchased the Broughton interest and also the other stock outstanding. Soon thereafter he became president of the corporation, a post he held until his death on July 14, 1951. In 1915,

Howell Lindsay Smith, the eldest son of Dr. Smith, joined the Company as secretary, and in 1916, William Oliver Smith, the second son, became treasurer. On May 1, 1923, Joseph H. Hardison, previously managing partner in the Hardison-Cox Lumber Company of Lovett, Georgia, and Dr. Smith's son-in-law, became vice president in charge of production. In 1930, Charles Lee Smith, Jr., the youngest son of Dr. Smith, joined the company as assistant secretary and became secretary on the resignation of Howell Lindsay Smith in 1934.

With the accession of Dr. Smith, there began a new era in the life of the company. Doubtless this was what was desired by the original partnership, Mr. Broughton and Mr. Edwards. With the weight of their years resting heavy on their shoulders, they knew their life expectancy was much briefer than that necessary for the accomplishment of a major undertaking. The work to be done required the vigor and enterprise, the initiative and resourcefulness of a young man with much of his life before him, one whose wide interest in religious, social, and political affairs would bring him in contact and friendly relations with the state's ablest and most influential men, a man ready to join with them in the conduct of the business as he found it; not just any young man, but one of ability, business acumen, sagacity, wisdom and vision, all necessary qualities in making and executing plans, and with the strength of body and the expectancy of years required to get the job done.

Just such a man was Dr. Charles Lee Smith, then in his prime—barely 41 years old. He worked from the very first in complete harmony with the other officers of the corporation, a fact made easy by the full and mutual confidence that they had in each other. An unusual fact is that during the years they worked together, every motion made before the board of directors was passed unanimously. The minutes of the directors show that the remarkable development of the company that began at this time was due chiefly to the plans proposed by Dr. Smith and the means he suggested for carrying them out.

One of the first acts of the corporation was the purchase of a lot, 212-214-216 S. Salisbury Street, 70 by 212 feet. Here was erected a two-story building designed especially for a printing plant, with 21,000 square feet of space, fitted with the best and most modern equipment. Hardly two decades had passed, however, before even this space was proving to be inadequate to meet the expanding volume of the business. The property at 107-109 West Hargett Street, then owned by Dr. Smith, was secured. This building and that of the company adjoined at the rear, so it was simply a matter of removing the partition walls to convert the two buildings into one, so far as the operation of the plant was concerned. In 1926, at the

Hargett Street entrance, the company opened a complete office furniture and supply store. This continues in operation at this location until the present day.

In 1911, the company added a steel die and copper plate engraving department, enabling it to meet the growing demand for this type of work. This department still flourishes.

On May 1, 1921, the company had a strike as a result of a nationwide movement known as the Forty-four (instead of forty-eight) Hour Week for workers in the printing trades.

A member of the company some years later furnished the following statement:

"The company operated as a union or closed shop for many years prior to 1921, when, on May 1, it broke definitely with the various printing unions on the question of the forty-eight hour work week. This was a national and not a local issue, and it can be truthfully said that despite this break and the ensuing bitter strife, the company has never had a dispute with its employees on any local question, or on any wage or working condition that hasn't been settled on a mutually satisfactory basis.

"From 1921 until 1933, it operated as a non-union plant, and since 1933 as an 'open shop,' employing both union and non-union members without regard to their affiliations."

This statement is still true today. The company is equally proud of the fact that, in addition to celebrating its 100th anniversary, half of that century has been free from any labor troubles.

An important milestone in the company's history was reached in 1927 with the installation of lithographic equipment, becoming one of the first, if not *the* first, in the Southeast to enter this field. With the advent of this equipment, the company entered the bank stationery field. The importance of this work to the company was brought home forcibly by that period of bank failures and liquidations that began in North Carolina in 1931 and culminated in the nationwide bank holiday proclaimed by President Roosevelt in 1933.

In this period of depression, beginning in 1928, the company needed all the courage and enterprise it could muster to weather the storm. They had lost almost all of the State printing; three years later they lost heavily in money deposited in banks that failed, and in accounts receivable from customers. These things, together with the loss of work from the banks mentioned earlier, created a situation from which the company did not fully recover until 1939.

However, the company did not look back. It kept its face forward. Despite the difficulties of these years, the officers continued their policy of replacing old and obsolescent equipment with that which was new and modern; they still retained the ideal with which the company began—to serve their customers with the best in material and workmanship. As a result, with the upsurge of business that began in 1940, they were well prepared to meet the demands and opportunities for service.

We come now to the years of World War II. The loss of key men began in 1940, when William Oliver Smith was called back into service. He was by no means the last, the company contributing a total of 18 men, most of whom returned and resumed their duties with the company.

During this period, despite the loss of many key men, those left behind, plus a number of women added for the emergency, set a most outstanding record in producing a large volume of printed matter for every department of the United States government and some twenty camps and forts in the Carolinas and Virginia.

It held direct contracts with the U.S. Government Printing Office for the period 1942-1945, and never turned down a demand or failed to deliver when and as promised. It can vouch for the fact that this was the "writingest" army ever, for among other things in only three years it produced over four million boxes of stationery for the various camps, using both lithography and engraving in the process.

It also answered every call of its established customers and was able to meet successfully many new and unusual demands.

One such demand was made of it by the State of North Carolina. The company had been a state contractor on a very limited scale since 1927. Due to the exigencies of the war, another contractor to the state was unable to carry out its contract. Edwards & Broughton assumed that contract in addition to its own, and carried it through to a successful conclusion.

Thus we come to the year 1946, and the 75th anniversary of the company. It had weathered two wars, and the most severe depression in the history of the country. It had had its good times and bad, but the future looked bright as it converted to a peacetime basis, adding new machinery that had been unavailable during the war years, and the officers looked forward to the future with enthusiasm and optimism.

* * * *

(The foregoing information has been condensed from the book, *A History of Printing in North Carolina*, published by Edwards & Broughton Company in 1946 on the occasion of its 75th anniversary. For a fuller account the reader is referred to this scholarly work, written by George Washington Paschal.)

* * * *

As the company entered the final quarter of its first century, the officers were: Dr. Charles Lee Smith, President; Joseph Hammond

Hardison, Vice President; Charles Lee Smith, Jr., Secretary; and William Oliver Smith, Treasurer.

It was about this time that the company entered a field of printing absolutely new to it—that of telephone directories. It willingly accepted the challenge, and this is now a large part of the company's volume. During 1970, it produced and mailed over 650,000 directories.

Dr. Charles Lee Smith died on July 14, 1951, only six weeks before his 86th birthday. A full statement of his contributions to the State of North Carolina as well as to his company will be found in his biography appearing elsewhere in this appendix. He was succeeded as president by his son, William Oliver Smith. Charles Lee Smith, Jr., became secretary-treasurer.

The decades of the 1950's and the 1960's represent, perhaps, the period of the greatest growth for the company. Early in the 1950's, due to the normal expansion of the company's business and the addition of many new customers, it found itself badly in need of additional space for its operations. The officers were not to be hurried, however. The location they were seeking had to meet their exact requirements. Such a location they found at 1821 North Boulevard, and in August 1957, 50 years almost to the day from the time it occupied the building on Salisbury Street, they moved their entire printing operation into a brand-new building at this location. Containing over 40,000 square feet of plant area alone, the building was designed and fitted perfectly with the elevation of the land. The lower level, overlooking a spacious lawn fronting the south lane of North Boulevard, contains the executive offices and accounting department, as well as storage space and lounges. The entire upper level is devoted solely to the printing, mailing and shipping operations, as well as extensive paper storage facilities. There are also offices for those directly involved with production, as well as a snack room for employees. There is a railroad at the back door, facilitating the delivery of paper stock, which the company receives by the car load. There is also easy access to the main north and south and east and west highways. There is ample parking both for customers and employees. The location is only five minutes from downtown Raleigh.

It is interesting to note in passing that this monumental move from the old location was made without missing a single day's production or a single deadline on any job.

It was about this time that Paul F. Hoch, a son-in-law of J. H. Hardison, entered the company as assistant secretary-treasurer and assistant superintendent of production, after several years as a salesman.

Upon becoming settled in its new location, the company immediately began the installation of new equipment. Perhaps the largest single piece of equipment in the history of the company went into operation in May of 1959. This was a web rotary offset press capable of delivering a 16-page form folded and ready for binding at speeds up to 20,000 per hour. Another unit has since been added, doubling the capacity of this press, and enabling it to print forms in two colors.

With the installation of this press, an event of considerable importance to the company took place. After a period of about 35 years, it once again began printing the *Biblical Recorder*. In 1901. when the Baptist State Convention took over ownership from Edwards & Broughton, the circulation was about 8,000. Today it is over 90,000 each week, and gaining steadily.

In January 1960 William Oliver Smith, then president of the company, and Mrs. Smith were on a voyage to Europe. On January 17, Mr. Smith died suddenly while they were still at sea. Upon Mr. Smith's death, Joseph H. Hardison assumed the presidency of the company. Other officers at this time were: Charles Lee Smith, Jr., vice president; Paul F. Hoch, treasurer; and William Oliver Smith, Jr., secretary.

Perhaps the greatest change in the printing industry in recent years has been the change from letterpress to offset printing. To keep pace with this trend, the company has, in addition to the web press mentioned earlier, installed two 2-color and one single color offset presses of the newest and most modern design. In addition a new camera with the latest in automatic developing equipment has been put in operation.

Other departments of the company have likewise kept pace. In the composing room, two new Blue Streak high speed linotypes have been installed. This department operates a battery of eight linotypes, four of them equipped with teletype setters.

To meet the expanding volume of its publication work, much new binding equipment was added, such as a Perfect binding machine. For those not familiar, the *Readers Digest* and pocket books are examples of this type of binding. Also added was an automatic gang stitcher, capable of collating, stapling and trimming publications to a maximum number of pages practical with this type of binding. The bindery is also equipped adequately with high speed cutting machines.

The mailing department boasts a high speed automatic mailing machine, for the company mails as well as prints its various publications and telephone directories. Nearly three quarters of a million pieces are mailed monthly.

A letterpress department is still maintained for those desiring this type of printing, but is gradually being phased out.

The company maintains an art department, staffed by three full-time commercial artists, thus enabling it to offer its customers complete design service from rough sketches of the original idea to finished art. It is no idle boast, therefore, that the company advertises itself as one of the most complete and modern shops in the southeast.

Adjoining property has been acquired to take care of any future expansion of the company.

On January 1, 1971, the officers of the company were: J. H. Hardison, chairman of the board; Charles Lee Smith, Jr., president; Paul F. Hoch, vice president in charge of production; and William Oliver Smith, secretary-treasurer.

Thus the Edwards & Broughton Company comes to the end of its first century, a century filled with progress as well as with frustration. From a small beginning it has survived wars and depressions to become a leader in its field. As a new century for it dawns, it looks forward to the future with confidence, not content to rest on its past accomplishments, but eager and ready to face and meet whatever challenge the coming years may hold for it.

BIOGRAPHIES

CORNELIUS BRYANT EDWARDS

Cornelius Bryant Edwards was born in Franklin County, North Carolina, on July 16, 1844. His parents were honest, respectable people; his father was superintendent of a large plantation, near Louisburg, which had a slave population of about fifty.

Here Cornelius and his two younger brothers, J. F., and E. W., and a sister, lived until he was twelve years old. Of these years he retained many vivid memories, most of which were pleasant. He liked to tell of his wandering around the place with his brothers and the Negro boys of their age, fishing, hunting rabbits, gathering and eating cherries, and wild plums and strawberries and other wild fruits, which he thought much better than the tame.

He used to recount stories of the Christmas revelries when in the large fireplace of the "Great House" a roaring fire with a big Yule log was kept burning, and the happy servants assembled to bring their Christmas greetings and received each his or her share of the eggnog prepared by their Master, after which they carried him on their shoulders in joyous procession around and around the house and brought him back and seated him in his big armchair.

Mr. Edwards also remembered Uncle Isham and Aunt Sophia, to whose cabin he used to go to hear stories, mostly "Bre'r Rabbit stories"—"Bre'r Rabbit in the Pea Patch, Races between Bre'r Fox and Mr. Terrapin, How the Bear Lost His Tail, and many others afterwards told by Joel Chandler Harris."

One incident in connection with Uncle Isham and Aunt Sophia made a deep and painful impression on his boyhood mind, and he often told it. The couple had a son named Fenner, about seventeen years old, who was an incorrigible thief, "appropriating to his own use such articles as suited his fancy." Following the custom of many of the larger slaveholders of the day with thieving or immoral servants, when there were no prisons for such offenders, his master sold him to a slave dealer. One day as Cornelius and his two younger brothers were lying in the shade of a large oak near Uncle Isham's cabin, they saw two horsemen riding up. One proved to be the Master, the other a slave dealer. To the surprise of the boys they went straight to the cabin and called out the boy, examined him to test his physical soundness, then tied his hands behind his back and rode away with him. While all this was going on the astounded parents of the boy were begging and weeping and pleading that their son might remain with them, the mother getting on her knees and seeking to grasp those of her master and the buyer; but all was of no avail. The boy was driven away and the parents never saw or heard of him again. The incident made so deep an impression of horror on the mind of young Cornelius that even in his later years he declared that it was worse than what happened to "Uncle Tom" in the story.

It was in these years, 1844-57, that the young Cornelius received all the education in the schools that he ever received. Of this he speaks jokingly in a letter in which was enclosed a contribution to the Alumni Association of the University of North Carolina. "I am not an alumnus of any college," said he, "as I graduated from a log school house in Franklin County in 1857, and later from a printing office in Raleigh in 1865."

This experience of his early years, his lack of educational advantages, gave him a deep sympathy for the boys of North Carolina whose opportunities for education until well into the present century were no better than his. He often said words for their encouragement, telling of a "printer's devil" (W. W. Holden) who became governor, and of Abe Lincoln and Andrew Johnson each of whom became president of our country, of others who became chief justices of our state, and another who became a college president (Braxton Craven), all of whom became great despite poor educational advantages. In many published articles he manifested his interest in the educationally underprivileged boys in our state, but perhaps most comprehensively in "A Word to the Boys," which appeared in *Charity and Children* in June 1906, and attracted much attention. In beginning this article he said:

"I feel like writing a word for the encouragement of the boys of our state who will not have the opportunity of a higher education than our free schools are able to furnish them. It is not the college graduates that necessarily reach the top of the ladder in obtaining distinction in their chosen vocation, but it is the young men who set their mark high and use every energy within their power to reach the goal—who live uprightly and burn the midnight oil."

Late in the year 1856 or early in 1857 the Edwards family moved from Franklin to Wake County. They first came to the Falls of the Neuse, where about 1855 a paper mill had been built, in which it was expected that Cornelius would work. But failing to secure the desired employment either there or in another paper mill which had, for some years been in operation on Crabtree Creek, the family moved to Milburnie, at which another and larger paper mill had also been constructed, and like the others made paper of rags, "wood fibre not having been discovered." It was in this mill that Cornelius, described as a boy of twelve years, began to work, and worked for four years, as a "second hand or back-tender." This was before the days of child labor laws, but events proved that the lad suffered nothing in mind or body from that labor. The hours were long, the hands working in two shifts of twelve hours each, six days in the week, under the superintendency of James D. Royster, grandfather of Dr. Hubert A. Royster. The following paragraph from a statement made by Mr. Edwards in 1924 indicates both working conditions and nature of the product:

"The Milburnie mill ran from Sunday night at twelve o'clock until Saturday night at twelve o'clock, not violating the Sabbath day. They made paper for State papers that gave them orders and had a standing order for all they could make for the *New York Times*, in size 23 x 33 inches, that being the size of two leaves of that paper at the present time."

There is a note of satisfaction in all Mr. Edwards' reference to his work as a boy in this mill, and one of his deepest resentments was against that officer of a regiment of the 14th corps of Sherman's army, who coming into Raleigh by the Tarboro road set fire to that fine property, worth at least $200,000. Although the officer who started the fire was punished by General Schofield, that did not restore the building, the loss of which ruined Milburnie as a manufacturing town.

In the spring of 1861, when war seemed inevitable, Edwards left the paper mill and came to Raleigh with a young friend, W. B. W. Williams, both expecting to volunteer for military service in Ramseur's Battery of Artillery. Williams was accepted and in 1862 was killed in the battle of Williamsburg. On account of size and age, Edwards, being only seventeen years of age, was rejected. After this he made cartridges for a few months, and then became an apprentice in a printing office under Rev. T. S. Mott, who published the *Church Intelligencer*, an Episcopal paper. Beginning in the humble role of "office boy and copyholder," he soon began to acquire the printer's art by distributing type. Just how long he continued in this office is not known to the writer, but before September 9, 1863, he had become a "printer's devil" in the office of the *Daily Progress*, whose editor, John L. Pennington, had moved it from New Bern to Raleigh in 1862 to escape Burnside's occupation forces. His duties were still humble, one of them being to deliver papers to subscribers who came early for their supplies to the Old Market, near which was the office of the paper.

On the date mentioned above he was engaged in this task when a riotous mob gathered and proceeded to destroy the printing office of the *State Journal* also on Market Square, in retaliation for the wrecking on the night before of the office of the daily Raleigh *Standard* by a regiment of Georgia soldiers, temporarily encamped in Raleigh, because the *Standard* was advocating the Alexander H. Stephens peace movement. The office of the *Daily Progress*, which was also an advocate of the peace movement, had escaped the fury of the Georgia soldiers only because its lights were extinguished and the soldiers could not find it. But its proprietor, Mr. Pennington, not approving of the mob, sent his "devil" on the run to the Mansion, at the foot of Fayetteville Street for Governor Vance, who mounted his horse, which was standing saddled at the gate, and went on a gallop to the scene of the rioting. When Edwards' hasty feet had brought him back, Vance, having laid his coat and hat on a box on the sidewalk, already had the mob under control.

Since he was on the force of a newspaper Edwards was exempted from military service until January 1865, when Governor Vance refused to renew the exemption for the *Progress* and the *Standard*, because, says Edwards, they had favored the A. H. Stephens plan for peace. All the force of both those papers who were physically qualified were ordered into camp at Green's Mill, where the Raleigh water pumping station was later situated, and here they remained with only light duties, such as guarding a few Federal prisoners, until the approach of Sherman's army, when, says Edwards, "Our Commander-in-Chief, the Governor, left Raleigh so hastily that he failed to issue any orders to his pet command, the printers aforesaid." On learning this, Edwards continues, "we marched into the city late in the evening before the arrival of General Sherman on the morning of April 13, 1865, and disbanded without being paroled or 'paid off'."

The events of the surrender of Raleigh to the Federal forces and the period of their occupation of the city were well remembered by Edwards, and in later years his circumstantial accounts of them often appeared in the Raleigh papers of April 13, the anniversary of the surrender. He was present when the Federal troops first marched up Fayetteville Street and saw three members of Wheeler's cavalry which had been "infesting the city," take a stand on their mounts at the south gate of the Capitol; he was looking on when one of them emptied his pistol at the advancing column of his enemies and so forfeited his life when he was caught. Later he watched from the top of the Capitol the grand review of the Federal army by General Sherman and General Grant who had come to Raleigh for the purpose. The sight of so many troops, estimated to be 100,000, marching in billowing lines up Fayetteville Street, keeping time to the music of the army bands, was wonderful to him and the other spectators.

Three years later occurred an important event in the life of Mr. Edwards. On May 20, 1868, he married Miss Alice Robertson

28

Adams, daughter of William T. and Barbara Robertson Adams. Her father had come from Scotland to Brooklyn, N. Y., where she was born on March 6, 1847. Before the War Between the States the family moved to Raleigh. The married life of Mr. and Mrs. Edwards was singularly happy. Both in his youth and late in life he wrote verse about her, some of which is found in his Scrapbook. After her death in June 1925, he said: "We had lived together 57 years, and never an unkind word had passed between us." To them were born a son, C. B. Edwards, Jr., and two daughters, Bettie Camilla and Flora. The son, late in the last century, became superintendent of the firm of Edwards & Broughton, but died early leaving a widow and a son and several daughters. Miss Camilla was married to Mr. M. C. Chamblee of Raleigh on February 14, 1900. Soon thereafter they moved to Oxford, where she died in August 1919, being survived by her husband and two sons.

Though his schooling was meager, all in a log house and ending when he was twelve years of age, like many other men of natural ability, he acquired from his training as printer the mastery of a good, clear English style, and a disposition to write. Brief articles from his pen often appeared in the newspapers of Raleigh, and in his later years in other papers. His narrative and descriptive powers were great, and his stories and anecdotes are always readable and interesting. His "Early Recollections, Slaves and Slavery Days," gives a vivid impression of certain aspects of life on a plantation of fifty slaves. "What I Know about Paper-Making," has both a human and historical interest. If one would know how deep and miry was the mud in Raleigh's streets in the days of Vance and Jarvis, when "Fayetteville Street became a sea of mud," let him read "What I Know about a Serious Bus Mire-up in Raleigh." The reader of "How Milburnie Came within One Vote of Being Capital" can hardly fail to share Mr. Edwards' deep resentment of the methods that made Raleigh the site. "When Sherman Passed through Raleigh," became a classic with the Raleigh press, and for many years was reprinted with changing titles as often as April 13 came around. Of almost equal interest is his "Raleigh Newspapers during the War Between the States." One of his stories, "An Incident of Lincoln's First White House Reception," was published in the *Century Magazine* of August 1906. It was well received; and would doubtless have been regarded as one of the very best of the Lincoln stories had it appeared as originally written and set up in proof, a copy of which was sent to Mr. Edwards and is now in his Scrapbook. But yielding to the urgent desire of General R. F. Hoke, whose name was in the story, Mr. Edwards, much to the displeasure of the editor, omitted a paragraph that would have made Lincoln-worshipers shout for joy.

During all his life Mr. Edwards was also a good citizen—interested in his state and city. Under Republican Governor Russell as well as under Democratic Governor Aycock he served as a director of the State institution for the Deaf and Dumb and the Blind. He served as city alderman from 1882 to 1886, being a member of the "Reform Board of Aldermen" whose other members were such men as Charles E. Johnson, Benj. R. Lacy, F. M. Moring, Dr. Richard H. Lewis, G. Rosenthal, C. C. Barbee, Alfred Upchurch, and G. H. Andrews, who with the help of their mayor, W. H. Dodd, got Raleigh "out of the red" financially, and out of the mud and into decency physically, putting in waterworks and sewers and beginning the paving of the streets, and widening the sidewalks on the broader streets from 12 to 19 feet. During this period Mr. Edwards was chairman of the street committee. He was also chairman of the committee that secured the property of the Old Governor's Mansion for the Centennial School, and saved not only that property but also Nash and Moore squares from private exploitation by real estate dealers. He felt that when the High School was built it should have been located on the ample grounds of the Old Mansion, facing the Capitol.

Mr. Edwards was a member of two fraternal organizations. First he became a Mason. On June 11, 1867, he was initiated by the William G. Hill Lodge 218, A. F. & A. M. and on July 11, 1867, "was raised to the sublime degree of a Master Mason." He became a close student of the Manual and gained such knowledge of it "that he filled every place and station with marked distinction and ability." He became Master in 1890 and served two years; in 1920 he was granted Life Membership. In operative Masonry also he "wrought mightily," especially in his devotion to the Orphanage at Oxford. His burial was with Masonic rites by the W. G. Hill Lodge.

Mr. Edwards was also an Odd Fellow. He was initiated into the Manteo Lodge, No. 8, of Raleigh on February 13, 1870; became a member of the Grand Lodge in 1879, and was elected Grandmaster in 1886, and served two years. In September 1887, he was elected Representative from the Grand Lodge of North Carolina to the Sovereign Grand Lodge of the Independent Order of Odd Fellows, for a period of two years, and was elected for another period of two years in September 1892. He served a fifth year in the same capacity. Attendance at its meetings brought him to such distant cities as Los Angeles. In this high service he was influential, and it is said that it was through his efforts that Charles M. Busbee

was elected Grand Sire, which position no other North Carolinian
had held. He was one of the two, Hon. A. H. A. Williams of Oxford
being the other, who led in the founding in 1888 of the Odd Fellows
Orphans' Home in Goldsboro, the location recommended by Edwards
and Williams. For the first thirty years and longer he was one of
its directors. It was Mr. Edwards also who brought to the Home
its first three children, and he served it as treasurer for many years.
In February 1920, the Manteo Lodge celebrated with an appropriate
program the Golden Anniversary of his initiation. At the time he
was the only North Carolinian who had been an Odd Fellow for
fifty years. On the occasion he was presented with the Honorable
Veteran Jewel, which had before been given to only one other
North Carolina member of the order. The occasion received much
notice from the press, and called forth many warm expressions of
love and friendship for Mr. Edwards. At his burial a group of little
boys and girls from the Orphans Home was present. Probably
they knew him only from his picture which hangs in the Home,
but they had been told that he was their friend.

Many were the traits that went to make up Mr. Edwards' personality. He saw good in others and their enterprises and was co-
operative. He liked to have a part in undertakings that made for
the public good. An example was the State Fair. He gave words
of encouragement to its first promoters and took an interest in their
plans. He was an attendant at every Fair from the first in 1867
until his death, sixty-three in all, and at them all his printing company had an exhibit so long as he was a member of it.

His friendships were strong and lasting. This is illustrated by the
fact that it was by his initiative and representation that the N. B.
Broughton High School received its name in honor of his former
partner. This was in 1930. Mr. Broughton had died in May 1914,
but his virtues and services were fresh in Mr. Edwards' mind, and
he told them to the people of Raleigh in the public prints.

Akin to his friendship was his admiration for good men and
their services. It would be hard to find a more just appreciation
of a life devoted to ministering to others than is the sketch of Mr.
John T. Pullen, published by Mr. Edwards soon after the death of
him who did "so much to bless humanity."

He made his business minister to human welfare. If he saw a
child, even one of tender years, whom he could help by taking him
into his shop, he took him. One such apprentice, Robert C. Lawrence, afterwards one of the state's great lawyers, and devoted to
the service of his church, remembered Mr. Edwards' kindness all
his life.

"The real Edwards," said Mr. Lawrence in an article in the

News and Observer of May 18, 1940, "cropped out at noon time. When the whistle blew and the men poured from the rear entrance, there was always a tramp printer waiting for Edwards. This printer always needed a job, but first he needed a dollar or, maybe, only fifty cents. He always got it, for Edwards was a great-hearted man, and he put up with much of human frailty. When the demon rum got the best of one of his standbys (as sometimes happened) Edwards always went to see him, saw that he had every necessity, and had his job ready for him when he was ready to come back to work." On another occasion Mr. Lawrence said: "Many a poor drunkard can testify to his bounty and generosity." Not inconsistent with this is the fact that Mr. Edwards was an active and uncompromising enemy of the liquor traffic. Many prominent in business and social and political life spoke in warm appreciation of Mr. Edwards' kindness to them.

In the spring of 1910 he retired from business. On that occasion he was honored in a farewell service by his employees. Many of them had happy homes because he had taken them unskilled and made them into skilled laborers. In his remaining twenty-two years he did not lose his interest in the Company. Even in his last months, when his step was slow, the visitor to Raleigh not seldom found him on Hargett Street near the site of the building where he labored for so many years.

He died on February 29, 1932. His funeral was in the First Baptist Church of which he had been a member for fifty years. The chief address was by Dr. Charles F. Meserve, President of Shaw University. "Our dear departed brother," said he, "may best be described as one who loved his fellow man." He was buried in Oakwood Cemetery.

NEEDHAM BRYANT BROUGHTON

Needham Bryant Broughton was born on February 14, 1848, in a cottage still standing on a farm near U. S. Highway 70, a short distance to the eastward of Auburn, North Carolina. The main facts of his life, as gathered from numerous biographical sketches in such manuals as *Historical Raleigh*, are these:

He was the fifth child and youngest of four sons of Joseph and Mary Bagwell Broughton. In consideration of the rare physical development and accomplishments in life of these four, Senator Josiah William Bailey, writing in the *Biblical Recorder* of September 24, 1941, said:

"Altogether there are abundant evidences of native physical and intellectual strength; and, I must add, even though their parents

were poor—when poverty was the universal lot—one could not
look upon the physiques of these four men without reflecting that
when they were growing up their parents managed to provide
them abundantly with the food of big men—plenty of vitamins, calo-
ries, salts and fats, obtained, I suspect, from pork, rabbits, chickens,
pot liquor, blackberries, roasting ears, sweet potatoes, eggs, milk,
butter, molasses, corn bread, cornfield peas, turnips and the salad
thereof, and collards—the best diet yet devised by and for the
genus homo."

The father died in 1854, and two years later the mother with her
four sons and three daughters moved to Raleigh. The boy Needham
had already attended the common school near Auburn, and after
the arrival of the family in Raleigh, his mother sent him to the
common schools, the only kind that the capital city boasted in those
days, a few months each year for three years according to one
account, but for five years according to the statement found in
Sketches of Prominent Living North Carolinians, by Jerome Dowd,
published in 1888, probably based on information furnished by
Mr. Broughton.

At any rate, after he had finished school, and not yet thirteen
years old, in 1861, he found employment as an apprentice in the
office of the *Raleigh Register,* of which since 1856 Mr. John W.
Syme had been editor and proprietor. Probably his was a regular
apprenticeship according to the laws of the State then in force,
under which it is the obligation of the employer to teach the apprentice a trade. Mr. Syme seems to have been faithful to do this
for the young Broughton, until the disturbances of the War caused
the suspension of the *Raleigh Register* in 1864, which rendered it
necessary for him to find employment in another office in which
he might complete his learning of the trade. This he found under
John L. Pennington, editor and proprietor of the *Daily Progress.*
At this time C. B. Edwards was working in the same office, and
like Broughton seeking to become proficient in the art of printing.
Thus, these two laboring together, began that intimate acquaintance
which later resulted in their forming a partnership which was maintained with the greatest harmony and mutual appreciation and trust
for thirty-nine years.

The following summary of Broughton's activities in the next few
years is found in Mr. Dowd's sketch: Just after the War, work being
very slack in Raleigh, he went to Richmond, Virginia, and found
employment for about six months on the *Examiner.* From that
place he went to Washington City and obtained work on the *Congressional Globe,* staying here until the close of Congress in 1867.
Leaving this city in the month of August he went to Baltimore,

Philadelphia and then to New York City. Speaking of his first two weeks in the great metropolis, he says it was the severest trial of his life up to that time. For two weeks he searched in vain for work—his scanty means were exhausted, and just as he had almost departed he obtained one day's work on the *New York World*, and then two weeks on the *Herald*, and for three months following found constant employment on the same great paper. He then left that office to take a 'sit' on the *Rural New Yorker*, the great agricultural paper, which position he held until leaving New York City; in February 1869, he returned to the city of Raleigh, being just then twenty-one years of age.

"In May 1869, Mr. Broughton married Miss Caroline R. Lougee, daughter of Wm. H. Lougee, Esq., of the city of Raleigh. To this union have been given six children."

In what printing establishment Mr. Broughton worked in the next three years is not known to the writer, but that he was working is beyond question, since he was married and had to meet the expenses of a home. What is certain is that before September 1871, he was known as a good printer, industrious and honest. In matters involving money also men were willing to trust him, so that one of the able business men of Johnston County and Raleigh, Major William A. Smith, sold a printing plant to him and his fellow printer, Mr. C. B. Edwards, of like character, almost altogether on credit, and lent them one hundred dollars besides to help them get started.

To be menioned here is the division of labor between the two partners which gradually became definite. Mr. Broughton was in the front; Mr. Edwards in the back. Mr. Edwards was busy with printers and printing; Mr. Broughton, while helping with the printing as he had time, kept the accounts and dealt with the public, and solicited contracts. It was owing to this arrangement that Mr. Broughton was enabled to develop those qualities for leadership in civic and religious life with which nature had so richly endowed him—handsome personal appearance, an inviting and frank countenance, ease of bearing, manliness, courage, unaffectedness, and power in private conversation and in public speech, and an interest in the welfare of others, in particular that of little children.

Outside his office Mr. Broughton's chief interest was religion. It would be true to say that in matters which make for human welfare Mr. Broughton made little distinction between sacred and secular, and that all his labors for the promotion of the general good had a religious color and motive. For convenience, however, we may classify as religious those matters in which churches are chiefly concerned. Some account of Mr. Broughton's interest in religion in this sense follows.

On coming to Raleigh, a boy of eight years, he became a pupil in the Sunday school of the first Baptist Church, of which Dr. Thomas E. Skinner was then pastor. In 1864 he was baptized into the membership of this church by the pastor at that time, Dr. T. H. Pritchard. After his return from the North in 1869, he took his place again in the church, and after no long time was put in charge of a class of boys in the Sunday school, of which Colonel J. M. Heck was superintendent. In 1871 he was a representative of his church at the meeting of the Baptist State Convention, and though he was only twenty-three years old he was appointed recording secretary of that body, a position in which he served also in 1872, 1880, 1882-1913, inclusive, thirty-five years in all, and dying in 1914, left as a monument to his service the printed minutes of the Conventions of those years, which in form, content, style and arrangement are models of their kind.

It was in Sunday school work that Mr. Broughton rendered his greatest religious service and attained his greatest distinction. He entered a Sunday school when he was eight years old, and was put in charge of a class of boys when about the age of twenty-one. In 1876 he was made superintendent of the Sunday school of the church now known as the Tabernacle Baptist Church of Raleigh, in which a Sunday school had been organized soon after its constitution two years before.

The following statement and summary of Mr. Broughton's Sunday school work were taken from the *Biblical Recorder* of October 22, 1913, and June 3, 1914, and were written by the editor, Dr. Hight C. Moore:

"The service which Brother Broughton rendered as Sunday school superintendent constitutes not only the most brilliant chapter in his career, but also one of the brightest in the annals of his denomination and of the Christian world. When he took charge of the Tabernacle Sunday school the enrollment was seventy-five, and when last October he laid it down the enrollment was 1,257.

"During the years many thousands of pupils have been taught in its classes and there received impulses to higher living. Superintendent Broughton has been one of the alertest, most-up-to-date, sympathetic, energetic, and (best of all) spiritual of the men who ever marshaled a Sunday-school army and swung their columns into the front lines of the onward march. He has kept himself in complete touch with every pupil in his school from tiny toddler to sedate sire. He has bound his fellow workers to him as with cables of steel in common endeavor. He has organized his forces for outreaching, ingathering, and upbuilding, both numbers and in quality of work. He has stressed the discovery and development of his fellow officers and teachers. He has made and tested many and many a plan looking to the betterment of his school in interest and efficiency. He has scanned the whole horizon in search of suggestions that would help him in his task. He has gone forth into many parts of the state and of the country as the exponent and inspirer of the best in the Sunday school; and in consequence unnumbered schools have been thrilled by him into clearer vision of their duty and more energy for their Master. Highest of all, he has so wrought that every one in his school might amid the glory of its transfiguring summit see 'Jesus only.'

"Brother Broughton has indeed been a great Sunday-school man who has really done much pioneering in the last four decades. And it is pleasing to record the recognition that has come to him in the ministry whereunto he as much as any pastor has been called. For the past twenty years he has been Chairman of the Sunday School Committee of our Board of Missions and Sunday Schools, his wisdom and counsel having much to do with the great usefulness of this department. For a dozen or more years he has been one of the vice presidents of the Sunday School Board of the Southern Baptist Convention. For the past fifteen years he has been a member of the executive committee of the International Sunday School Association, and has thus been thrown officially with the leading Sunday school workers of North America. In 1906 he attended the World's Sunday School Convention in Rome, Italy, and was there made a member of the executive committee of that body. But amid all the honors that have come to him he has steadfastly devoted the most of his time, the strength of his thinking, and the richness of his life to the thousand and more pupils, who by registering themselves in his classes have said, 'Sir, we would see Jesus'."

In North Carolina Mr. Broughton joined in all movements to improve the Sunday schools. He was a regular attendant on the meetings of North Carolina Baptist State Sunday School Convention and was president of that body in 1881 and in 1891. He was also a member of the State Sunday School Convention (interdenominational) and its president for the year 1894-95.

However, Mr. Broughton's greatest accomplishment in promoting general interest in Sunday school work in North Carolina was the series of annual meetings known as the North Carolina Baptist Sunday School Chautauqua, which he instituted in 1893 and continued for eight years, those for 1893 and 1894 being at Mount Vernon Springs in Chatham County, those for 1895 and 1897 being at Red Springs, that for 1896 at Morehead City, those of 1898 and 1899 at Shelby, and that for 1900 at Lenoir, all or nearly all popular summer resorts. Like the famous institution after which it was named this Chautauqua had social, recreational and educational features, but the conception was Mr. Broughton's own; in fact, at first, the Chautauqua seems not to have been regarded with favor in official Baptist circles in the state. However, it proved extremely popular; in two years the number of attendants was too large for the hotel accommodations at Mt. Vernon Springs, and on this consideration other places were chosen. The meetings continued for five or six days during which was provided a program of lectures, demonstrations, round-table discussions, all admirably adapted by Broughton's master hand for the training of Sunday school workers in methods of teaching and management and the means of creating interest in that work. The entire program was carried through without hurry and yet expeditiously under Mr. Broughton's personal direction. One of the most popular instructional features was in music and songs suitable for Sunday schools, including the use of the organ and the fiddle and the bow, the latter being a surprising innovation at some of the places of meeting. At times the regular work of training was interrupted to make place for a sermon or lecture by some able leader. These were often heard by great throngs from the surrounding country.

In a year or two the Chautauqua revealed to the Baptists of North Carolina and other states of the South the need and value of such instruction as was given in its meetings and the desire of Sunday school teachers and officers for it. The demand could not be supplied by one assembly a year in a great state like ours. To meet the need thus revealed the Baptists of North Carolina, in April 1896, employed a Sunday school secretary whose duty it was to hold Sunday school institutes in all parts of the state. Other states of the South took like action—all in accord with the recommendation of the Southern Baptist Convention, which had awakened to a sense of the need. Thus began what is sometimes called the modern era of Sunday school work among Southern Baptists.

However, the Sunday school institutes lacked the social and recreational features of the Chautauqua. After the suspension of its meetings the need for them was strongly felt, and the result was the establishment of the place now known as Ridgecrest, which from small beginnings has grown to be one of the greatest religious assembly grounds in the country. Other like summer assembly grounds, to meet local or regional needs, have been established in other Southern states, and in 1945 the Northern Baptists began planning for a magnificent one of their own.

In the daily course of his life also Mr. Broughton manifested the same Christian qualities of mind and heart that brought him to the front in church and Sunday school. He was ever ready to hear the poor and needy and help them as he could. "I knew and associated with him in boyhood and was in business with him for about forty years," said Mr. C. B. Edwards: "I do not think there was a man in Raleigh who helped more young people than he did."

Mr. Edwards also said that he did not think there was a man who did more for the upbuilding of the city than Mr. Broughton, according to his means. Of his many services to his city, probably the most long continued and of most lasting benefit was in connection with the schools of Raleigh. According to a statement in a Raleigh paper of May 1930, Mr. Broughton was made a member of the city school board when it was organized in the 70's, and was later its chairman and continued to serve on it for many years. He was one of the Big Three—Dr. R. H. Lewis and Mayor Alf A. Thompson being the other two—who in the late 80's put the Raleigh schools on their way to their development. They secured from the General Assembly legislation providing for an eight-month school and taxes to support it—in a day when such taxation was very unpopular with many wealthier men. In recognition of his services in this way, and in response to a general demand of the citizens of Raleigh, the Needham Broughton High School was named in his honor in May 1930.

Mr. Broughton's interest in education extended beyond the public schools. From 1895 until his death he was a member of the board of trustees of Wake Forest College, and he had a prominent part in the organization of two educational institutions of Raleigh. One of these was what is now known as North Carolina State University. Though he was debarred by age from being a member of the Watauga Club, consisting of young men under thirty years, to which the establishment of the State Agricultural and Mechanical College (now N. C. State University) was particularly due, he was a powerful supporter of it, both with his counsel and influence with a reluctant General Assembly. The other institution in which he had a like interest was Meredith College, and he was a member of the boards of both institutions until his death. For eighteen years he also was a trustee of the Oxford Orphan Asylum (Oxford Orphanage since 1924), and found great joy in helping provide for orphan children. For some years he was a trustee of the State School for the Deaf and Dumb and the Blind.

For purely political affairs Mr. Broughton does not seem to have had much taste, but he served for a period as chairman of the executive committee of the Democratic party of his congressional district; he refused, however, to allow his name to be considered when his friends thought he might have been nominated for Representative in Congress. In 1900 he was elected to the state Senate, and had a part in the important educational legislation of that year. "In public duties that were not political he was, when called upon, always ready and always conspicuously strong and efficient."

In the spring of 1913 Mr. Broughton's health began to show signs of failure, and he was warned by his physicians that he must relax and recuperate. In October of that year he resigned his place as superintendent of the Sunday school of the Tabernacle Baptist Church. Though he continued in his position as president of the Edwards & Broughton Printing Company, he did not have the strength for regular work. The end came on May 26, 1914. "On Wednesday afternoon, May 27, an immense concourse of his friends," says the *Biblical Recorder* of June 3, 1914, "gathered in and around the auditorium of Tabernacle Church. Among them were the rich and poor of the city and of the State, the obscure and the prominent, the old and the young, white and black—all assembled in common grief and lamenting a friend to one and all. . . . Simple was the service just as he requested. It was conducted by his pastor, Rev. Charles E. Maddry, aided by Dr. T. W. O'Kelley and Dr. Livingston Johnson." The hymns were two of his favorites: "How Firm a Foundation," and "The Sweet By and By." The burial was in Oakwood Cemetery.

The following appreciation is from an obituary article by Rev. J. N. Cole, a Methodist minister, which appeared in the *Raleigh Christian Advocate*, shortly after Mr. Broughton's death.

"He blazed his own path through the forest into the open, where men took knowledge of him, and where he came to the place of command in the chief cities of the commonwealth. For years and years he was a man to be reckoned with in every great movement of his time. Hardly any cause in North Carolina felt safe without the support of Needham Broughton. There has hardly been an administration of the state government that has not at crucial times called for his service in matters of great moment; and there has been no movement for social betterment and uplift that has not felt his strong hand and the guidance of his superior wisdom. Without ever having seen a college during the years of his early struggles, he became a charter member of the boards of trustees of two of the largest colleges of the state, and by his wisdom and strength of influence hastened the day of their larger usefulness. During his entire career he put his strong personality back of the cause of the orphan. His service in the institution at Oxford was second to that of no other man in the state and was one of the supreme joys of his life. Probably more than any other man he had to do with the founding and building of one of the greatest churches of the state. As a worker in the Kingdom of God he was probably our chief citizen. As I have known men, I have known no other man who seemed to me to give so large and effective service to the cause of Christ in North Carolina as Needham Broughton. For thirty years as head of a great Sunday school he was our foremost worker in the field. . . . I regard him as our largest contributor to this cause."

The following is from the close of an editorial notice in the *Biblical Recorder*:

"In whatever he undertook Mr. Broughton was markedly efficient and successful. He has been quoted as giving the following formula for success: 'Faith in the Father, Son and Holy Ghost; identification with the church and its agencies and work; love of home and kindred; association with the best people; an earnest desire to serve others.' With these ideals ever before him, it is no wonder that his path was the path of the just, shining more and more unto the perfect day."

Among the many tributes paid to Mr. Broughton probably none is more just than this from an officer of the Junior Order of the American Mechanics, written in 1930 to support Mr. Edwards' suggestion that the high school be named for him:

"Mr. Broughton was a man of great native ability, an executive and a successful business man, who for nearly half a century was one of Raleigh's most public-spirited citizens, both in religious and civic life. There are many living who can recall his generous nature and his constant efforts for the benefit of the masses and his many benefactions to those in distress."

CHARLES LEE SMITH

Charles Lee Smith was born at his father's country home Wilton, Granville County, N. C., August 29, 1865. His father was Louis Turner Smith, a practicing physician in Granville County, formerly a surgeon in Lee's Army, Jackson's Corps, and later a physician and surgeon in Durham, N. C. His family is of English origin and came to North Carolina from Gloucester County, Va., about the beginning of the nineteenth century and settled in Granville County. His mother's name was Nannie Green Howell, and she also was from a Virginia family which came to Granville County about the same time as the Smiths. She numbered among her ancestors the Howells of Virginia, the Lockes of Rowan County, N. C., the Clarks of eastern North Carolina, the Bateses, and others. On both sides of his house are numerous ancestors who bore an honorable part in the war of the Revolution and in subsequent struggles.

Dr. Smith was reared in the country till about ten years of age, when his father moved to Durham where he established important business interests and had a large practice as a physician and surgeon. Here the son learned to share the duties and responsibilities of his father's business affairs. He was prepared for college in the Buchanan School, Luther T. Buchanan and Charles D. McIver, principals, entered Wake Forest in 1882, and was graduated in 1884.

At this stage in his career it was Dr. Smith's intention to study law. He was unexpectedly offered a position in the Raleigh Male Academy and accepting this was thus shunted off from the routine of a lawyer's life where the emoluments in a financial way may have been somewhat greater, but where in general usefulness to mankind his opportunities would have been vastly diminished. Dr. Smith taught in the Raleigh Male Academy a year; he became associate editor of the *Biblical Recorder* in 1885, and then, feeling his own need of a higher and more thorough training than could be had in North Carolina, went to Baltimore in January 1886, and entered the Johns Hopkins University. With the exception of a part of the year 1888 spent at the University of Halle, Germany, he remained in residence at the Johns Hopkins for the next five years and by sheer force of ability and scholarship filled successively the positions of University Scholar (1886-87), fellow in history and political science (1887-88), and received the degree of Doctor of Philosophy in 1889, was instructor in history and lecturer on sociology in the University (1888-91), and was at the same time secretary of the Baltimore Charity Organization Society, an office requiring much administrative ability and a wide knowledge of the history of the administration of poor laws in the past, and secretary of the National Conference of Charities and Correction in 1889-90.

After a brilliantly successful university course he was invited in January 1891, to occupy the chair of history and political science in William Jewell College, located at Liberty, Missouri. This position he continued to fill with credit to himself and profit to the institution till the close of the academic year 1904-05.

On July 21, 1905, Dr. Smith was unanimously chosen president of Mercer University, located at Macon, Georgia, as successor to Dr. P. D. Pollock, deceased. His inauguration took place on November 24, 1905, a day auspicious for the future of higher education in Georgia and among the Baptist institutions of the South. The occasion was made memorable also by the presence of eminent educators from other sections, including Dr. Ira Remsen, president of the Johns Hopkins, who made a most admirable address on the scientific spirit in education; of Professor Richard T. Ely of the University of Wisconsin, and of Professor Shailer Mathews of the University of Chicago, who also made addresses.

After one year he resigned the presidency of Mercer University and returned to Raleigh, North Carolina. A few months later he was invited by Mr. Edwards and Mr. Broughton to become a member of their firm. In May 1915, he was elected secretary and treasurer, becoming a joint owner of the Edwards & Broughton Printing Company with his two partners.

The History of Education in North Carolina

Although Smith, in September 1886, ceased to be a staff contributor to the *Biblical Recorder*, it was because he had agreed to write the educational history of his native state and in doing that, for more than a year he gave all the time he could spare from his university studies. Dr. Herbert B. Adams, the head of the department of History and Politics in the Johns Hopkins University, had been engaged by the United States Bureau of Education to edit a series of "Contributions to American Educational History." The first (*The College of William and Mary: A Contribution to the History of Higher Education, with Suggestions for Its National Promotion*, published in 1887) and the second (*Thomas Jefferson and The University of Virginia*, published in 1888) were by Dr. Adams. It was no small honor to Smith that he was chosen by his distinguished teacher to write the third of the series (*The History of Education in North Carolina*, published in 1888).

The United States Commissioner of Education, Hon. N. H. R. Dawson, in his letter of December 9, 1887, to the Secretary of the Interior, Hon. L. Q. C. Lamar, recommending the publication of this history said:

"It is an original and valuable contribution and deserves to be widely read. In this monograph Mr. Charles Lee Smith, who has been trained in historical methods at the Johns Hopkins University and now holds a fellowship in history and politics at that institution, gives the results of a thorough and careful study of the educational history of his native state.

"For North Carolina this is pioneer work. The history of education in that State has hitherto remained unwritten. . . . The sketch which is given of the University of North Carolina is the first full account of that institution which has ever been written. The writer thinks no institution of this country has a more honorable record, and it is claimed that in proportion to the number of its alumni

it stands second to none in the number of the distinguished public
men it has given to the State and Nation." (See pages 40-42 of
the Report of the Commissioner of Education for the year 1887-88.
Washington, Government Printing Office, 1889.)

In *Bibliographical Contributions,* edited by Justin Windsor, Li-
brarian, issued by the Library of Harvard University, 1895, the
"Bibliography of the Historical Literature of North Carolina, by
Stephen B. Weeks," is the following concerning Smith's history:

"The work is in a hitherto unexploited field. The materials for
it were quite abundant, but scattered; besides the general histories
of the State, Mr. Smith was the first to make use of the recently
published *Colonial Records:* Church and denominational histories,
local and town histories, sketches of particular periods, biographies,
public acts and laws of the State have been used. Many monographs,
catalogues, and reports have been brought into requisition in a
field new to Carolina—*Culturgeschichte.* The volume is the result
of much labor, of careful research, of painstaking sifting, and
thoughtful digestion of evidence."

Smith's history was published in 1888, and on March 28, 1889,
the Commissioner of Education, Mr. Dawson, wrote the author as
follows:

"I have been very much gratified at the reception of your monograph upon Education in North Carolina. The faculty of the University at Chapel Hill have passed a very complimentary resolution,
which has been sent to me, and the legislature of North Carolina
has presented me with a copy of the colonial records of the State.
It may be that I am reaping honors that you deserve."

In the 1889 volume of *The University of North Carolina Magazine* is found the following review of Smith's history by Dr. George
T. Winston, at that time professor of Latin and later president of
the University:

"This is the first systematic history ever written of education
in North Carolina, and it is the best answer yet made to the charge
of dense and degraded ignorance, so persistently and maliciously
made for half a century against the people of our State. While it
must be confessed that the public-school system was not efficient,
and that the masses were not well educated, yet private schools
were abundant, high schools and academies existed at many places,
and the University was founded one hundred years ago.

"Mr. Smith shows conclusively that recent writers, especially
Prof. John Fiske and Mr. Henry Cabot Lodge, have either willfully
or ignorantly wronged our ancestors most grossly. Fiske has declared that, 'Until just before the War for Independence, there was
not a single school, good or bad, in the whole colony. It need not

be added that the whole people were densely ignorant.' Lodge says: 'There was scarcely any means of education and no literature whatever.'

"Mr. Smith shows by the Colonial Records that schools did exist, that creditable libraries were established in several towns, and that the leading public men of the day were well educated and refined. A careful reading of the Colonial Records will show that the political and legislative papers produced by the North Carolina political leaders were not only superior in matter and in style to those of their English governors, but were a high order of excellence, capable of comparison with those produced in the other colonies.

"Mr. Smith has written with a heart given to North Carolina but equally to truth. The book is evidently the result of much labor and research, and its author has learned to study history by using original material. He has the happy mental balance which enables him to weigh calmly both sides of disputed questions. This is strikingly shown in his treatment of the Pool administration of the University during the period of Reconstruction. He is also gifted with appreciation of the picturesque and dramatic, as well as with the faculty of illuminating a subject by many lights from different distances focused upon one point. He has produced a truthful, impartial, and most interesting sketch of education, in all phases, in North Carolina. The subjects treated are: Education during the Colonial Period, the University, the Colleges, the Female Academies, the Male Academies, Education by the Friends, the Public Schools, the Normal and Graded Schools, the Teachers' Assembly.

"The sketch of the University is admirably written, and no doubt it will be a surprising revelation to students of education in the North when they read of the great work and great influence for nearly a century of our noble institution. The sketch contains a dozen excellent engravings of the University buildings and halls. In behalf of the University, we thank Mr. Smith and the Commissioner of Education."

The Raleigh *News and Observer* and many other important periodicals of this and other states published long appreciative reviews and, although twenty thousand copies of the history were published, the demand was such that the edition was soon exhausted. Both the author and the Commissioner of Education received many letters commending the publication.

A Significant Academic Event

Probably the most noteworthy single event in Smith's academic career, evincing the high esteem in which he was held by distinguished educators, many of them his personal friends, was his

29

inauguration as president of Mercer University, Friday, November 24, 1905. Full reports of the exercises, furnished by the Associated Press and special correspondents, were published by leading papers throughout the country. A New York paper said "It is safe to say that never before had there been so brilliant an academic occasion in Georgia or the South."

In the afternoon, preceding the formal inauguration exercises that evening, there was a banquet at which talks were made by representatives from a number of institutions. At seven-thirty p.m., an imposing academic procession composed of students, alumni, faculty, delegates from colleges and universities, Mercer trustees, state and city officials, the Governor of Georgia and President Smith entered the City Auditorium where an audience of thirty-five hundred were seated.

After addresses of welcome by Governor Terrell, Chancellor Hill, of the University of Georgia, and others, Dr. Smith delivered his inaugural address. Following this, addresses were made by President Ira Remsen, of the Johns Hopkins University; Professor Richard T. Ely, of the University of Wisconsin; and Professor Shailer Mathews, of the University of Chicago. A full account of the proceedings, including all of the addresses, was published in the *Quarterly Bulletin of Mercer University*, December 1905.

Besides the universities represented by speakers on the program, delegates were present from the following institutions: University of South Carolina: Professors Patterson Wardlaw and H. C. Davis; Southern Baptist Theological Seminary: Professor W. O. Carver; Yale University; Mr. W. J. Tilson; University of Georgia: Professor S. V. Sanford; Emory College: Professor F. C. Brown (later professor of English in Duke University); Shorter College: President T. J. Simmons and Professor J. H. Simmons; Georgia School of Technology: President K. G. Matheson; Alabama Polytechnic Institute: Professor J. E. Wiatt; Monroe College: President C. H. S. Jackson and Professor O. A. Thaxton; University of Iowa: Dr. Herbert E. Truax; Massachusetts Institute of Technology: Mr. Wallace E. McCaw; Wesleyan Female College: Professors J. C. Hinton and C. R. Forster; Georgia Normal and Industrial College: President M. M. Parks; South Carolina Military Academy: Major St. James Cummings; Stevens Institute of Technology: Mr. Crawford Wheatley; Tubman School: Professor T. H. Garrett; Cox College: Professor William Cox.

More than one hundred congratulatory letters were received from colleges and universities, and many from former colleagues and students, and other esteemed friends of Dr. Smith. Because of references to the career of Dr. Smith, whom they had known and

esteemed for many years, special mention is made of their letters:
Dr. James G. Clark, William Jewell College; Dr. Charles E. Taylor,
Wake Forest College; President Charles D. McIver, North Carolina
College for Women; General Julian S. Carr and·Hon. James H.
Southgate, Durham; Professor Charles M. Andrews, Bryn Mawr
College; President John H. Finley, The College of the City of New
York; Professor John Spencer Bassett, Trinity College (now Duke
University); Professor Charles A. Ellwood, University of Missouri
(later a distinguished member of the Duke University faculty);
and Professor Clarence A. Cannon, Stephens College, who later
became a lawyer and entered politics.

"A Scholar's Library"

In his later years in his travels to many countries, Dr. Smith
gathered rare and important books for his library. This collection
grew from a small but impressive collection during his academic
years to a library of some 7,000 volumes. It delighted him to show
them to interested visitors; and no one ever went away without an
enhanced appreciation of the literature of our own and past centuries.
It was his desire that his collection should be more than mere show
pieces; but that they should be kept together as a unit library. To
this end he donated it to Wake Forest University, his alma mater.
Today it is housed in a special rare book room in the library of
the University.

On the evening of October 20, 1941, his gift having been accepted by the College, President Thurman Kitchin and professors
representing departments of the College visited Dr. Smith to express
their appreciation of his gift. When they had assembled in his
library, he addressed them as follows:

"President Kitchin, it gives me pleasure to welcome to my library
you and the members of your faculty, who honor me by this visit,
that you may become acquainted with my intimate friends, these
books, which are destined to be permanently domiciled in Wake
Forest College. They are cherished companions, and I sincerely
hope that you and your successors for all time will esteem them as
friends. It is a great satisfaction to know that this library will be
safe-guarded as a separate unit, so that future generations can have
a realistic example of a comprehensive private library of the first
half of the twentieth century. Should these books be placed on
shelves with thousands of other books, they would lose their identity
as an independent library, and the institution possessing them would
lose the opportunity to preserve a unique evidence of the home life
of this period. A home with a library of personally selected books
tells its own story of culture, or the want of culture.

"In this connection, I venture to add that in appraising a library, its value does not primarily depend upon the number of volumes but on the importance and character of its books. The development of a significant library—one that shows scholarly understanding and cultural appreciation—demands a careful study of literary and historical values, and an intelligent discrimination in selecting rare and worthwhile books.

"It is encouraging to note that in recent years several able and distinguished citizens of North Carolina have made collections of books on special subjects and periods, the most important being Caroliniana and incunabula. Fortunately, some of these collections have been secured by the college and university libraries of our State. Probably it was well that the early collectors gathered books of special North Carolina interest. Certainly the late Dr. Stephen B. Weeks, my affectionately remembered friend, the able author of many valuable monographs on the history of our State, deserves the gratitude of all North Carolinians for his tireless and successful efforts in gathering from near and far the large and valuable collection of Caroliniana which our State University was wise enough to purchase. I happen to know that at this time there are several citizens of our State who are widening the scope of their collections and creating libraries of a character which entitles them to be recognized as discriminating bibliophiles.

"There are many avenues of pleasure open to the bibliophile but nothing delights him more than to secure a rare book of exceptional association interest—a presentation copy from a great author to a distinguished friend, or a volume from a famous scholar's library with his bookplate and marginal annotations. The satisfaction of possession is enhanced if the book was printed on paper of superior quality and beautifully bound in finest leather. An aesthetic lover of books is conscious of a most pleasurable thrill when reading the pages of such a treasure. Just here let me say, that few things in life have given me as much pleasure as collecting books, and when this library passes into the keeping of my alma mater, I can ask no greater reward than to be remembered as one of her devoted sons and as an ardent bibliophile, who, through many years and in many countries, personally selected these volumes.

"Beginning with an incunabulum published seven years before Columbus discovered America, you will find on these shelves volumes printed by the master makers of books, illustrated by famous artists, bound by great binders and carrying dates from the fifteenth century to the present time. A large number have the bookplates of distinguished men, and many are first editions inscribed by authors.

"With the gift of my library, I am including my autograph

collection consisting of manuscripts, documents, and letters. The College has guaranteed to keep perpetually the autograph collection and the books safely in a separate, suitably furnished room connected with the general library."

Dr. Smith was married on October 24, 1889, at High Point, N. C. to Miss Sallie Lindsay Jones, daughter of Dr. William Oliver Jones and Elizabeth Clay (Lindsay) Jones, and they had three sons, Howell Lindsay, William Oliver, and Charles Lee, Jr., and a daughter, Katherine Clark [Mrs. Joseph Hammond Hardison].

In 1931 Mrs. Smith died. He later married Miss Celeste Henkel of Statesville in 1934. She was deceased in 1935 and he then married Miss Carr Antoinette Vaughn of Franklin, Virginia in 1937.

Dr. Smith was a charter member of the Raleigh History Club, a group of 18 men who gathered monthly for a presentation of a scholarly paper. Dr. Smith remained president and the largest stock holder of Edwards & Broughton Co. until the time of his death, July 14, 1951. He was a member of the First Baptist Church and is buried in Oakwood Cemetery at Raleigh, N. C.

JOSEPH HAMMOND HARDISON

Joseph Hammond Hardison, printing company executive; b. Wadesboro, N. C., Jan. 31, 1897, son of William Cameron and Harriet Bennett Hardison. Student UNC, 1913-16; m. Katherine Clark Smith, June 7, 1918; Children: Katherine Smith (Mrs. Robert Vaughn Lamb); Sarah Locke (Mrs. Paul Frederick Hoch); Joseph Hammond, Jr. With Coxe-Bennett Lumber Co., Wadesboro, N. C., 1916-18; Managing partner Hardison-Coxe Lumber Co., Wrightsville, Ga., 1919-23; Vice president Edwards & Broughton Co., Raleigh, N. C., 1923-60, president 1960-69, chairman of the board 1969-; president Smith-Hardison Investment Co. 1956-60, Vice president 1960-; president Printing Industry of the Carolinas 1946-47; director Raleigh Little Theatre 1951-53; president Community Chest 1953-54; director Raleigh United Fund 1954-; Carolinas United Fund 1955-; trustee Rex Hospital 1955-66; director Rex Hospital Foundation 1966, president 1967-68; named "Outstanding Citizen" city of Raleigh 1968; served from pfc to 2d lt., U.S. Army 1918-19, AEF; Neuse Argonne Ribbon; Confederate Memorial Medal; member Draft Board No. 93 1958, Chm. 1971; Kappa Sigma, Omicron Delta Kappa; Church of the Good Shepherd (Episcopal), treasurer 1947-58, senior warden 1957-58; clubs: Civitan, president 1946-47; Carolina Country Club, Raleigh; Executives Club, president 1954-55; home: 915 Holt Drive, office: 1821 North Blvd., Raleigh, N. C.

WILLIAM OLIVER SMITH

William Oliver Smith, b. August 28, 1893, Liberty, Mo. Son of Charles Lee Smith and Sallie Lindsay (Jones) Smith. Moved to Macon, Ga., 1905, and to Raleigh, N. C., 1906. Educated in the grammar schools and high school of Raleigh, and at the University of North Carolina (A.B. 1916). Employed by Edwards & Broughton Company July 1916. Entered 1st Officers Training Camp, Ft. Oglethorpe, Ga., May 14, 1917. Commissioned 2nd Lieutenant Infantry Aug. 15, 1917. Ordered to Camp Jackson, S. C., Sept. 1917 and assigned to Co. B 316 M.G. Bn. 81st "Wildcat" Div., Oct. 1917 transferred to Co. D 318th M.G. Bn. Jan. 1918 promoted to 1st Lieutenant Infantry. Sailed for France July 31, 1918. Landed France Aug. 15, 1918. Served Vosges Mts. Sector, Oct. 1918 and Meuse-Argonne Offensive, Nov. 1, 1918. Wounded and captured, Haudiomont, France, Nov. 10, 1918, and hospitalized at Stuttgart, Germany. Discharged from hospital and returned to France Dec. 1, 1918. Returned to United States, Newport News, Va., June 20, 1918. Discharged Camp Jackson, S. C., July 15, 1918. Decorated with D.S.C., Croix de Guerre with Palm, Purple Heart and Victory Medal. Re joined Edwards & Broughton Co. Aug. 19, 1919. Served as treasurer 1919-1951; president 1951 until his death in 1960. Member U.S. Army Organized Reserves and served as adjutant 321st Inf. 81st Div. Passed through the grades to Major Inf. Volunteered Sept. 1940 and ordered to Camp Stewart, Ga., Nov. 6, 1940. July 1942 ordered to Norfolk, Va., as Executive Officer Norfolk Region, Anti-Aircraft Artillery Command—later Chief Operations Officer and Inspector Instructor, Commanded Norfolk Region Provisional Training Bn. A.A.A.C., Camp Pendleton, Va. Placed in Inactive Reserve Feb. 1944 and returned to Edwards & Broughton Co.

Member: Kappa Sigma Fraternity, American Legion, 40 & 8, Legion of Valor (National Commander 1955), U.S. Army Organized Reserves, NOMA (president), Executives Club, Carolina Master Printers Association, PICA, Society of the Cincinnnati (member of standing committee), Sons of the American Revolution (president, treasurer, and National Trustee), Member and Deacon, First Baptist Church, Raleigh.

Married Vandelia Elizabeth Drew Oct. 26, 1921. Children: William Oliver Smith, Jr., and Vandelia Drew Smith.

Died at sea while on the way to Europe on Jan. 17, 1960, and buried in Oakwood Cemetery, Raleigh, N. C.

HOWELL LINDSAY SMITH

Howell Lindsay Smith, b. High Point, N. C., July 31, 1890. Son of Charles Lee Smith and Sallie Lindsay (Jones) Smith, then residing in Liberty, Mo. Educated in private schools and William Jewell College, Liberty, Mo.; Mercer University, Macon, Ga.; and University of North Carolina (Law School 1909-1911). Admitted to North Carolina Bar 1911. Entered 1st Officers Training Camp, Ft. Oglethorpe, Ga., May 1917; Commissioned 2nd Lieutenant Infantry, August 1917; ordered to Camp Jackson, S. C., September 1917, and assigned to 324th Infantry, 81st "Wildcat" Div.; January 1918 promoted to 1st Lieutenant Infantry. Sailed for France July 1918. Served in Vosges Mts. Sector, October 1918. Transferred to 38th Infantry, 3rd Div., and served in the Army of Occupation (Germany) 1918-1919. Returned to United States and was discharged July 1919. Returned to Edwards & Broughton Printing Company September 1919. With that Company 1914-1937 (secretary 1920-1937).

Member: Kappa Sigma Fraternity, American Legion, 40 & 8, and Capital Club.

Died July 12, 1952, and buried in Raleigh, North Carolina.

CHARLES LEE SMITH, JR.

Charles Lee Smith, Jr., b. High Point, N. C., January 31, 1907. Son of Charles Lee Smith and Sallie Lindsay (Jones) Smith. Home: Raleigh, N. C. since birth. Student, Murphey School, Raleigh, N. C.; graduated Woodberry Forest School, Orange, Va., 1926; graduated University of North Carolina (A.B.) 1930. Joined Edwards & Broughton Company, September 1930. Secretary 1934-1940, Secretary-Treasurer 1940-1942, 1946-1960; Vice President 1960-1970, currently President. Volunteered in Army, Fort Bragg, N. C., December 5, 1942. Commissioned 2nd Lt. Antiaircraft Artillery, Camp Davis, May 25, 1944. Separated Camp Chaffee, Ark., April 22, 1946. Member Zeta Psi Fraternity, President of Chapter 1929-30; Terpsichorean Club, President, 1935; Raleigh Sales and Marketing Executives Club; Printing Industry of the Carolinas, former Director; Civitan Club; Nine O'Clock Cotillion Club, Secretary and Treasurer; North Carolina State Art Society, Secretary and Treasurer; First Baptist Church, Past Chairman Board of Deacons, Raleigh, N. C.

Married Mary Virginia Camp, Franklin, Va., November 23, 1940. Children: Mary Lindsay (Mrs. Major Charles Newsom, III); Charlotte Camp (Mrs. John Ward Purrington); Charles Lee Smith III.

PAUL F. HOCH

Paul F. Hoch, b. Poughkeepsie, N. Y., June 22, 1918. Son of Mary E. Maroldt and O. E. Hoch. Educated in schools in New York State. Graduated North Carolina State College 1940 with B.S. in engineering. Special Course in Quality Control in Magnetic Ink, Rochester Institute of Technology 1960. Served in armed forces as 1st lieutenant 1941-1945. Saw service with paratroopers in Panama, Africa, Sicily, Italy, France, and Belgium. Jumped into Southern France. Participated in Battle of the Bulge. Test jumped out of glider in tow. Engineer with Federal Government 1945-46. Vice president Eastern North Carolina Engineering Company 1946-1948. Edwards & Broughton Company, eastern representative 1948-1960; assistant treasurer 1957-1960; treasurer 1960-1970; vice president 1970-. One of the first to introduce magnetic ink in North Carolina and a charter member of National organization of Bank Stationers Association, Inc.

Married Sarah Locke Hardison January 1, 1944. Children: Paul Frederick Hoch, Jr., and Lindsay Bennett Hoch.

WILLIAM OLIVER SMITH, JR.

William Oliver Smith, Jr., b. Raleigh, North Carolina, April 9, 1929. Son of William Oliver Smith and Vandelia Elizabeth Drew Smith. Student Ravenscroft Episcopal Day School, Hayes Barton Grammar School, Needham B. Broughton High School, Oak Ridge Military Institute. Graduate University of North Carolina, Chapel Hill, N. C. (Member Kappa Sigma at UNC). Graduate student, University of Innsbruck, Innsbruck, Austria. Printing Management course, Carnegie Tech. Served two years United States Marine Corps, attaining rank of sergeant. Joined Edwards & Broughton Co. 1957 in office supply department; Assistant Secretary-Treasurer 1959; Secretary-Treasurer 1970. Member Church of the Good Shepherd, Brotherhood of St. Andrew; Charter member North Raleigh Exchange Club, Director since 1969; Raleigh Chamber of Commerce; Sons of the American Revolution; North Carolina Society of the Cincinnati; Raleigh Post No. 1 American Legion; Raleigh Toastmasters Club.

Married Margaret Miller Maxwell, June, 1962. One child, Margaret Oliver.

LIST OF EMPLOYEES

Name	Department	Year Employed by Edwards & Broughton Co.
Aan, Albert P.	Linotype	1962
Aharon, Andrew F., Jr.	Shipping	1968
Aharon, Sue	Litho	1970
Allen, Charlie U.	Litho	1964
Allen, Harry Braxton	Job Press	1930
Alley, J. Wallace	Litho	1953
Alston, Ruby Lee	Bindery	1969
Amos, William E.	Office Supplies	1964
Austin, William	Office Supplies	1969
Baker, Allen L.	Linotype	1925
Baker, Charles Edward, Jr.	Composing Room	1970
Bagley, Calvin	Job Press	1954
Bagley, Willie Leon, Jr.	Composing Room	1949
Barker, William O.	Litho	1970
Barrow, James N.	Composing Room (Foreman)	1926
Beasley, Roy Donald	Litho	1962
Beckwith, Hattie	Office Supplies	1969
Benfield, Jack	Litho (Foreman)	1951
Blankenship, James E.	Litho	1962
Bost, Carolyn Brewer	Mailing	1970
Brannock, T. Pat	Litho	1927
Brannan, Marie Womble	Bindery	1921
Brixon, William Pierce, Jr.	Office	1970
Brown, William L.	Engraving	1951
Buckner, Reba Sanderson	Clerical	1970
Cahoon, Nancy Bray	Teletype	1967
Carswell, Claude L.	Linotype	1966
Carter, Luther E.	Bindery	1970
Cobb, Lequita Hartsell	Bookkeeping	1968
Council, Lynn	Janitor	1966
Cotton, Tommie L.	Litho	1967
Cunningham, Donald	Shipping	1970
Daniels, J. W.	Cylinder Press (Foreman)	1937
Dees, William R.	Office Supply	1970
Dickens, Lillie O.	Bindery	1944
Dillard, Pamala Ehrens	Bindery	1969
Donnelly, Marjorie Maddrey	Office Manager	1937
Dupree, Walter Wayne	Litho	1969

Name	Department	Year Employed by Edwards & Broughton Co.
Dupree, William Oscar	Linotype	1948
Easterling, Eli F.	Office Supply	1970
Ellington, L. B.	Linotype	1959
Ellington, Norman L.	Litho	1969
Goodwin, Ernest O'Dell	Composing Room	1954
Graham, Thomas J., Jr.	Proofroom (Foreman)	1934
Grissom, Thomas C.	Linotype	1940
Hagwood, Vivian O.	Litho	1944
Hagwood, William Henry	Composing Room	1954
Hall, Grace Ann	Mailing	1967
Hall, Delton	Bindery (Foreman)	1968
Hamilton, Ernest Edward	Bindery	1951
Hamilton, Deborah A.	Secretarial	1969
Hardison, Joseph H.	Officer	1923
Hare, Myra Cochran	Proofroom	1969
Harris, James T.	Bindery	1966
Harris, Oscar Lee	Litho	1966
Hatcher, Ray Franklin	Litho	1959
Hendley, Richard E.	Office Supply	1970
Hendricks, Mack, Jr.	Litho	1963
Hill, George F., Jr.	Art Director	1956
Hill, Roosevelt	Janitor	1945
Hoch, Paul F.	Officer	1948
Hodge, Robert C.	Composing Room	1959
Holloway, Lottie O.	Engraving	1954
Holmes, Rebecca Ann	Mailing	1969
Horton, Charles Massie	Litho	1960
Inman, Christine Peddy	Bindery	1968
Inman, Frank M., Jr.	Composing Room	1939
Jackson, Willie	Bindery	1957
Jernigan, Dale Ann	Artist	1965
Jones, Billie Bussey	Secretarial	1969
Jones, Dassie Melvin	Office Supply	1970
Jones, James Rufus	Bindery	1969
Kelly, Edna P.	Engraving	1965
Lambert, Ervin Glenn	Job Press	1952
Lambert, James R., Jr.	Job Press	1970
Lancaster, Barbara Aan	Proofroom	1970
Lancaster, J. Michael	Proofroom	1960

Name	Department	Year Employed by Edwards & Broughton Co.
Lee, Ernest	Litho	1959
Lee, Proctor S.	Litho	1955
Leonard, Arch Perry	Bindery	1968
Long, Fred W.	Litho	1969
Limer, Charles R.	Chief Stock Clerk	1954
McVickers, Charles T., Jr.	Shipping	1968
McVickers, Charles Thomas	Accountant	1967
Maness, Thomas L.	Sales Representative	1966
Marcom, C. B.	Mailing (Foreman)	1960
Matheson, Marvin L.	Bindery	1964
McCauley, Andrew M.	Composing Room	1957
McDonald, Charles (Tom)	Litho	1954
McKenzie, Margaret W.	Bindery	1966
McMillien, Robert Wade	Bindery	1968
Mills, W. Hardy	Litho	1950
Monroe, William	Janitor	1945
Morgan, Linda Faye	Check Room	1969
Morgan, Velma Love	Check Room (Foreman)	1938
Morris, Callie Margaret	Bindery	1970
Munns, Wilbur L.	Linotype	1928
Myers, Sandra M.	Check Room	1970
Odette, Samuel J.	Shipping	1970
Olson, George A.	Sales Representative	1953
Pace, Kathryn	Clerical	1970
Parker, Bruce E.	Engraving (Foreman)	1961
Parker, Joyce P.	Proofroom	1970
Phelps, Joseph F.	Sales Representative	1947
Poole, Bessie W.	Office Supplies	1917
Poole, Ronie Wilkins	Bindery	1938
Rand, Phyllis A.	Office Supply	1970
Ringrose, Helen	Office Supply	1970
Robinson, Charlie	Litho	1948
Rogers, Robert	Bindery	1970
Russell, Donald Neal	Composing Room	1968
Sauls, Charlotte Fish	Bookkeeping	1968
Sawyer, James Edward	Litho	1967
Scarboro, Robert Lee III	Composing Room	1968
Seagroves, Ervin Lee	Mailing	1969
Seeley, Horace I.	Office	1963

Name	Department	*Year Employed by Edwards & Broughton Co.*
Settle, Linwood E.	Engraving	1968
Shell, Howard T.	Officer Supply (Manager)	1969
Sides, Jo Anna	Secretarial	1971
Smith, Charles Lee, Jr.	Officer	1930
Smith, Lassie Marshall	Quality Control	1967
Smith, Ross, Jr.	Litho	1969
Smith, William Oliver, Jr.	Officer	1957
Stephenson, Annie Ruth	Bindery	1966
Stephenson, William D.	Bindery	1960
Suggs, Charles H.	Composing Room	1956
Thompson, Otis	Mailing	1968
Thompson, Paul	Mailing	1968
Thompson, Peggy C.	Check Room	1966
Thompson, Roy	Mailing	1969
Thompson, Willie, Jr.	Stock Room	1969
Turnage, Lloyd, Jr.	Artist	1961
Upchurch, Charles	Office Supplies	1962
Vick, Geraldine	Proofroom	1970
Vick, Linda P.	Bindery	1970
Wade, Judith T.	Secretarial	1968
Watkins, George T.	Office Supply	1966
Watson, Linda Barbour	Bookkeeping	1964
Wells, Donna	Check Room	1970
Wells, Juanita Sauls	Secretarial	1968
Whitfield, John	Office Supply	1970
Whitley, David	Litho	1969
Whitley, Janice Dew	Teletype	1956
Williams, Alphonzo	Litho	1968
Williams, Maxine	Office Supplies	1961
Williams, O. A.	Bindery	1922
Willis, Ruth	Engraving	1924
Wyatt, Maud Hall	Check Room	1963
Young, Katherine	Bindery	1968
Young, Zelma	Bindery	1922